Twilight Rebels

Twilight Rebels

by Keith Wilkerson

New Leaf Press

Green Forest, Arkansas

NEW LEAF PRESS EDITION
1991

Library of Congress Catalog Number: 91-60940

ISBN: 0-89221-206-3

Cover design by Richard Nakamoto

With thanks:
To the two pollywogs of my Pooh years, Andrew Loveall and Sean Goller.

And to the extraordinary vision of Lawrence Hallum, long-time superintendent of Cookson Hills Boys Ranch and Christian School near Tahlequah, Oklahoma. May those who read this book and follow in his footsteps never forget the thousands of good kids who merely don't have anybody—as our world turns ever more selfish in these dangerous latter days.

So many of us were twilight rebels, rescued by someone obedient enough to care in the early hours of our insurrection.

Preface

Filled with an urgency that she did not understand, "Lord, be with my grandson," interceded the old lady in the midnight's stillness. "Father, You made him and You have a great purpose for his life. Watch over him, protect him from evil. Show him the plan You have for his life."

Her room was silent.

"Lord," prayed the woman. "I don't understand Your ways. My time on earth is almost over, yet You do not take me. Why? I'm in constant pain. My husband has gone on ahead of me. And now, I just wait for death in this place. Why do You withhold it from me? O Father, I so long to see Your face. I ache to come to heaven with You. I can barely move. What possible good thing is there left for me to do here? I am so frustrated, so alone, so useless. Only You are there. What do You have for me to do for You?"

In the night's stillness, the old woman suddenly was filled with an urgency: *Pray for that grandson. Intercede for that special child that you love so.*

"Father," breathed the old woman, her voice filled with great awe. "Be with my little grandson. Fill him with joy and wisdom, Father! Guide him! Send him the right people to guide his footsteps. He's even more alone than I, so Lord, give him a special family—a supernatural and mighty family. Give him a mighty angel who will hover over him and keep any evil from befalling him. Surround him with your power and might, O Lord. Protect him, Father. Lift him up and cover him with Your might...send him a special angelic guardian..."

Her prayer drifted on into the night.

Twilight Rebels

Of course, Teddy and Tadpole weren't really brothers. Growing up at a ranch for throwaway kids, the two had just adopted each other and started telling people they were siblings when Teddy was thirteen and Tadpole was six.

But, although Teddy seemingly liked to remember otherwise, there had been no Ouachita Hills Boys' Ranch or Tad early in his life.

Teddy had arrived at the ranch a wary, feisty thirteen-year-old with thick glasses, curly blond hair and a police record that included car theft, narcotics possession, credit card theft, and solicitation.

Tall and physically mature for his age, he had easily passed for a skinny fifteen or even an immature seventeen.

He was the sort of boys' ranch kid who caught visitors' attention. He obviously needed to be mothered. Behind his curls were big brown eyes in search of a family—friendly, inscrutable eyes that the visitor kept seeking out, eyes filled with humor, wit and mischief, yet hiding unspoken hurt.

Those dark, friendly, wary eyes betrayed his streetwise façade, his junior-high swagger. No, it was obvious, he was no punk, no killer, no Artful Dodger. In his adolescently self-conscious

---

smile you saw potential. His awkward, trim body spoke of the outdoors and a not-so-distant childhood among people who had loved him, who had nurtured his spirit—and who'd had a future planned for their young heir.

But there was also a gauntness to his face that told of a boy who had smoked too many cigarettes, who had lost everyone he loved, who had missed a lot of meals and...and who had experienced too much of the seamy side of life too early.

Yet, to assume that Teddy was simply a poor victim was to fall for part of his savvy act; many of his troubles were his own making. A number of times, instead of trusting those who'd taken an interest in him, he had insisted on tackling life alone. The little scrapper was an effective con artist, but not a real pro — more a checkers player forced into playing chess, a survivor, undirected when he needed someone to guide him ... betrayed too many times by strangers he trusted.

He was not an orphan, although the stability of his early life had ended when his loving grandmother had died. No, Teddy was a throwaway, abandoned at age ten by the enigmatic, impulsive thrill-addict who was his mother—a woman who had snatched him away from the relatives who would have cared for him.

      ✐   ✐   ✐

Behind thick glasses, Teddy had stared out the car window on the long, autumn drive through the Ozark foothills to the boys' ranch.

Silently, he had remembered ....

"Allen," had asked the lady juvenile referee—using the false name that he had given police, "am I to understand that this is your first time before a judge?"

"Yes, ma'am," Teddy had lied.

"Where are your parents?"

"I don't know," he responded truthfully, pushing his glasses up on his nose. "My mom's off somewhere and I've never seen my dad."

The woman flipped through his file. "Allen, are you really seventeen years old?"

Stoically, thirteen-year-old Teddy nodded—lying. He was barely an eighth grader.

"It says here you were found in the possession of a stolen Diners Club card, that you were passing yourself off as Daniel Ross Dundee, age twenty, by using stolen identification and that you defrauded the bus line by use of a forged instrument. That means, you used the credit card to buy a ticket."

Teddy didn't say anything.

"Well?" asked the woman.

Teddy shrugged. Nervously, he pulled a cigarette pack out of his pocket and, unsuccessfully, tried to display nonchalance. But his shaking hands betrayed his terror. The woman sighed inwardly. She had seen too many others like him: unwanted kids unable to quietly just find some productive niche—any-thing—in a society content to ignore them. "Do you have relatives?"

"I used to live with my Uncle Willem and Aunt Minnie in New Mexico until I ..." Teddy stammered. "... 'til my cousin Janny got killed." He shrugged, offering no further explanation. Blankly, he drew on his cigarette and pushed his glasses against his forehead.

"What about your mother?"

"She stole me from my aunt and uncle when I was a kid, back when Grandma died. Trixie—that's my mom—she promised me all sorts of stuff and took me with her and these boyfriends and then dumped me in Denver, then Reno and Galveston ...." He blew a cloud of smoke and attempted to stare impassively—

steely-eyed—as if the incredible words he'd just uttered meant nothing to him. Instead, he just looked like a very scared boy, certainly younger than the seventeen years he claimed to be.

The woman looked at him strangely and tossed him a note pad. "Write down the name of any relative who would be interested in coming to get you, and their telephone number if you know it."

Slowly, awkwardly, Teddy scrawled his Uncle Willem's name and number.

The woman picked up a telephone.

Teddy stared impassively at his shoes as she dialed. He lit another cigarette.

"Hello, Rev. Willem Behre?" She listened. Then, "May I speak to him, please?" Teddy grinned to himself, fingering his cigarette lighter. His cousin Hans had probably answered the phone out in the barn.

"Rev. Behre?" asked the woman. "My name is Patricia Cupertino. I'm a juvenile referee with the Wichita, Kansas, Juvenile Court. I have someone who wants to talk to you."

She handed Teddy the phone. "Uncle Will," stammered the startled Teddy, clutching the phone to his ear. "Hi...Hi! How are you doing?"

On the other end, there was silence, then over the hundreds of miles, a pained, perhaps too-dramatic sigh. "Well, Teddy Bear," muttered his uncle, "just where are you now?"

Teddy looked up at Mrs. Cupertino. He shoved his glasses against his forehead "Kansas. Can I come back and live with you?" The boy's voice was newly high and strident—pleading. Mrs. Cupertino watched his expressionless eyes as he listened to his uncle.

"Well, it's a long story," whined Teddy, taking a nervous drag on his just lit cigarette—but not inhaling. Anxiously, he ground out the butt in the ashtray at Mrs. Cupertino's fingertips. "I've had a bad time. When I get home, we'll talk about it."

"Let me talk to him," said the woman. Abruptly, she took the phone. "Rev. Behre," she said. "Patricia Cupertino again. I'm afraid that Allen is in quite a bit of trouble. Can you provide him with legal counsel?"

She listened, then tapped the top of her desk with her pencil in irritation. She glared at Teddy. "Well, Reverend," she said, "whatever his name is, he is being charged as an adult on multiple counts of grand theft and fraud by use of forgery in New York, Minnesota, Kansas and several provinces in Canada. He ran up some pretty incredible bills on some credit cards he apparently took in a robbery."

Teddy sank down in his chair. That was the last thing he needed his preacher uncle to know.

"No," the woman said. "We thought he was seventeen years old." She was silent. She listened. "I see. Do you want to talk to him again?" Her face grim, she scowled at Teddy with one eyebrow raised high and handed him the phone.

"Theophilus?" said Uncle Will. "I can't come to Kansas and I couldn't pay for a lawyer this time if I could come. Are you guilty of all these things?"

Teddy cupped the telephone mouthpiece and turned his back to Mrs. Cupertino. "Nossir. Well, maybe the credit card stuff. I stole that from this pervert. But, I didn't do any, you know, stuff with him."

As if Uncle Willem hadn't heard him, "No matter what we did for you," intoned the man, "you were destined to turn out just like your mother."

Teddy's eyes began to fill with tears. He blinked and kept his back to Mrs. Cupertino. "I didn't know what to do." he pleaded, his voice low—defeated. "Let me come home."

"You could have done a lot of other things," said his uncle distantly. "A great many things."

The line was silent.

Teddy didn't ask again.

"Your probation officer waited months and months before turning you in. We kept thinking you'd show up. I'm going to call him and see what he thinks we ought to do. But I think you ought to go to a really strict reform school or whatever it takes this time. Do you understand me?"

"Yessir."

"May God be merciful to your soul, Teddy Bear. You don't know what you've put us through. We were afraid that you were dead. Now, I think that would have been better."

The thirteen-year-old winced and fumbled for another cigarette.   •

"You're just like your mother," said his uncle. "You did a really fine thing, getting my sons on drugs."

Teddy's head spun. That wasn't true. He took off his glasses. He hadn't done anything like that. "Can I talk to Hans?"

"No." There was a long pause. "I better call ...what was your probation officer's name? Octavio?"

"Gene Ortega."

There was another long pause.

"May God be with you," said his uncle. "And may He have mercy on your soul. Goodbye, Teddy Bear."

And then Uncle Will hung up.

Teddy held the receiver to his ear and listened to the dead line. He looked at Mrs. Cupertino and handed her the phone. His eyes were wet. With both hands, he made a slow, careful production of putting his glasses back on. "My probation officer's going to call you," he growled.

"So, you *have* been in trouble before!" she accused, her eyes narrow. "Allen." She curled her lip as if spitting an obscenity.

"Young man, I don't understand how you think I can help you when you lie to me. You're not seventeen, you're only thirteen. And your name is Theophilus. Your uncle calls you Teddy."

The boy slouched. He blew a cloud of smoke.

"Don't you want anyone to help you, young man?"

Teddy shoved his glasses up on his nose. "I don't care," he monotoned impassively. But he was crying inside: Being treated like this just wasn't fair...he wasn't a criminal. He was a good kid. His grandmother had taught him right.

He blinked away tears and pushed his glasses up his greasy nose.

That night, two older boys were put into his cell and tried to force him to bob for cigarette butts in the toilet. He fought with them until one almost broke his nose on the toilet rim.

Bloody, Teddy was taken to a solitary cell in the juvenile facility where he patched his crunched glasses back together with adhesive tape.

Juvenile Hall had been crowded with young drug couriers and a few scared sixteen-year-olds recovering from having wrecked their cars, sullen seventeen-year-old shoplifters, even one tattooed, prissy twelve-year-old caught in a burglary. But mostly the place was packed with young "clockers"—kids selling small amounts of drugs for older pushers.

Teddy spent most of his time ignoring the other kids and reading old *Time* magazines and *National Geographics*. There was one night counselor named Raymond who found out why Teddy'd been arrested—at least how he'd stolen the credit cards—and started taunting him with a variety of "I'm just curious ..." questions.

The first day, Teddy had made friends with one of the two adult trusties, long-term prisoners who helped with janitorial duties. Jack was a short hunchback—misshapen and badly cross-eyed. He sort of slunk around, always seeming to be watching out behind his back. Aaron, on the other hand, acted like he was in charge, carrying a clipboard, bumming cigarettes from the kids, listening to their complaints, promising results.

Jack had gotten upset when he saw a cafeteria worker offering Teddy a cigarette at dinner.

"Don't take no more cigarettes from that con," he said that evening as he came through mopping the floor. Through the bars, he gave Teddy a pack. "You give that con back his cigarette at breakfast and don't you take no more, you hear?"

"Why?"

"You want to be his woman?" asked Jack.

"Do what?" exclaimed Teddy. "No way."

"I didn't think so. Then, don't you take no cigarettes, no candy, no nothing from none of them cons. You do and one day they gonna give you a bill. They gonna say you owe them four packs. When you can't pay, they gonna let you off easy, they gonna let you be their woman. If you refuse, they gonna say they'll kill you if you don't pay them back."

Scared, Teddy glanced at the pack Jack had given him.

The man gave him a steely stare. "I first joined the system when I was 16, but I was a lot smaller than you." His one good eye stayed fixed on the boy—the other stared off to the left as usual, seemingly keeping watch. "Don't you worry about Jack. I won't give you no bill."

So, lying in bed, Teddy had smoked cigarettes until they gave him a headache. He stuck the pack in his front shirt pocket and grinned at himself in the polished steel plate over the toilet. The cigarettes made him look considerably tougher.

✐   ✐   ✐

Outside of the little town of Los Cerrillos, New Mexico, a frail, white-haired woman stiffly attempted to re-pot the brilliant orange daisy hybrids she had bought at the nearby Wal-Mart.

In the morning's twilight, Miriam Julian rubbed her arthritic hands in frustration and began to cry. "O God," she whispered. "How good You are to those who are pure. But me! I am such a disappointment to You. Even still, You bless me!

"Now," she whispered. "Father, please ease the pain of this terrible arthritis. I just want to get these daisies into bigger pots before they wither and die. Their roots are all bound up—and they need more dirt, more room to grow..."

Her own words caught her by surprise. Stunned, her eyes glanced in the bedroom window at her still-sleeping six-year-old grandson. On a piano sat a school photo of a one-time favorite piano student, a boy called Teddy Bear.

"O Father," she whispered, tears filling her eyes, her heart in sudden anguish. "My grandson's roots are bound up, too. He needs room to grow, too, doesn't he?" Trembling at the truth she did not want to consider, she wiped her cheek with a thin, frail wrist, smudging her face with the black potting soil.

"What am I to do, Lord?" she whispered. "He has no one else. I can't send him to strangers."

Her grandson had been abandoned at birth by his unwed mother, Miriam's only daughter—a confused, tortured girl who lived in Nashville, Tennessee. Jeanne had such terrible problems of her own, more than she could cope with daily. She could not manage this tender little boy that Miriam had nurtured since his first hour of life.

Now, "I am all he has ever known! Where else could Thaddeus go, Lord?" whispered the old woman. And her heart almost burst with the pain of the answer. *Ouachita Hills Boys' Ranch.*

Miriam and her late husband had helped found the refuge for homeless kids who had not run into trouble with the law. They had given the ranch one hundred acres near Siloam Springs, Arkansas—beautiful, rolling acres of wooded hills along the twisting, scenic Buffalo River.

Leroy MacDonald, another of her former piano students had come to them with his dream for a refuge for good kids with nowhere to go in a society increasingly too selfish and inwardly directed to care about young discards.

"Ours is a throwaway society," young Leroy MacDonald had proclaimed at their church. "We discard more usable garbage than any society in history. We spend more for the bottle that perfume comes in than for the perfume itself—then when it's empty, we toss it out rather than go to the messy bother of refilling it."

Now, there were no orphans at Leroy's ranch. Most of the kids were throwaways—unwanted, inconvenient burdens, fortunate not to have been aborted, but unlucky to have been born into such a society so consumed with its self-gratification.

Miriam fumbled with her daisy pots.

The answer was too obvious. She could no longer try to take care of herself or her little grandson—particularly after falling and breaking her hip for the third time last winter. She and her husband had made arrangements long ago to spend their final years at the University Towers in Fayetteville, Arkansas.

It was a well-planned retirement center in which residents had their own apartments and balconies—and all sorts of electronic gadgets that brought nurses and staff instantly if needed. Money had been put into a trust long ago for Miriam to go to University Towers. She had just been procrastinating the move—over a thousand miles from her New Mexico buttes and desert.

But now, it was time, she could see. Thaddeus needed to put his young, tender roots down into the fertile soil of the nearby Ouachita Hills ranch.

Tears filled the old woman's eyes. Her fragile shoulders shook with grief. "O Lord," she pleaded. "You have made the way. You have held the doors open. You are so kind, so loving, so caring. Now, please give me the strength to walk through Your doors."

In the morning twilight's sun, she watched the stirring Thaddeus. The bright, empathetic first grader rubbed his eyes and squinted out the window at his grandmother.

"Lord," prayed the old woman silently. "Give him a special friend. A good friend. A protector. A guardian. Send Thaddeus an extraordinary friend who will care about him and love him."

As she prayed the sudden, spontaneous request, Miriam was filled with a sudden and wonderful peace. It was a strange sort of prayer—but it came from deep within her heart and from her understanding of this complex little boy who cared so deeply about everything. He sensed other people's pain. He would be adrift without a special friend who needed his love.

"Yes, Lord," she whispered in awe. "A remarkable friend who will take our Thaddeus under his wing and let our little boy love him. Send us someone who will love Thaddeus like You love Thaddeus and like I do." There was no thunderclap, no booming voice from heaven, but Miriam knew that her request had been heard—and miraculously granted.

And she did not doubt—or wonder just where such a child would come from, for ours is not a society that instills in modern youngsters the taking of responsibility for one another. Where, in a generation tutored by television to meet only its own cravings, would such a guardian come from? Miriam did not nurture these thoughts.

Instead, she rested in the peaceful assurance that the great God who had created the world, who had delivered Israel and had been her gentle Provider for almost eighty years would again do the impossible.

A smiling man stood as thirteen-year-old Teddy swaggered into the interrogation room, a cigarette dangling from his young lips. The grinning man was immense—maybe six-feet, nine-inches and three hundred pounds. His thighs were as big as the boy's chest. His mountainous shoulders drooped with the neglected muscles of a football coach in the off-season. He appeared to be maybe thirty or forty years old, Teddy couldn't tell.

The man smiled openly—naively—much too friendly for Teddy. The man's big grey eyes held the suspicious thirteen-year-old's, giving the increasingly paranoid kid an uncomfortable feeling that the boy did not control what was going on. For the longest time, the smiling man's eyes held the boy's. Anxiously, Teddy glanced away, poking his glasses up on his nose with his middle finger.

Studying the floor, Teddy tried to ignore the burden of the smiling man's gaze on him.

Then, "Hi, Theophilus!" the man boomed stepping forward, snatching Teddy's hand and pumping it vigorously. Grinning, the man tried to hold eye contact, but Teddy refused—looking away, examining the tabletop and the law enforcement posters on the wall.

For a long thirty seconds, the man watched the boy's every reaction. He waited patiently—for what, Teddy did not know—and continued grinning stupidly. Teddy furtively glanced at him, again recoiling from the strange, too-eager, so-friendly eyes.

The man gestured broadly at a chair. "Sit down, my friend." Shaken, Teddy obeyed.

Wide-eyed, the man continued to grin—his big eyes studying Teddy. Apparently he was waiting for something—Teddy couldn't imagine what.

"Well, praise God," the man exclaimed, opening a file.

The thirteen-year-old relaxed in his chair. Okay, that made sense: the guy was some sort of a religious fanatic. *Great,* snickered the boy to himself. Before he would be able to get out of the room, he would have to fake some kind of miraculous religious conversion. But, Teddy knew, smiling to himself—he could do it. He'd already been "saved" three times now.

Grinning like a Cheshire cat, the man leaned his chair back on two legs and continued to study Teddy's face, then his file. Teddy would look away, then would glance back to see that the man was watching him instead of reading the papers. Grinning, the man would squint and turn a page. "You've been a pretty busy boy," he said finally.

Teddy tensed, unsure what that meant.

"Do you want to tell me about it?" prompted the man, his goofy smile increasingly hard to take.

"What's there to tell?" exclaimed Teddy, too loudly, defensively, his voice cracking. Embarrassed, he ducked his head, shoved his glasses against his forehead and fumbled for another cigarette. He flicked his lighter and studied the floor.

"Do you play football?" asked the man.

Teddy guffawed to himself. He'd encountered this type before—weight-lifting mental dwarfs. If you didn't play football, they looked at you with some sort of stupid superiority: Real men play football, boy; what are you a sissy-boy? For sure, Teddy wouldn't admit that he played the piano. "I hate it," he retorted, his voice too high. "It's an ignorant game. I'd rather just kill people. I killed my cousin Janny, you know." He stared poker-faced at the startled man.

"Do you like to kill people?" smiled the man.

"You bet. Guts and gore between my teeth. Babies on my bayonet. Watch 'em squirm and cry and die." Blowing a smoke ring, Teddy stared at the ceiling. "You ever kill anybody?"

"No, I haven't," laughed the man, returning to the file. He closed his eyes and sighed deeply. Then, as if wanting to start the interview all over again, he opened his eyes and smiled at Teddy again, with that simpleton smile of before, the macho, blank, trusting eyes.

Teddy leaned back. Grinning, "Who are you?" asked the thirteen-year-old.

"My name is Leroy MacDonald," said the man softly, almost warily. "Many years ago back in Santa Fe, New Mexico, your grandmother, Madeline Behre, and I were very good friends when I needed a friend." He paused and examined the file. "Theophilus, how long have you been here?"

"Three stinking weeks," said the boy. "You gonna get me out?" They had been long weeks—with the ever-present probability of physical violence, the paranoia of being closed in by the bars, the urine stench of the place, and the lights that stayed on twenty-four hours. He'd lost three fights and his jacket.

Now, sitting across from this MacDonald, Teddy fought a sudden rush of hope. Desperately, he squinted at the man.

"I had quite a time getting copies of your birth certificate," the man was saying. He held up a facsimile of Teddy's Austrian papers. "Do you read German?"

"No," mumbled the boy, frustratedly. MacDonald seemed stupid enough that perhaps a display of submissive humility might do the trick. Teddy bit his lip and grinned shyly at the man.

"Neither do I," said the man, laughing out loud. "But I do understand one thing if you're to do battle for the cause of Christ."

"Huh?" exclaimed Teddy. MacDonald smiled, pleased at getting Teddy's attention. The thirteen-year-old mentally kicked himself. This guy was weird—too unpredictable to mess with. "Being born in Austria has its down side," the man was saying. "You'll never be able to become president of the United States. You and Henry Kissinger. However, you can be a missionary in a lot of countries that won't accept an American passport. You're a U.S. citizen, but you can apply for dual citizenship and have an Austrian passport, too. Austria is neutral, you know—like Switzerland."

Teddy nervously lit another cigarette. This guy was very strange, strange, strange. He was playing games Teddy couldn't figure out.

"Do you understand how much trouble you're in, Teddy Bear?"

"No," answered the boy.

"Do you realize that the juvenile referee has recommended that you be tried as an adult? You put a deputy in the hospital when they took you off of that bus. You had to be subdued by force. You'll be one of the youngest kids ever sent to the Kansas State Prison Farm if you are certified as an adult and convicted. I personally can't believe that in this state they would do that to a thirteen-year-old. I guess it's because you don't look or act like any thirteen-year-old. They say you're dangerous and completely incorrigible."

Teddy smiled, mysteriously.

Dangerous. And the youngest. He'd be famous. Like Billy the Kid.

"Seems that you owe various credit card companies, airlines, hotels and so forth about $7,000," MacDonald was saying. "Do you have any idea of how you can pay them back?"

Teddy snorted. "They can't do nothin' to me. Stick their $7,000. I didn't spend no $7,000. That guy that I heisted the wallet from is just trying to get out of his bill. What can they do to me? I'm under-age."

"They can press charges. They can have you declared incorrigible and certified as an adult because of your long record of arrests. They can send you to jail until a hearing when you are twenty-one years old. Do you like it here? Are you ready to spend the rest of your childhood here?"

"It's not bad," rasped Teddy, his voice suddenly hoarse. He grimaced, then squinted. MacDonald's eyes were troubled, staring at the boy's face, as if for the first time. Grimacing in seeming pain, MacDonald looked down at the file. "Well, let's see here. You have been picked up by police in Colorado, Wyoming, Nevada.... What did you think of the Anchor of Hope Christian Home in, where was it? Armstrong, Texas?"

"It was okay," Teddy mumbled. "I got awful behind in school, though. When I went to live with my uncle in New Mexico, I had to go back to the second grade. That was humiliating."

"Hmmmmmmmm," said the man. "They're supported by the Corpus Christi area Bible Churches. Very interested in the Book of Revelation. Not what you were raised in, was it?"

Teddy shrugged. "My grandmother was some kind of crazy Pentecostal. My Aunt Minnie, she says she wasn't even saved. They made me get prayed-through and baptized again. And the Anchor of Hope people made me do it all over their way one more time."

The man laughed—and flipped through the folder. "How are you going to pay back that $7,000?"

Tensely, Teddy jerked his head, shaking his hair out of his eyes, looking MacDonald squarely in the eye.

MacDonald blinked back, trying to affect the same goofy stare of before.

"I could work, I mean, I used to have a pretty good paper route. I know a lot about sheep and calves. I helped my Uncle

Will build the barn. I can drive nails better than my cousins. I mean, better than Hans. Janny's dead."

MacDonald nodded, studying Teddy intently.

"I'm good at computers," continued the boy, uncomfortable under the man's gaze. "They had one in the Boys' Club in New York and they let me play with it. I wrote a video game, but the computer wasn't sophisticated enough to make the gremlins work like they should have. I beat it every time, but nobody else could."

"Computer programming," nodded MacDonald, flipping Teddy's file open, then closed. "That's a high-paying field. We've got a computer in the administration building. If you're good enough, maybe you can get it to behave for me. It's always eating all our files. We keep hard copies of everything because the thing is so unreliable." He chuckled.

Teddy stared at the tabletop. He glanced up and tried to chuckle, too—but didn't manage. Suddenly, he was shaking, trembling. Ashamed, he tried to hide that he was crying. He put his forehead down on the table and puffed on the smouldering butt of his cigarette.

"I came to look you over for the last time, maybe, before you disappear into the prison system, Teddy," said MacDonald gently. "I'm the superintendent of a boys' ranch."

Not responding, Teddy pressed his forehead against the cold tabletop.

The man reached over and gently tousled the thirteen-year-old's hair. "I'm the superintendent of the Ouachita Hills Boys' Ranch and Christian School near Fayetteville, Arkansas. We take in good kids whose parents can't take care of them anymore. We seldom take bad kids—the ones referred through the courts—mostly because they're too much to handle. Troubled kids disrupt what we're trying to do. I wish I had enough time to work with hard cases like you, but I don't. There are too many good kids out there who need love and a home."

Teddy sniffled and shivered. Why hadn't his grandmother known about this ranch? Why hadn't she arranged for him to go to something like it? He sniffled, gritting his teeth.

"What did I say?" asked MacDonald, softly, concerned.

"Nothing," whispered Teddy, trembling. He jerked upright and shook his long curls out of his face. But, then, he felt himself crying again. Determinedly poking at his glasses, he turned his face away.

MacDonald seemed surprised. He fumbled with Teddy's file. "This says that at age ten you were tested at the Southern Wyoming Diagnostic Center and showed possible retardation."

He flipped a page, glancing up to grin at Teddy—who was staring at him in disbelief. "Just kidding," laughed MacDonald. "Testing showed you have superior intelligence. At age eleven, after multiple encounters with authorities, you were placed in custody of the Texas State Department of Human Services. Psychiatric evaluation found criminal tendencies and ambitions. Child talked proudly of alcohol and drug abuse, of participating in larceny, fraud, grand theft auto."

MacDonald squinted at Teddy. "At age twelve, runaway, violating terms of transfer to the New Mexico Welfare Department and resulting in revocation of Texas probation." He put down the file. "It doesn't look too good, Teddy Bear," he said. He sighed, then smiled blankly. "As far as the State of Kansas is concerned, you're a multiple offender who wasted a lot of their staff's time by giving them aliases and claiming to be seventeen. This sheet says you bragged to cellmates of 'participating in armed robbery, murder, truancy, assault, purse-snatching, drug and alcohol abuse and repeated fraud through illegal use of credit cards.'"

Teddy considered lighting up another cigarette.

"They're going to lock you up and think they've done society a big favor," said MacDonald. "They've got claims on you from all over everywhere. They'd like to make an example of you. The press will jump all over this one—an incorrigible thirteen-year-old who proves that juvenile courts are a failure."

"Jerks," snickered Teddy. "I'm not a criminal. And I hardly used their stinking credit cards. Plus, I'm just a kid. I'm only thirteen years old."

"Did you do all these things?"

"I didn't spend no $7,000. But, I did some of that other stuff. What was I supposed to do? I'm just a kid, man. I can't work."

"This says you've charged $6,983.67 with credit cards you stole while you were turning a trick."

"That's a sick lie!" bellowed Teddy. "I let that guy pick me up, but I didn't do any of the stuff he wanted." Teddy's eyes flashed. "I'm not that way. Trixie, she's my mother, she was a pro, so I know all about that kind of stuff and I just thought I'd try to get some money. But that guy was really disgusting and I wouldn't do any of that stuff—I vomited all over the guy. I stole his wallet, like my mom used to do all the time, and I got out of there."

"Mmmm ..." said MacDonald, staring at the file.

Teddy frowned, confused, as—again—the simpleton, the do-gooder looked up and grinned.

"Come on, man," Teddy exclaimed, the anger returning. "I didn't do anything. How can you sit there and smile at me? All my life, I been pushed around by my crazy mother and relatives who didn't want me." The thirteen-year-old's own voice sounded foreign to him, more hysterical than he wanted it to. Teddy jumped up again and in a fury stalked around the room. "Come on," he whined. "Just let me go to your ranch, man. Let's cut all the crap."

MacDonald looked sad, as if he were extremely disappointed. Then, he stood up, too.

Teddy gawked, then snorted. It didn't matter if the guy was leaving. He was a jerk.

"I'm sorry, Teddy Bear." MacDonald said softly. "I'll do what I can to see that you get good help."

Suddenly, panicking, "You better not leave me here!" exclaimed Teddy, not believing the guy really would walk out on him. "You said my grandmother helped you. Well, I need you to help me, man! Get me out of here!"

MacDonald smiled, placidly, blankly. "I'd like to help you. But you would be a lot bigger problem than we can handle. You're lucky, however. You've got a very good probation officer back in Santa Fe, Gene Ortega. He's really interested in what happens to you. I'm going to tell him about a really good program in Oklahoma called the Bethesda Boys' Ranch. It's for kids like you who have been in serious trouble. Maybe he and I together can pull the strings to get you in there."

"I'm no con!" exclaimed Teddy. "This is the first time I've ever been in a real jail, except for Galveston and Cheyenne and they didn't even lock me up then, except to hold me while they looked for Trixie and stuff."

"Teddy," said MacDonald. "You're a mess. You need a program that will help you admit to yourself that you didn't have to do any of these things that you're charged with. Your uncle says you turned his sons onto drugs and that one of them fell off a cliff and died after smoking hashish with you. I'm sorry, but I can't let you ruin my program."

"Don't go," Teddy whimpered, cringing against the wall. "Janny didn't do drugs. That was a lie. He and Hans thought it was funny to act like they were high, but we didn't do hardly any dope—just maybe once or twice. Janny, he wasn't on anything when we—when he got killed."

MacDonald paused. "I'll do my best to help you, Teddy Bear. But you've seen too much, son. You wouldn't like it with us."

"Don't go," whispered Teddy. "I'll be good. I can. I have lots of times."

MacDonald stared at him. "Teddy, I would be taking an immense risk. You'd have to swear to yourself and Almighty God that you won't ever do anything illegal, including theft, shoplifting, hustling, airline hijacking, genocide or atomic war. That's the sort of vow I had to make when I was just a few years older than you."

Teddy stared at him.

"That's what I had to do," repeated MacDonald. "And it wasn't easy. I still have to pay for things, because sometimes, you just can't undo damage."

"I swear it," said Teddy. "I'll do it. I never wanted to steal stuff. And I ain't gay."

MacDonald stared at him. Teddy struggled to maintain eye contact. Then, self-consciously, the boy stared at the floor. "I swear I'm not conning you. I'm not really scared of prison. I'd survive. I'd probably like it." Unable to control himself, Teddy felt tears on his face again. Ashamed, he dramatically yanked out his cigarettes and threw them on the table. "See, I'll stop smoking—I'm not hooked! I can be good. I'll behave. I can. I will."

MacDonald watched him.

In frustration, "You knew my Grandma," blurted Teddy in frustration. "She helped you, you said. Well, I know nobody wants me to be their son. But at your place, maybe it could be almost as good. It could be like I was your kid."

MacDonald smiled broadly at him—realizing that the kid was completely desperate.

Was he desperate enough to change?

Or did he need to hit bottom? *Should a thirteen-year-old have to hit bottom?*

MacDonald studied him, grinning. Teddy grimaced in frustration. He was fighting back tears.

Was this remorse? Or just more of the act?

"Okay," said Leroy, "tell me what you've promised me."

Astonished, Teddy looked up. "That I'll be good. I won't do nothing illegal again, ever. No matter what. And I'll be like a son to you. I won't smoke. I won't cuss. I won't steal nothing. I won't get no girls pregnant."

"It's not going to be easy," said MacDonald. "Being good isn't as easy as being bad. You'll have to work at it. And with you, you'll have to tell the truth even when you know you could improve matters with a well-constructed lie."

"Oh, yeah, I know. I won't lie. Not ever again."

"You may only get one chance like this in your whole life, Teddy Bear. It's up to you whether you're going to make it this one last time."

"Yessir. I know. Absolutely. I'll make it work this time."

"You'll be on tight, tight probation. The first time you let me down, the first time you pull *anything*, you're coming right back here."

"Yessir," barked Teddy. "Can I smoke one last cigarette?"

"No," said MacDonald.

"Hey," exclaimed the thirteen-year-old, shoving his glasses up on his nose. Dramatically, he dug out his lighter and slammed it down on the tabletop. "No problem. I've quit. For good. No more."

Teddy waved at Jack as he followed MacDonald out of the sheriff's office. The trusty smiled, the gaps in his teeth showing.

✐   ✐   ✐

Carefully, Teddy steered clear of his two new roommates at Ouachita Boys' Ranch, particularly a deaf first grader named

Leslie Brady who had an almost impossible-to-understand speech defect. Little Les had made it clear he wanted to be great friends.

But Teddy coldly gave him a wide berth.

The thirteen-year-old remained aloof—but not distant enough not to give Les a nickname that stuck immediately: "Sluggo." Les liked the name—which amused Teddy.

But he and Sluggo did not become immediate friends.

As far as Teddy was concerned, the teen-age girls that made up half of the population of the "boys' ranch" were the extraordinary thing about the place. They were beautiful, friendly and everywhere. Within days, he was in the mainstream of the ranch's junior-high soap opera.

"What's wrong with Brenda?" asked one of the ladies in the kitchen. Teddy—out in the cafeteria, sweeping—eavesdropped unseen.

"Oh, she's all upset about that cute new guy, Teddy Behre," said a girl Teddy didn't recognize. "He was going with Sherrie, then he liked Cindy. But, Brenda sat with him in chapel. That's why Cindy ran off Sunday night. Now, Teddy likes Angie, her best friend."

"*Teddy Bear?* Isn't he that delinquent Leroy brought back from Kansas who has been in so much trouble with the police? I heard he was a runaway and stole thousands of dollars when he took some credit cards."

"Nah. He's really nice and he's only thirteen. But, he'll be fourteen in December. And he's sooooooo dreamy. His name isn't really Teddy Bear. It's *Theophilus.* Like in the Bible. Theophilus Behre." The girl mispronounced his last name to sound like "BAY-ur," which was incorrect. It actually sounded just like "bear."

Teddy grinned. His new girlfriend, Angie, was from Idaho, one of the only states he hadn't been to. She was great—

enthusiastic, full of energy, friendly to everybody. And she loved hanging on his arm. They were instant friends before they became "steadies."

The ranch had all sorts of rules: boyfriend-girlfriends were required to keep air space between them at all times. The only contact permitted was hand-holding and only after the boy asked permission from the girl's houseparents. Kissing was officially prohibited—which meant that lovebirds had to sneak around to do any serious lip-locking. Getting caught meant serious penalties, including forced separation.

Asking permission to hold hands consisted of the couple presenting themselves to the girl's housefather and requesting if they could "go" together—"go steady."

There were no romances permitted between kids in the same cottage—all of which were built on the same floor plan with three four-bunk bedrooms for the boys on the right of a big living room and three for the girls on the other side. The rationale: *you can't date your sister*. The ranch attempted to duplicate family life as closely as possible.

The night before, Teddy and Angie had presented themselves to her "dad" to ask to go together. "You again?" exclaimed Mr. Darley, Angie's housefather. "I thought you were going with Sherry. Or was it our little Ruthie?"

"Cindy. But we broke up," said Teddy, poking his glasses up on his nose.

The man nodded somberly. "Why should I trust you with one of my other girls? You're obviously a cad."

Angie giggled. The man fought a smile. He glowered at Teddy, who could tell he was enjoying every bit of it.

"I'll stick with Angie. We really like each other. We'll go together for a long time."

"Hmmmmmm. I don't know if I'd like that. Why don't you just be friends? Then, if you prove to me that your intentions are honorable, I'll give you permission."

"Oh, my intentions are *very* honorable."

"Well, you two come back Saturday. We'll talk about it then."

There were no orphans at the ranch. Most of the kids were throwaways like Teddy. Whenever Ouachita Hills Boys' Ranch staff members were invited to speak at churches or civic clubs, they preached about the growing problem of discarded kids, thundering that if the country couldn't take responsibility for its own future, it was headed for ruin.

The ranch made aggressive efforts to adopt out any youngsters clear of custodial claims—but prospective adoptive parents generally refused boys older than five, girls older than two, babies with handicaps, toddlers with disabilities, black kids, Oriental kids, Indian kids, Mexican kids or any combination thereof. The prime adoption candidate was a blond, blue-eyed, male, infant orphan—an incredible rarity since on the black market, desperate prospective parents would pay tens of thousands of dollars for such a child. So, few ever made it to the ranch—which instead gave refuge to children like Les, a hearing-impaired, speech-handicapped throwaway.

Yet the Christian ranch was a far, far better place than any state-run institution. In those crime academies—of which Teddy was an alumnus—there was little attempt made to teach kids any values, except the shallow disappointments of humanism. Most of the places were just warehouses for discarded offspring.

The vast majority of Ouachita Hills youngsters were there "temporarily." Tots were dropped off by weeping widowers who visited once a month and paid whatever tuition they could afford...or hyperactive kindergartners enrolled by hard-faced single mothers who couldn't take anymore and did not know how to enforce any sort of discipline.

Others were dropped off at the administration building without a word by parents who sped away as their four-year-old in the driveway screamed, or by stepfathers who had decided to do something about the unruly seven-year-olds who bore previous husbands' names, or by grandparents who couldn't bear up to admissions of defeat—and frequently by neighbors who found themselves stuck with abandoned twelve-year-olds whose parents had moved away without a word.

✐   ✐   ✐

A new first grader was assigned the bunk over Teddy's bed the day after the thirteen-year-old got contact lenses.

Carefully putting his battered old glasses in his top drawer, Teddy laid out all the contact-lens cleaning paraphernalia and was completely civil to his new roommate as he warned the kid never to touch any of his stuff.

The new boy was a rosy-cheeked six-year-old with bright, flashing brown eyes and curly blond hair—and an insecure smile that proclaimed a quick mind, but many yet-unresolved questions about himself.

He was readily cooperative and eager to please. Too eager, Teddy thought.

He wanted to be mothered.

Teddy was not interested.

The macho eighth grader had no intention of coddling some delicate little boy.

Teddy joked to Angie that he'd been given another "ankle biter" for a roomie—and it wasn't fair. He'd wanted somebody his own age. She told him about the time she'd had to share a room with two babies that a preacher had brought in.

Teddy grinned and self-consciously pushed his glasses up on his nose—glasses which were no longer there. He snickered at Angie and laughed.

"What's his name?" she asked.

"Thaddeus," chuckled Teddy. "Almost as bad as Theophilus. I'm going to have to find him a nickname."

"Oh, him," exclaimed Angie. She had daily chores in the ranch office. "He's from New Mexico, just like you."

"Really? Where in New Mexico?"

"I don't know."

Thaddeus's first night, the little boy wanted to talk.

Before the lights went out, Teddy meticulously cleaned his contact lenses for the third time that day. Thaddeus excitedly told Teddy and Sluggo all about helping his grandmother move into a nursing home in nearby Fayetteville.

"I came here because God told her that this was the place for me," said the six-year-old.

Teddy winced at him. "Right. God. You bet," he muttered under his breath.

When the lights were turned off, Sluggo rolled over and dozed off—because talking ended for him at "lights out." He followed conversation only by reading lips—impossible in the dark.

As Sluggo began snoring loudly, "My grandma really does love me," the new kid asserted in the dark, "but she can't hardly see anymore because of her cataracts and she can't fix meals because of her arthritis. And she keeps breaking her hip. One morning, we talked it over and decided it would be best if we both went to places where good people would take care of us."

Then, the little boy got quiet.

Teddy rolled over and was about to go to sleep, when: "Can we turn the light on?" whispered Thaddeus. "I'd kind of like that, please."

"No," snorted Teddy derisively.

"Please?"

"No!"

"Then, can I sleep with you?"

"WHAT? No way."

"*Please?*"

"Forget it."

"Then, can I sleep on the floor beside you?" There was a plaintive lilt to the six-year-old's voice that struck an unexpected chord with Teddy. "Why?" he asked gruffly.

"You know," said Thaddeus, bravely, his voice wavering just a bit, "monsters and stuff. They might get me."

"Monsters?" chortled Teddy. "You're too big for that. Look at Sluggo. He's already asleep. He's not afraid of any monsters."

Thaddeus began to whimper.

In irritation, Teddy turned on his flashlight. "Do you see any monsters? How are they going to get in here?"

The newcomer buried his face in his pillow, crying pitifully.

"Hey," said Teddy. "Look at me."

Thaddeus peered at him, sniffling.

"There are no monsters. Do you see any?"

The first grader shook his head.

Teddy turned out the light. As he laid back, he realized the kid had somehow scooted down onto the floor beside him. "I know you're there. Get in your bed. You'll catch a cold on the floor."

"What's it to you?" retorted Thaddeus tearfully. "You don't even care if I get eaten by a monster."

"Don't be crazy. *There are no monsters!* Get in your bed."

"Can I sleep in your bed with you?"

"Are you kidding? No."

The little boy began sobbing again. Teddy smirked. He could think of lots of times he'd cried himself to sleep. *It'd be good for the little sissy.*

But in the darkness, Teddy remembered being scared to death at a very dark and dirty foster home...being terrified at the diagnostic center in Wyoming...aching with loneliness under dark bridges...shivering in abandoned cars...hiding in trash dumpsters.

Surprising himself, "Get in," he ordered Thaddeus. "But, I'm warning you. You better keep to yourself."

In a flash, Thaddeus was in bed, warm and little against him. Almost immediately the little guy was asleep.

Teddy lay awake for quite some time, uncomfortable with the gentle child snuggled against him. Carefully, he scooted away— and fell asleep with one foot on the floor.

But in the wee hours, Teddy dreamed of a dark night not so long ago...*On a Greyhound bus somewhere near Rocky Mountains National Park, Colorado, ten-year-old Teddy had sat next to his drunken mother, hugging a dirty sack that had contained everything he owned in the world.*

A woman younger than Trixie boarded, lugging two toddlers. As his mom snored, Teddy had watched, hypnotized by the family. The toddlers adored their mother, snuggling her and obeying her whispered requests. They were well-scrubbed, well-fed and much-loved.

Teddy leaned over against Trixie and hugged her, waking her. She slapped him and told him to get back into his own seat.

Sniffling, he tried to read an Archie comic book he'd stolen from a newsstand at the last bus station. Then, the bus driver once again announced that everybody was going to have to get off the bus at the next station while the driver took a break. Tired passengers began gathering their belongings.

In a panicked, frenzy, the toddlers' young mother began grabbing scattered toys and clothes. And, before he realized what he was doing, Teddy was down on the floor helping her.

"Thank you, so much," she said to Teddy with a helpless smile. "Could you carry Kevin?"

Teddy happily picked up the older boy. And on a more crowded bus, they all rode on into Denver, Kevin up in Teddy's lap, Trixie coughing by the window, Kevin's mother whispering to three-year-old Travis.

For a while, Teddy drew silly pictures that held Kevin's interest. Then, Kevin took it and scribbled on Teddy's pad while Ted admired the work.

At one stop, Teddy almost missed re-boarding the bus while buying Kevin and his mother cans of pop from an outdoor vending machine. Then, Kevin sat on Teddy's knee and drank Dr. Pepper from a can and shared a candy bar from his mother's purse.

Outside of Boulder, Teddy and Kevin were playing a game in which the toddler dropped his pen between the seats, Teddy made a surprised face, Kevin giggled and crawled into the aisle to retrieve the pen.

"How old are these three?" asked a lady across the aisle.

"Which one?" asked the little boys' mother. Teddy turned and grinned, delighted that the woman thought he was part of the family.

Minutes later, Kevin, Travis and their mom disboarded outside of Denver. The four-year-old wailed loudly as his mother dragged him down the aisle.

"Daddy!" Kevin had called, tearfully.

The bus pulled out. Teddy had sat back, his eyes moist, his heart heavy.

Now, Teddy blinked at the ceiling. He squinted in the dark at Thaddeus. That was a weird name. The kid would have to become Tad.

Tadpole.

Miriam awoke confused in the darkness of the Fayetteville retirement center. "Father," she prayed silently. "I need peace. Help me. Help me." Suddenly, she was humming a simple, haunting tune that one of her young piano students had written once upon a time:

"Holy Spirit, help me ease my mind now ....
"Thank You, Father, as I speak the thought I know
"That You are there all around me
"I know that You're here where I'm walking.
As I wander through the valley of the shadow of death,
I fear no evil, for I know and have great joy—
"That You are there all around me
"I know that You're here where I'm walking."

"Yes," she whispered. But suddenly in the midnight darkness, she found herself again assaulted by confusion and turmoil. Why was she here in this strange place so far from her home? Who were these people? What was happening? Where was little Thaddeus? Where had they taken him? "Father," she cried out silently. "What have they done with my little grandson? Protect him, Mighty Father! You alone are his strength and his protection. He is all alone! Lord God, our Creator, build for him an island in the raging sea and set him on it, protected and loved." Again, she was filled with peace. "Yes, Lord," she whispered. "Thank You."

Then, the terror returned.

"Lord God!" she cried out silently. "Banish this fear gripping my heart. Let no bad thing touch me or Thaddeus! Surround him with Your mighty angels. Father, I can do nothing here! Nothing! But You are there with him. Protect him in Your mighty way."

Miles away, Thaddeus stirred in his sleep.

There was a peaceful grin on his face. And one arm hugged his new thirteen-year-old Teddy Bear. That morning, Teddy began calling the new kid by his new nickname. Thaddeus took to it instantly—introducing himself to his teachers in his new classes at school as "Tadpole."

At lunch, the six-year-old excitedly spotted Teddy in the cafeteria line and charged over to stand with him.

"Who's this, your little brother?" guffawed a ninth grader in line behind Teddy.

The two brown-eyed, curly-haired blond roommates squinted at each other, then at the older boy.

"Hey," growled Teddy. "Yeah, this is my little brother Tad. I'm Ted. You got a problem with that, big mouth?"

"You look just alike," snickered the ninth grader.

Teddy grinned, putting his arms around the shorter boy's chest, hugging him under the armpits. "I bet you've never even been to New Mexico."

Tad looked up at Teddy in surprise.

"I been to Canada," defended the ninth grader.

"What a doofus!" exclaimed Teddy, swinging Tad in the air. "I said New Mexico, not Mexico. Tadpole here and me, we're from New Mexico, the forty-seventh state of the Union. I bet you didn't even know that New Mexico was part of the Confederacy.

"Huh?" exclaimed the older boy.

"What a loser!" snickered Teddy. "New Mexico was occupied by Texas during the Civil War. We became part of the South. Tadpole and me, we're southern boys from New Mexico!"

✐   ✐   ✐

"Bear," yelled Tad, bursting into their room. Behind him, Sluggo bolted in, excited. Both were caked with mud. "Bear, come down to the bat cave!"

Teddy looked up from his homework.

"Thi' guy fwom the new'paper in Tulsa ih' here an' we went with 'im," exclaimed Sluggo. *This guy from the newspaper in Tulsa is here and we went in with him.*

"They need kids in the pictures," exclaimed Tad. "Come on. The cave is neat."

Excitedly, Sluggo nodded his agreement.

"Did you guys get your picture taken?" drawled Teddy.

"Naw yet. CumOW!" answered Sluggo. *Not yet. Come on!*

"The cave's great," repeated Tad enthusiastically. "You have to crawl in the mud on your stomach, then you come to this river and it's cold and you have to wade. And there's little salamanders."

"Yeah, an' they' bwind!" exclaimed Les. *Yeah, and they're blind.*

"We came back to get you. Come on," pleaded Tad. "We'll show you. The newspaper guy's still in there."

Behind the thrilled pair, Teddy jogged. Both first graders rattled off all the things they were going to show him:

• the sleeping bats—which you weren't supposed to touch—
• the big room with the stalagtite hanging from the ceiling,
• the blind salamanders, the ladder....

The entrance gate was about 18-inches square—and although usually locked, it was wide open.

"That' 'cuz ifu can' squeeze thwu', you woon be able ge' pas' Fat Man's Agony 'nyway. Da's dis cwack you have do cwaw thwu' do get to da wake." explained Sluggo. *That's because if you can't squeeze through, you wouldn't be able to get past Fat Man's Agony anyway. That's this crack you have to crawl through to get to the lake.*

Tadpole and Sluggo led the way. Behind the excited little guys, Teddy crept down a damp, muddy bank. The low ceiling was covered with tiny crystals, which Sluggo cautioned Teddy not to touch. They could hear the voices of the others echoing in the distant depths of one of the bigger rooms.

"We gotta follow the river!" Tad exclaimed, pointing his light down into a boggy-looking pit at the bottom of the bank. "Stay on the side where it's shallow."

Teddy shone his light on the water, but didn't see any salamanders.

"Come ow!" enthused Sluggo, the water up to his knees.

As the boys slogged through the muck, "Ted Beah, ih guy Jay ih cawwin' Tabpole 'Gayboy' at 'choo'," volunteered Sluggo: *Teddy Bear, this guy Jay is calling Tadpole 'Gayboy' at school.* Since Sluggo had to read lips, he turned and held his flashlight so that it illuminated Ted's face—so he could see Teddy's mouth and "hear" what Teddy had to say in response.

"Oh, yeah?" mused Teddy, stopping and peering up at the ceiling.

"Eh'bo'y eh ha' 'tawtid it, too. You be'ah bea' Jay *UP* sin' you 'i bwuvver," declared Sluggo: *Everybody else has started it, too. You better beat Jay up since you're his brother.*

"Yeah?" drawled the thirteen-year-old. "Well, I don't know."

"Jay' *MEAN* an' geh'n fights," said Sluggo: *Jay's mean and gets in fights.*

"You don't say?" said Teddy. He squinted at Tad, who was uncharacteristically silent.

"You cah beah'im up *easy*, Ted' Beah" said Sluggo: *You can beat him up easy, Teddy Bear.*

Tadpole looked up hopefully.

"Well ..." hedged Teddy, startled by the sincere request he saw in Tad's eyes—and knowing he could hardly go beat up a first grade bully.

The other kids' voices faded in the distance. "Come on," gestured Tadpole urgently. "Sluggo, I know where they're at—

the big room." Ahead in the mud, Sluggo was already down on his knees, scooting into a dark tunnel.

"Where is he going?" exclaimed Teddy.

"The big room. Come on," nudged Tad. "First, we gotta get through Fat Man's Agony."

They must have crawled for five minutes—down on their stomachs in gooey mud when just ahead of Teddy, six-year-old Tad turned and stopped.

"Bear," he whispered. "Am I gay?" The first grader's voice was high, worried.

Stunned by the question, Teddy paused.

"*GAY?*" he exclaimed, tensing. Suddenly wary of who might be listening, he sat back and clunked his head on the low ceiling.

"Dang, Tadpole," he said. "That's a stupid question."

Immense hurt welled up in the littler boy's eyes.

No, you're not gay," said Teddy softly, quickly. "That's one thing you're *not*. You're too little to know anything about that kind of stuff."

"Sluggo says I won't fight Jay because I'm gay," said Tadpole, softly. "Sluggo says I'm a girl."

"Sluggo said that? Well, he doesn't know. You're not gay."

Tadpole sniffled in the darkness. "Why did he say that?"

"Tadpole," said Teddy impatiently. "You're not gay. Believe me, I know what gay is and you're not. Just because you won't fight somebody doesn't make you gay. That's stupid. Sluggo is too ignorant to know even what it means. Do you understand me?"

Tadpole nodded in Teddy's flashlight beam. But he looked unconvinced.

"Listen," said Teddy, "I'm a lot older than you are and I've been around stuff, you know? Some people say that gays are okay and all that. But the ones I've been around like little boys and are really, really sick. They want you to walk around naked when their friends come around so they can all look at you and get weird with each other. They do disgusting stuff that I'm not even going to tell you."

"Wow," whispered the first grader.

Ahead of the two, Sluggo began hooting loudly that he'd reached the bat cave. "Come on," urged Teddy.

Minutes later, standing in the spacious room, Teddy began inspecting the sleeping mammals clutching onto ledges on the side walls.

"Don't touch 'em," instructed Tad. "They might have rabies."

The next room was enormous—even had a lake. Inner tubes and a pump waited on the bank in case you wanted to kick across to an island with large stalactites and stalagmites.

As Sluggo jumped in with an inner tube and began hooting at Ted and Tad to join him, "Did you do it?" asked Tad softly.

"What?"

"Do disgusting stuff?"

Teddy's eyes narrowed threateningly. "No. Don't you ever tell anybody I told you about that stuff."

"I won't," promised Tadpole.

"I hated those people," muttered Teddy. "I wanted to kill them. And I never, ever, wanted to be like any of them."

"Yeah," whispered Tad. "I know."

"Listen," said Teddy. "You're not that way. Not at all. And you never will be."

Tad grinned. And he attacked his brother. Whooping, the two wrestled in the mud, tickling each other—Teddy pinning the first grader's knee to his forehead, then letting him go. Yelling, Tadpole jumped into the lake, shouting at Sluggo to bring the inner tube back.

On the other side of the lake the soaked boys found a small room where, when they shone their flashlights at the ceiling for several minutes then turned them off, some of the tiny stalactites would glow. Then they paddled back across.

Sluggo's wet flashlight began to go dim.

Shivering, Teddy suggested they'd better catch up to the newspaper photographer and the other kids.

"Right," whispered the wet, trembling Tadpole. And off the chilled trio marched.

Teddy began to sense something was wrong when the shivering Sluggo paused a long time at the top of a long bank. Teddy flashed his dimming light along the opposite wall.

"Haven't we been here before?" asked the thirteen-year-old.

Sluggo suddenly began to cry.

"Hey," exclaimed Teddy. "What's the matter with you?"

"We'ah lost," blubbered the kid, losing his composure completely. "An' I'm cold!"

Teddy frowned. "Hmmmmmmmm," he said. "Let's do jumping jacks. Come on —" He jumped into calisthenic position. "You two turn off your lights. We'll just use mine to save the batteries. Come on, jumping jacks—1, 2, 3, and 4 ..."

"No," wept Sluggo in his usual semi-intelligible babble. He huddled next to Tadpole. "I can't. If I turn out my light, I can't hear you. We're gonna die. We're gonna starve to death in here and rot."

Teddy snickered. He punched the shivering, worried Tadpole in the shoulder. "Look who the sissy is," he whispered. "All right! Jumping jacks. Come on! This works. I used to do it when I was really freezing. Come on!"

Like some kind of insane, subterranean aerobics instructor, Teddy cajoled the first graders into running in place, touching their toes, then bouncing wildly.

Their spirits lifted considerably, they ran up and down the rocky bank until they were panting and laughing. Fortunately, the cave was a constant seventy-two degrees.

But the feeling of being lost was not good. "This ain't that big a cave," Teddy mused as the three poked through a new, unfamiliar room. "Plus, when we don't show up for supper, they'll start looking for us."

He studied the situation, then dug a pen out of his back pocket and peeled off his still-damp T-shirt. He began tearing his shirt into strips.

"Wha' you doin'?" exclaimed Sluggo.

"We gotta tear this up into little pieces. Then, we gotta put little arrows on each piece. Here, I'll tear, you make arrows."

Excitedly, Tadpole agreed, peeling off his shirt, too and tearing it into strips.

"Wha' for?" protested Sluggo.

"Everywhere we go, we'll put down pieces, showing which way we went before."

The marker system worked. With Sluggo worrying that it was against the rules to leave the cave all littered up, the three boys worked their way back to Fat Man's Agony and back outside. They showed up at their cottage just before dinner, all three covered with mud—Tad riding on Teddy's bare shoulders.

"We got lost in the cave!" yelled the excited first grader. "And Teddy Bear saved us!" Sluggo bellowed his agreement.

"What happened to you?" exclaimed Mrs. Gilliam, their house mom.

"The newspaper photographer went off and left us in the bat cave," shrugged Teddy, crossing his arms self-consciously. "But we got out okay. No big deal."

"Teddy Bear saved us," hooted Tad again.

The next day at lunch, Teddy wandered over to the grade school playground. Tadpole spotted him and jumped off the merry-go-round. *"Bear!"* he trumpeted, running over.

"Hey," said Teddy, glancing around conspiratorially. "Look at the water tower. Stare at it."

The six-year-old did. Sluggo charged up and belted out greetings.

"Hey. Stare at the water tower," said Teddy. "Which one is Jay? Both of you stare at the water tower and tell me what he looks like. Don't look at him. Stare at the water tower."

"He'a wun nock'n' peopah offa 'wings," pronounced Les: *He's the one knocking people off the swings.* Tadpole pointed.

Teddy casually turned. Climbing to the top of the swings was an enormous first grader with dingy, reddish hair. He was bellowing like a bull moose and trying to catch a laughing, evading second grader.

"Okay," said Teddy. "You two go back to the merry-go-round and stay there no matter what happens."

The younger boys obeyed.

Casually, Teddy strolled over to the swings. "Hey, Jay," he greeted cheerfully.

"Get away from here," yelled the kid. "I'm the troll and I'll gobble you up."

"I'm a warrior angel," said Teddy. "I'll turn you into a pillar of salt if you give me any trouble."

Jay stared at him incredulously.

"I heard about something you did to my little brother and I thought I better warn you," said the thirteen-year-old. "You know what I mean?"

"HUH?" said Jay. "Who are you?"

"I'm Tadpole's big brother, Teddy Bear, and he's really upset with you. I'd watch it if I were you.

"YOU're Teddy Bear?" guffawed Jay, climbing up to the safety of the top bar. "Teddy Bear! Teddy Bear!"

Teddy stared nonchalantly at the sky.

"Jay, I don't think you know how dangerous ol' Tad is. He's my little brother and you *know* that I killed a guy once. Shoot," Teddy spat dramatically on the ground. "There was this time once when Tad kept bein' picked on and we almost couldn't stop him from killing that guy."

Jay was staring at Teddy with a furrowed brow. He glanced around and spotted Tadpole and Sluggo staring at the water tower.

"Man, our family's got terrible tempers," said Teddy. "Why, one time back in New Mexico, I saw Tadpole kill a horse with a two-by-four just 'cuz the thing bucked him off. Shoot, you make my little brother Tadpole mad and there's no telling what'll happen to you in your sleep, you know, after it's dark? You know what I mean? After lights out? I mean, do you have any idea of the kind of stuff that can get you? Do you always look under your bed? Or in the closet?"

Trembling, Jay didn't say anything.

Solemnly shaking his head, Teddy spat again. "Be sure to look under your bed tonight," he drawled. "But the best thing you could do is to leave Tadpole alone. He's my brother, you know. *And in our family, we kill people.*"

Then Teddy strolled off.

That night, Tad's fighting lessons began. Teddy was immensely relieved to find that Tadpole was left-handed, just like Teddy. "Us lefties have a great advantage," Ted instructed. "Nobody can figure out how to fight us. It's like we come on backwards. Square off."

Grinning, Tad held up his fists. Sluggo followed suit. Aloofly, their newest roommate, a kid named Clive Simpson, watched from his bunk.

"I don't have to fight," offered Tad, confidently. "God will fight my battles for me."

"Uh, right," said Teddy. "Look, if I wanted to punch you in the stomach, all I'd have to do is *wham!*" Suddenly, he jabbed Tadpole in the gut—but not hard enough to hurt. "You were wide open, like a barn door. Here, stand like this:"

He turned so that his shoulder faced the six-year-old. His left fist was clenched in front of his stomach. His right fist was in front of his face. "Now, watch your right elbow. You can block anything with it, too. And use your knee. Pull it up to block. What's gonna hurt you most, getting hit in the stomach or in the knee?"

"'Tomack," blurted Sluggo, taking up the stance.

Tad winced. Humoring Teddy, he adopted the stance, but, "I'm not going to have to do anything to Jay," he said confidently. "God fights my battles, just like He did Jehoshaphat's in the Bible. I just have to praise Him and watch Him be God."

"Right," said Teddy. "But in case He doesn't send in a company of angels, let's be ready, huh? Standing sideways gives Jay no target at all. He can't hit your stomach without swinging all the way around where you can—*wham!*—just knock his lights out. He can't hit your ribs, because your elbow is going to block it. He can't hit your face, because this fist is right up there."

Tadpole squinted and held the stance—although he obviously thought it was unnecessary.

"Okay," said Teddy. "I'm gonna be Jay. I'm gonna try to hit you. Dance with me. If I move, you move. Give me no target no matter where I go."

Taking up a more traditional boxer stance, Teddy began moving around Tad, who stood still, a foolish look on his face.

"Come on, Tadpole, get off your heels. Come on, bounce. Stand on this part of your foot." Teddy patted the ball of his own foot. "Come on. Sluggo can do it. See? Duck and dodge. Come on, Tad."

The three bounced together, Sluggo enthusiastic, Tadpole patronizing his big brother.

"That's it," said Teddy. "Now, watch this:"

Slowly, he waved his right fist, then awkwardly swung it at Tadpole. The first grader ducked. Then, out of nowhere, Teddy slammed his left fist into the boy's face.

"HEY!" protested Tadpole.

"That's your secret weapon, Lefty," said Teddy. "Get his attention with a right, then whallop him with your deadly left. Jay'll never figure it out. Fighters just aren't used to anything coming from the left. They just can't accept that somebody's gonna blast them from the wrong side. It looks too crazy and awkward."

Accommodatingly, Tadpole practiced the right jab, then the left haymaker. Around and around Teddy and Sluggo danced. The older boy faked out the first grader every time.

"Okay," said Teddy. "Watch." He charged Sluggo, grabbing the deaf kid's right fist, then pushing him backwards while fanning his face with left jabs.

"That'll just blow his socks off," said Teddy. "Jay's gonna expect you to be scared. So, you attack. You jam his good arm up into his shoulder and let him have it with your left. It doesn't matter which way he's turned. If he's turned the other way, just hammer him in the back of the head."

Tadpole practiced the attack.

"Wow," said Clive. "The little twerp can do that one."

"Shut up," said Teddy. "Okay, Tadpole, we gotta practice this every day. I gave Jay a scare today, but in about a week, he'll challenge you to fight. And you're going to plaster him and make yourself a reputation. You're gonna show 'em that nobody messes around with Ted Behre's little brother."

After lights out, "Teddy Bear?" whispered Tadpole, leaning down from his bunk. "We're not supposed to fight. God fights our battles for us."

"Well," snickered Teddy. "Sometime you gotta stick up for yourself. In times like that, God'll help you win. You can't lose. Who started this fight?"

"Jay did."

"Who kept making fun of you?"

"Jay."

"Who wanted there to be peace?"

"Me."

"So, who is right?"

"I don't know."

"You are," said Teddy. "You, Tadpole. Are you gonna start anything if Jay leaves you alone?"

"No. I want to be friends."

"So, he'll be starting the trouble and you'll be ending it."

"Jesus said to turn the other cheek."

"Yeah," Teddy retorted. "But He didn't say you can't blow them away if they hit you a second time."

"Hey, why don't you guys go to sleep?" complained Clive.

"Shut up, Preppie," said Teddy.

That night Teddy had a dream he'd had before. Tonight, it was vivid in detail—and troubling.

Teddy—standing atop Mexico's great Aztec Pyramid of the Sun—frowned solemnly, his head held high. In front of him, from a tilted couch atop the pyramid, an old man received a vast crowd's adoration. He turned weakly and looked in sur-

prise at the boy. "Well, Xocoy," the old man rasped. There was an aged cynicism in his voice. "You came."

Teddy sat down on a ceremonial pedestal. He glanced almost disdainfully at the Indians. "Why did you waste your time here, Dad?" His young, high voice was strident with emotion. "Why can't we change it? I'll go back and we'll do stuff again and pick somewhere better. I'll stay and we'll do great stuff together."

The old man suddenly coughed—a deep, rattling rasp. "Don't you know who you are?" he rasped.

"What?" demanded Teddy.

"You are the fulfillment of the great prophecies. You will be the mighty one who leads the final rebellion."

"No," rasped Teddy, his voice a terrified whisper.

And then he awoke.

His dorm was silent—except for the sounds of Clive's, Tadpole's and Sluggo's breathing.

What did such a dream mean?

Troubled, he lay awake—staring at the ceiling and trying to figure it out.

⬿   ⬿   ⬿

He was on his way to lunch when he saw the mob of little kids headed around in back of the gymnasium. No teachers were in sight. He clutched his books and sprinted for the back of the gym. There, in a wide, dusty circle out back, stood Jay and an ashen-faced Tadpole.

A defiant Sluggo was standing beside Tad, staring down the large Jay and flashing karate punches in the air. A couple of eleven-year-olds from Jay's cottage were trying to officiate, briefing everybody that there would be no groin punching, no kicking, no biting ....

Then they stepped back. Sluggo was dragged back by somebody.

"I don't want to fight," Tadpole announced, his high voice clear. "You'll have to hit me first."

Older kids hooted. Jay was obviously the heavy favorite. He was twice Tadpole's size. Sluggo shoved his way back to the front, bobbing up and down, babbling his support for his roomie. The older boys grabbed him again.

Jay began to make fun of Tadpole, pretending to be a monkey, then let loose with a baboon scream and swung, clobbering Tad on the side of the head.

Stunned, Teddy's little brother tottered.

Sluggo howled, trying to wrestle away from the bigger boys. Then, he hooted victoriously as Teddy Bear was suddenly there.

Teddy grabbed Sluggo by the collar and held his arms to his side.

Tadpole struggled to his feet, tears flowing. He looked at Teddy.

"You cannot lose," whispered the older boy.

Tadpole nodded. Then, slowly, deliberately, he turned his head and presented Jay with a second cheek.

Jay began making train noises and, with the crowd cheering, he swung again, knocking Tadpole to the ground. The six-year-old didn't get up this time.

One hand firmly grasping the loudly weeping Sluggo's collar, Teddy pushed kids aside. Sluggo babbled unintelligible advice as Teddy gently helped Tad to his feet. Kids jeered. Tears dripped down the dusty first grader's chin.

"Come on, tough guy," Teddy whispered to his little brother. "Okay, Tadpole, now's your chance. You've proved your point. Now watch your stance. Remember your moves. Try not to kill him."

"He' mean. He dohn' fi' faih," howled Sluggo: *He's mean He doesn't fight fair.*

"Sluggo's right," agreed Teddy loudly, for the other kids to hear. "Tadpole, you and me, we don't put up with bullies. So, it's time for you to put an end to this punk for everybody's sake. Your cause is right. You are the peacemaker."

Tad stood, dropping into his much-practiced stance. Loudly, "You aren't ever going to pick on anybody else, Jay," Tadpole pronounced, his high voice wavering.

The crowd roared with laughter. Teddy growled loudly and crossed his arms. Sluggo yammered incomprehensible oaths. Then, just like Teddy had coached him. Tadpole gripped both fists under his chin. His eyes on Jay, he bowed. *"Ichi, ni, san, shi,"* he declared aloud. The kids quieted, nobody knowing that the words were just "One, two, three, four," in Japanese.

Jay cautiously squared off.

Then, instead of holding his guard up, Tadpole went into a stance clenching both fists down at his waist.

Teddy groaned.

"You stupid Gayboy," sneered Jay. "Why don't you cry?"

Then—as if in slow motion—Tadpole swung an awkward right. Jay hooted and ducked. And to everyone's amazement, Jay stumbled over his own feet. He grabbed at Tad's wrist, but pitched face-forward into the dust.

Just like he had practiced, Tadpole beautifully punched multiple times with months of pent-up fury. But he did not touch Jay—who was sprawled on the ground.

Sluggo whooped in delight.

Struggling to his knees, Jay held his nose in pain, crying. Blood dripped from between his fingers.

A twelve-year-old housebrother bent over Jay. "He says his nose is broke," the sixth grader announced. "It wasn't fair. Tadpole's arms were too long."

"Here comes a teacher!" yelled somebody.

As the kids scattered, Teddy grabbed Tadpole and headed through the woods to their house. In the bathroom, he ran water on a washcloth and grabbed a bar of soap. Then, he ducked into their room. "Take off your shirt," he ordered.

Tadpole complied, Sluggo devotedly helping him.

And sitting on the bunk, Teddy quickly removed the dirt and dust of the playground. Sluggo tried to comb Tad's hair as Teddy inspected him. There were no bruises.

"Smooth down your hair and put on another shirt, then go watch TV," Teddy ordered. "Do you hurt anywhere?"

"No. I won, didn't I?"

"Yes. And everybody knows it. He quit. I was proud of you."

"So wa' I," pronounced Sluggo in determined seriousness. He fanned the air with punches. "You wea'y show'm, di'n't he, Ted Beah?"

Teddy grunted an incomprehensible answer.

The next day, Teddy was called into the ranch director's office. Behind his desk glowered the grade school principal. In a chair sat a red-faced Tadpole and a beaming Sluggo between Mr. Gilliam, and Jay's housefather, Mr. Gorley.

"Hey, Tadpole, Sluggo," said Teddy. He smiled at everyone.

"Hi, Beah," croaked Sluggo.

"What's going on here?" asked MacDonald, calmly.

"What do you mean?"

"Your first grade roommate here almost killed the playground bully yesterday," said MacDonald. "Are you going to tell me you don't know anything about it?"

Teddy glanced at Tadpole, who stared at his feet, grinning.

"Oh, that," said Teddy. "Tad never hit him. Jay just fell down. No kidding. Jay was calling him 'Gayboy' and people were saying Tad was a homo because he wouldn't fight and they were picking on him, so I just showed Tad a few things to do in case Jay ever punched him."

"Just what did you teach him?" asked MacDonald darkly. "Gerald LaGrange has a black eye and a broken nose. Little Thaddeus Grey here doesn't even have a scratch. Gene Gilliam didn't even know there'd been a fight."

"Tad le' Jay hit'm fuss," piped up Leslie. "Then, Tad tun' udda' cheek juss wike Jesus."

"You should hear the story the teachers are telling," said the grade school principal. "The rumor is that your little room-mates have become karate experts. Les has been telling his teacher he knows how to break boards."

"He can," admitted Teddy.

"What did you teach these two?" repeated MacDonald.

"Well," said Teddy. "A little Okinawan self-defense."

"Okinawan?" exploded MacDonald. "What, karate? Ju-jitsu? Ninjitsu? Did you give them guns, too?"

"They don't know any complicated kicks," said Teddy. "See, back when I used to live in this old hotel in New York City, I needed to know what to do if anybody gave me any trouble, so I took lessons at the Boys' Club."

"Have you got a degreed belt?" demanded MacDonald.

"Brown," said Teddy. "I was given an honorary brown, but I really hadn't earned it. I don't know all the *kata* and formal *kumite,* but I wear brown. Plus, I didn't like to fight browns in tournaments. I had to quit when my teacher went to New Jersey and the subway didn't go there."

The adults stared at the boys.

Teddy blinked penitently, shrugging self-consciously.

MacDonald stared at him. He turned to the principal.

"Okay, thanks, Jack," he said.

The man stalked to the door. Gilliam and Gorley stood, too. Teddy turned to go.

"Teddy Bear, Tadpole, stay put," said MacDonald.

After the others were gone, MacDonald motioned for Teddy to sit down. Ted plopped down on the sofa.

"Well, Theophilus, you're all full of surprises, aren't you? Mrs. Gilliam says you know how to play the piano."

Teddy grinned and nodded. "Only classical stuff," he said.

MacDonald didn't smile.

"I couldn't let Tadpole here be made fun of," blurted Teddy. "He was crying about it at night and stuff. I had to teach him how to fight. But, believe me, he can hold his own."

"Thaddeus has been telling people that you two are brothers. Mr. Gorley thinks you really are. I know otherwise. What's this all about?"

"Well," said Teddy, slowly. "We've just kind of adopted each other. I've always wanted to have a brother. So, me and Tadpole we thought we'd be brothers. My cousin Janny had a big brother, Hans, and he taught us stuff and looked out for us and stuff. Their dad was going to adopt me, but didn't want to after Janny ... you know, died."

"We're not really brothers. It's a lie, isn' it?" blurted Tadpole. He began to sniffle. "We shouldn't tell people that should we?"

MacDonald looked at the first grader. "Come here...*Tadpole,*" he said. He glanced at Teddy. He took the little boy into his lap. "Thaddeus, do you love Teddy Bear like a brother?"

Tadpole grinned widely and nodded with enthusiasm.

MacDonald lifted an eyebrow and looked at Teddy. "Teddy Bear, do you love Tadpole?"

"How do you mean?" asked the older boy, warily. "We're not weird or anything. We're not...you know."

"That's good," said MacDonald. "Do you love Tadpole like you would a little brother?"

"I would, I mean, if he really were," growled Teddy, "But, well..."

"But you don't love anybody?" probed MacDonald.

The macho Teddy grinned, then grimaced as he saw Tadpole's horror—shock and betrayal all over his face. "I mean," blurted Teddy, "Okay, if I were to, you know, love anybody in the world it would be Tadpole. Tad is different. You know, Tad and me, we been through stuff together. You know what I mean ...."

Immense hurt in his eyes, Tad began to blubber.

Squirming, "Hey ..." hedged Teddy, grimacing uncomfortably at the first grader. "Okay! Yeah, I love you," he exclaimed. Assuringly, he winked at the boy, then squinted self-consciously at Leroy.

Tad beamed, pleased.

MacDonald nodded, thoughtfully.

"Well," the superintendent said. "You know, I'm in charge here and if you guys want to be brothers, I say you are brothers. Neither one of you has anybody who will object. I believe Tad's grandmother will be quite pleased. So, you are brothers."

A chill of excitement went up Teddy's back.

"Forever?" exclaimed Tadpole.

MacDonald looked inquiringly at Teddy. "You're taking on quite a commitment, Teddy Bear. Maybe this isn't what you have in mind."

Teddy, tingling all over, grinned, wrinkling his nose at Tad. "Forever," Teddy Bear announced dramatically into the first grader's earnest, brown eyes. "And I mean that. You understand me, kiddo?"

The six-year-old whooped.

       ✐   ✐   ✐

That night, Tadpole waited until Sluggo and Clive were asleep, then climbed down with Teddy. His head on Teddy's chest, he fell asleep.

And in the midnight darkness, Teddy dreamed again.

Standing atop the great Aztec Pyramid of the Sun, he frowned solemnly, his head held high. On a couch in front of him, old Quetzalcoatl received the vast crowd's adoration. He turned weakly and looked in surprise at Teddy. "Well, Xocoy," the old man rasped. "Don't you know who you are?"

Teddy awoke.

Staring at the ceiling, he glanced at Tad, still dozing peacefully beside him. Teddy felt for the first time a realization of the deep protectiveness, the intense guardianship, that he felt for the boy.

Was it because for so many years he had ached—longed—for somebody to watch out for him? Now, if he couldn't have a dad, at least he could be one for this incredible kid.

Was it normal? Teddy winced, worried.

Was it "weird"?

In the midnight stillness, Teddy wrestled with terrible doubts. For, despite his glib assurances to Tadpole, Ted had deep, serious concerns of being weird—if not sexually, then perhaps something equally unimaginable and terrifying.

Maybe, he had worried a number of times, he was secretly a super-sicko psycho.

Now, in the night's stillness, Teddy had a sudden realization: *He would never hurt Tadpole. No, he had been sent to help the little boy.*

Sent?

Gently, Teddy rested his hand on the boy's curly head and knew the child's well-being was far too important for Teddy to ever injure him.

Teddy knew he would never betray this one's trust.

No, Teddy understood deep within himself: *This one is important.*

Four hundred people crowded into the circus tent on the boys' ranch playground. The first speaker at the seventeenth annual Ouachita Hills Evangelism Conference was waxing eloquent.

Teddy and a dozen other boys, including, Clive, Sluggo and Tadpole were pulling chairs off of a flatbed truck, loading them onto a forklift, then setting up rows on the edge of the tent. Teddy had jogged after the forklift about five times when he decided to just hop a ride.

The adult running the little tractor—which was actually a front-end loader with a forklift attachment—didn't see Teddy. He touched the foot pedal that brought down the boom. The folding arms sank onto Teddy's foot.

Teddy screamed and toppled off, his foot pinned, his head bouncing off the hard ground. The audience stood, gawking as the tractor dragged Teddy twenty feet before the counselor realized what was going on. He lifted the forklift arm and people Teddy didn't know were tugging off his shoe and putting a rolled-up suit coat under his battered head.

Within minutes, his foot had swelled to twice normal.

It should have hurt.

But Teddy was unconscious.

Filled with an urgency that she did not understand, "Lord, be with Thaddeus," whispered Miriam Julian in the retirement center. "Father, I don't know what's wrong, but I sense a terrible thing.

"Lord...it's not Thaddeus, is it? It's his friend, this older boy that so fills his life—this one Thaddeus calls Teddy. Why do I feel such fear for this boy, Lord? Father, fear is never from you. So, I denounce this dark dread, this horror of death that fills my heart with such emptiness and...hopelessness. You are my hope, O Lord. You are my joy. You so love my little Thaddeus—

and this boy who Leroy says needs Thaddeus to be his little brother.

"Well, Lord, You made this Teddy and You have a great purpose for his life. Now, watch over this Teddy, Father, protect him from this great evil that I believe wishes to overtake him. Father, show him the plan You have for his life."

Her room was silent.

Miriam smiled.

"O Father," she whispered. "O Lord, you gave Thaddeus this big brother. Now, Father, let Thaddeus show this boy the only true reason for living. Let Thaddeus know the joy of leading Teddy to know You."

Teddy reeled into painful consciousness.

Tadpole was hugging his chest and crying hysterically. He stuck an ear to Teddy's ribs, listening for a heartbeat. People were yelling. Sluggo was screaming and jumping up and down on the bleachers.

People were crowding around so close that Teddy couldn't breathe. One of the houseparents began pulling Tad away. Then, people were carrying Teddy outside as Tad screamed.

"It's okay!" Teddy would remember Mr. MacDonald yelling over the chaos as he lifted the hysterical Tadpole into the ambulance where Teddy lay. "He's gonna be all right!" assured the man.

Teddy gritted his teeth and tried to grin at his little brother, who knelt down beside him, his face white with fear. Then, trying to be brave, Teddy tried not to scream as a medic pulled off his sock. The world began swirling again. Adults he didn't know leaned into his face.

"Father," prayed Miriam Julian. "I don't understand Your ways. I certainly don't understand what is going on tonight that

I am filled with such urgency for my little Thaddeus's Teddy Bear. But protect that boy's life, O Lord.

"Spare him, O Lord.

"You sent him to us for a special reason—and in response to our great need. Now, protect and strengthen that boy. Lord, give Thaddeus great strength and understanding—and faith! Lord, build up my grandson's faith!

"Let this be a good time in which my grandson sees Your miraculous ways!"

"Jesus, heal my big brother," Teddy heard the tearful Tadpole weeping beside him. The little boy's hands were clasped together as he prayed. "Make Teddy's foot okay, please. Make it quit hurting. And make his head okay, too. Don't let his brain be messed up like that kid he told me about in Texas."

"Hey, Tadpole!" whispered Teddy, between clenched teeth. He jerked his tortured foot out of somebody's hand. It slid down and hit the cot. Teddy screamed in agony, passing out again.

A blue light flashed over the Emergency Room door. "Dear, Jesus," whispered Tad. "We're here. Let Teddy be okay."

Adults were rushing around—picking up the gurney and rushing the wheeled cot down a hallway. "Bear," whispered Tad.

People milled in a little room.

"Hey, Tadpole," whispered Ted.

"Jesus," prayed the little boy. "Make Bear's head okay and make his foot healed, too, amen." He stared at Teddy, a pleased look on his face.

As Ted's foot began to burn, he screamed. More adults scurried around in the swirl as other adults talked and filled out paperwork. Mr. MacDonald put his hands on Tad's shoulders and bent into Teddy's face. A nurse whispered assurances as she took an x-ray with a little portable machine.

A doctor came into the curtained-off area where Teddy lay on a bed. Tadpole was gingerly massaging his foot.

"Is your name really Teddy Behre?" asked the doctor squinting over Teddy's chart.

"You bet," exclaimed little Tad, his voice high and filled with pride.

"How old are you?"

"Eight."

"I meant him."

"Oh," said Tad. "He's gonna be fifteen in December."

"Hmmmmm," said the man, looking at the x-rays. "You must be Tadpole. I understand you are brothers." He pushed his glasses up on his nose. "Well, Tadpole, I think he's going to live. Nothing's broken. I thought I saw a nasty cut on your head, but I see it was just a scratch. What happened, anyway?"

Teddy didn't move. His little brother smiled mystically.

Teddy's foot had burned and throbbed and stung like a thousand little needles were pushing out right after Tad had prayed. Now, it was numb. The swelling was going down.

The room no longer whirled, either. Teddy didn't even feel light-headed. "Where's my shoe?" he rasped.

That evening, he strolled back into the tent with Tadpole sitting on his shoulders. Surprised at himself, he turned various shades of crimson as four hundred people stood and applauded.

From his shoulders, Tad cheered and gently hugged his brother's tender skull. Sluggo bounced on the bleachers, hooting his delight as the roar rose from the crowd.

     ✐   ✐   ✐

"My time on earth seemingly is over," whispered Miriam in the darkness. "Yet, You do not take me. Why? I am in constant pain. Now, I am blind. My beloved husband has gone on ahead of me. I just wait for death in this place. Why do You withhold it from me? O Father, I so long to see Your face. I ache to come to heaven with You. Yet...yet, You do not choose to take me. Why"

She paused. "I am old. I am blind. I can barely move. What possible good thing is there left for me to do. Father? In this nursing home, I am so alone. Only You are there. So, what do You have for me to do for You?"

In the night's stillness, the old woman suddenly was filled with an answer: *Pray for those boys. Intercede for those special children that I sent you.*

"O Father," breathed Miriam, her voice filled with great awe. In the dark stillness, she gripped her eyes shut in intensity. "Thank you, Lord," she whispered. But how was she to pray?

For them, came the answer. "I have never even met this Teddy that Thaddeus talks about so," she whispered. "I know he is a miracle. You sent him, Lord. You brought him to us.

"O Lord, I do not understand Your ways. But be with my little grandson. Fill Thaddeus with joy and wisdom, Father! Do the same with Teddy Bear. Guide him! Send him the right people to guide his footsteps as he guides Thaddeus'. Those little boys are even more alone than I am, so, Lord, give them a special assurance of Your presence—a supernatural and mighty reassurance that You are all around them. Give them angels who will hover over them and keep any evil from befalling them ..."

She paused. Angels? "O Father," she whispered. "Did You send us an angel? Is this Teddy Bear an angel?" She was filled with a strange excitement—but no assurance.

"Or is he just a boy who needs ...." she paused. "Prayer. And someone to love him." She softly began to sing to herself.

Tired from football practice, Teddy plodded down the hall and slammed into his room. Leroy—who Teddy thought was in Alaska opening a new ranch there—looked up in surprise. He was sitting on Teddy's bed, reading one of Teddy's notebooks.

"Howdy," said Teddy, throwing down his helmet and cleats.

"Hi," said MacDonald. As the boy peeled off his filthy shoulder pads, Leroy gave Teddy the same too-naive grin from their first meeting in the Kansas jail. "So, you're playing ball?"

"Yeah." Teddy gave him a wry grin. "Us tough guys have to stand up for America, apple pie and motherhood, you know."

"You left this in the cafeteria." MacDonald thumbed through the notebook. "It's good."

With relief, Teddy noted the spiral was only a recent version of his novel—not one of his personal diaries, which might have had incriminating admissions about some of the girls.

"Do you read everybody's stuff?"

"This one said 'Science.' I opened it to see how you were doing. I don't know what this is, but it's not science."

Teddy sat down on Tadpole's bunk.

"It's a little rough," mused MacDonald. "But you've got talent. I think you might just be a writer when you get older. You ought to get this typed up and printed in a youth magazine."

"Yeah? It's gonna be a best-seller. I'm gonna be rich. Me and Tad will go live in California—maybe on the beach."

MacDonald stood up. He tossed the notebook onto Teddy's bunk. He chuckled.

"Interesting," he mused. It's about an angel sent to take care of a very important kid destined to become a world leader. Who's it really about?"

"Nobody."

"Oh, yeah?" MacDonald chuckled.

In the muggy evening, a sweaty Teddy put his shoulders onto the handlebars of his bicycle and shot down into the cool river valley that nestled the ranch's church camp.

Throughout the summer, the ranch hosted week-long sessions of a wilderness camp in the woods down by the scenic Buffalo River, a camp popular with churches throughout Oklahoma, Missouri and Arkansas.

At his own tenth-grade week, Teddy had met a dark-eyed girl named Phoebe Jane from a large church in Tulsa. She had awakened something in him.

Phoebe had long, dark hair, a knowing smile and a wry wit. She was smart. She and Teddy seemed to think on the same wave-length, too—constantly anticipating each other's reactions and finishing each other's sentences.

She liked Teddy. And he was consumed with her.

It was different than ever before, he knew. Phoebe wasn't into the social scene of being seen with some popular dude so that all the other girls would whisper in envy. She deeply cared about him. She did not flinch as he haltingly told her bits and pieces of his nightmarish childhood. For long hours sitting on a flat boulder down by the river, he told her everything. About Janny. About his grandmother, Madeline Behre. About Wyoming. And Chuck. And Dobson. And the credit cards.

As he poured out his hurts, she understood—telling him of the terrible year when her mother had fought off cancer...the long nights of holding her mom's frail, weakened body and crying with her when her dad could not handle the terror.

"My father is...kind and good," Phoebe had said hesitantly. "He may not like you at first, though. He was really worried about me coming up here—that I might fall for some delinquent from the boys ranch..." She smiled, her eyes distant, then giggled, grabbing Teddy's hand. "I never disobey my father. I love him very much. So, we may have to be kind of...wise—"

Teddy nodded. "I go to church with Leroy in town. We can tell him I'm from the church in Fayetteville. It's true."

The final night of ninth grade week, the camp's teams had a tournament—the old Password game with Bible words. Teddy and Phoebe represented their team.

It had been wonderful.

They won every round as the entire camp applauded—awed and thrilled by the well-liked couple.

Phoebe legitimized Teddy. The preachers for the first time saw that there was depth to the young cassanova. In the Password tournament, while the other contestants needed three and four clues, Teddy and Phoebe never needed more than a single turn.

"Strong," hinted Ted, glancing at the answer.

"Samson," knew Phoebe.

Then, handed the next word, "Garden," prompted Phoebe.

"Eden," knew Teddy.

"Mary," offered Teddy.

"Magdelene," responded Phoebe.

At chapel that evening, most of the kids responded to the final, emotional altar call. Teddy and Phoebe did not.

Instead, they held hands through the multiple verses of the invitation hymn, "Just As I Am," and knew what the other was thinking: That Teddy would go when he was ready. And that Phoebe was already a sincere believer—and did not need to make any public demonstration in response to the desperate pleas of a visiting youth evangelist.

✐   ✐   ✐

At first they wrote daily letters. Then, it stabilized down to twice a week. Excitedly, Teddy ripped open his mail and read her words over and over.

Then, Phoebe wrote that her dad would be driving the church bus to come get their congregation's fourth-grade campers that Saturday morning—and that she was coming along.

And so, Teddy had gotten permission to visit Tadpole and Sluggo at camp—and stay in their cabin Friday night.

❦   *❦*   *❦*

The valley's timber-scented air rushed around him. The rough asphalt bounced his rattling, dusty bike. A scarlet and indigo sky turned the camp cafeteria pink, its wooden roof a dark violet. Teddy shot down toward the chapel and gripped his brake handles.

He slowed to a stop, panting, his cheeks flushed in the cooling air, his head clear, his mind alert.

He could hear singing inside. He locked his bike to the flagpole and put on a windbreaker as he strolled into the chapel.

"Teddy Bear," exclaimed a big, red-haired ten-year-old wandering out of the men's room. "Hey, when'd you get here?"

It was Jay. Teddy put a finger to his lips.

"I want to surprise my brother," he said. "What's going on in here?"

"You don't know about Sluggo?" guffawed Jay.

Blankly, Teddy shook his head.

"He got adopted yesterday. Some dummies from a church in Springfield came and wanted to meet the deaf boy. He got all excited and started doing that dumb finger-talking with them. He's gone."

Stunned, Teddy stared at Jay.

"You're lying."

"No way. Ask anybody. He's gone. And ol' Tad acts like he's responsible. He's been praying all week that Sluggo could get adopted and be somebody's stinkin' kid. Now, he's praying that his real mom comes and gets him."

"Where is he? Inside here?"

"You ain't gonna believe it," snickered Jay. "They have prayer meeting every night."

"Who?"

"Anybody who wants to come. But Tad's one of the worst ones."

Teddy pushed open the chapel door and the two stepped into the darkened sanctuary. Softly, fourth graders were singing a reverent chorus. Several lifted their hands, palms upward, their faces turned toward the ceiling. They rocked slowly, blissful smiles growing balmy. The volume of the song grew.

"What are they doing?" whispered Teddy. The song grew in intensity. No one seemed to be leading. Older kids—the camp counselors—slowly began standing. Jay and Teddy lumbered up as the song went up a half-step in key.

"They do this every night," whispered Jay. "Even Tad's doing it. They raise their hands and everything. Even Tad."

"Praise You, Jesus," whispered a fourteen- or fifteen-year-old counselor in front of Teddy. The kid—from a church in Fayetteville—seemed oblivious to a very cute girl next to him who was trembling, her face contorted in joy, tears streaming down her cheeks. "Thank You, Father," she whispered.

Someone on the other side of the aisle started singing another chorus. Immediately, everybody joined in.

Teddy realized for the first time that somebody was playing an electronic piano—or maybe a synthesizer. He peered toward the front and picked out a half-dozen musicians—a chubby boy caressing a violin, a gaunt, head-shaking girl sawing a cello, another kid standing and almost dancing as he trilled a haunting harmony on a flute.

"Just wait 'til they all start getting excited," snickered Jay, rolling his eyes knowingly. "They all do it. Instead of canoeing, they stand on the riverbank and witness to strangers and hand out tracts. It's downright embarrassing. Tad's one of the worst of them. I'm sure glad you got here, I've been going crazy. You an' me, we don't believe this stuff, do we?"

Teddy frowned. He looked down the rows near him for Tadpole. The song ended, but the standing kids didn't stop singing. Swaying, they lifted up a haunting, spontaneous blend of melody.

Teddy shivered, a chill going down his spine. Nobody was singing the same thing. Everybody just seemed to be harmonizing in minor keys with everybody else, singing short phrases and nonsense syllables. It was rich and genuine—downright heavenly.

Jay snickered, his head bowed, looking sideways at Teddy. "Well?" Jay whispered. "What do you think? How would you like to be stuck up here all week with everybody acting so dang religious?"

Teddy shrugged. Then the chapel was silent.

"Keep your head down," whispered Jay. "Or they'll start praying for us or all run over here and lay hands on us or something weird."

Quietly, Teddy kept his head bowed.

"Tadpole was one of the first to start getting so fanatical," whispered Jay, leaning against Teddy. "Your own dang brother."

Then, seemingly from nowhere, an enthusiastic Tadpole slipped in beside Teddy. "Hey," he greeted, hugging Ted. Jay winced as Teddy hugged the boy back. Tadpole held up a rumpled song sheet.

"What are you doing?" whispered Teddy.

"We're just praising God and getting people saved," said Tad, grinning.

"Yeah?" mumbled Teddy, fumbling with the sheet. He stole a side glance at the nine-year-old. Tadpole started belting out a determined soprano, his gaze toward the front steady, his jaw resolute. He didn't look at all disturbed that Sluggo had been adopted.

Teddy glanced down at his song sheet. Maybe Tad was growing up. That wasn't fair. Perhaps Teddy had figured Tadpole would be like Peter Pan somehow—always a little boy.

Teddy started singing along. Each song seemed to repeat interminably. Jay caught Teddy's eye and rolled his eyes.

Teddy sang three more songs. Then, as the chapel quieted, Teddy fumbled, then went out to check on his bike. In a pool of light from the porch light, he knelt, making a pretense of examining the grimy chain.

Tadpole bolted outside. "Ain't it neat?" enthused the boy.

Teddy plinked a couple of spokes and dug in the bag that hung from his saddle. He pulled out a spoke wrench. and made a great show of tightening one loose spoke. "It's a little strange," he responded.

"Hey, Bear," said Tadpole. "You're like the dad I never had. I love you a whole lot."

His eyes moist, Teddy slowly put the wrench back in the bag. "Don't get mushy on me, kid," he muttered, attempting humor. "Jay told me about Sluggo. We're gonna miss him. What are we gonna do without our best buddy?"

Tadpole knelt beside him.

"You okay?" asked Teddy.

Suddenly, emotionally, Tadpole embraced his brother.

Feeling just a bit awkward, Teddy hesitated, then hugged him back. Then slowly, he stood and hoisted him up, just as he had when Tadpole was little. Tad wrapped his legs around Teddy's stomach and rested his head on his shoulder. When he was little, he would melt into Teddy like that, his ear to Teddy's chest, listening to his heartbeat.

"You are getting enormous," said Ted. "How much do you weigh?"

"Eighty."

"How tall are you?"

"I don't know," said Tadpole, his cheek wet against Teddy's neck.

"Tell me what's going on."

"Bear," whispered Tad excitedly. "God listens to us—and does stuff that I ask him to do. I started praying Tuesday that Sluggo would finally get adopted—and he's gone. Then, I prayed all day today that you'd come see all this. And I'm praying that we can go live with my mom." He jumped down. "Come on."

They took seats on the back row. Jay came back and scooted in beside Teddy. "I told you he was were as nutty as the rest," the red-haired boy chortled, too loud.

Tadpole glanced at him in irritation.

As the song service continued, Teddy let his mind wander. With his housefather's permission, he had bicycled 70 miles since early morning, taking a wide loop through the Mark Twain National Forest's southern arm, even taking ten miles of gravel detour where the highway was being straightened.

Then, in irritation, he'd found himself on busy Arkansas 33. The road was narrow, the trucks enormous. Most slowed to pass, but some swerved close to show their dislike of anybody on their highway. Watching them on the tiny rear-view mirror on his sunglasses, Teddy had "wobbled" into their path several times just as they swerved—sending them into wide arcs across the center line, their brakes hissing, their horns blaring.

It was a dangerous game of chicken.

Teddy looked up. The kids were forming circles. He followed Tadpole to the nearest group. Jay sat down and nudged Teddy while whispering to another fourth-grader. Tadpole glared at him.

A Tulsa counselor named Michael Veale, who was maybe a year older than Teddy,was ordering the circles in the front to move further apart. Then, he turned his attention to the back. Teddy glanced solemnly at Tadpole. Jay giggled something rude.

"You!" said Veale into the podium microphone. "I want you up here." Teddy grinned at Jay, who solemnly stared at the door—pretending he didn't hear. "You," bawled Veale.

Teddy elbowed Jay and guffawed.

"YOU!" said Veale.

The room grew still.

"Jay," snickered Teddy. "You better do what he says."

"Teddy Bear!" yelled Veale. "Do I have to drag you up here?"

Stunned, Teddy stared up at the counselor, who grinned and pointed at a gap in one of the front circles.

"Me?" Teddy asked meekly.

Grinning, Veale nodded. The fourth graders gawked, waiting to see if Teddy would cooperate.

"I'm coming," muttered Ted, standing. He glanced back at Tadpole, who grinned in delighted approval.

Teddy sat down in the first group, rattled, irritated. The kids—mostly teen counselors and kitchen workers—began praying quietly, their eyes closed, words muffled.

Teddy frowned, his brow wrinkled.

A squirrelly-looking junior high schooler with greasy hair and a Hawaiian shirt started talking:

"Jesus, we just love You and praise You for Your infinite goodness and power and love and for the joy that You fill us with. I thank You that You can take a lazy guy like me and give me a good summer job doing exactly what I like and a beautiful, loving mom who doesn't care if I forget to clip my toenails."

The kids in the circle all giggled.

"Praise Jesus. Thank You, Lord. Hallelujah," they all whispered in a soft hubbub. The squirrelly kid prayed on: "And Father, I know Teddy Bear doesn't understand what's going on, but we praise You that he got on that bicycle of his and couldn't do anything else with his evening but come out here, because You know how Tad loves the socks off of him and wants him to be filled with Your joy and peace.

"Father, I ask You to soften Teddy's heart and let him come to You, asking questions and wanting answers.

"Jesus, I ask You to start doing powerful things with Tadpole's big brother so that he can't sit still until he knows the fullness of life that submission to Your will brings—"

Teddy carefully glanced around the group. None of the kids was watching him. All were smiling and praying mumbled agreement and soft adoration to the Almighty.

"— and open Teddy Bear's cynical, inquiring mind to seek You, oh, Father. Jesus, we all really thank You and we praise You for everything You've done this week, for healing Donna's back, for easing Tracy's sunburn pain. God, You are so great, so good, so loving …"

The squirrel began listing miracles, healings and interventions that had happened, were occurring or that he was sure God would bring about.

Teddy glanced back at the rear group. A bowed Tadpole looked up and smiled serenely at him, then returned to the joint supplications.

Teddy glanced around the chapel. He looked back at Tadpole again, who didn't look up this time. The squirrel prayed on. Teddy leaned back, resting his eyes. He jumped as somebody brushed his knee. The group was moving in on a fat girl, placing their hands on her head. Teddy sat back and watched.

A teen boy with an unchanged voice beseeched God to fix the girl's chronic knee, to make it new, to let her dance and run—

The prayers continued.

Teddy quietly got up and walked outside.

He stepped onto the back patio overlooking the river. He turned, knowing Tadpole was on his heel.

"Well." Teddy sat down on the steps. "What has happened to you, dude?"

"From the top?" asked Tadpole, almost laughing aloud as if with private joke that he was dying to tell.

"In your own words," drawled Teddy.

"Who else's words would I use?" twanged Tadpole in an imitation of Teddy's favorite Groucho Marx voice, tapping on an invisible cigar. He trembled in anticipation.

Teddy leaned back and stared at him expectantly.

Tad grinned.

"Uh, Tadpole," said Teddy. "Those guys in there remind me of weirdo cults that I have heard about. They're 'way too interested that I do something or other—I don't know what. You need to understand I am not interested in becoming a zombie."

Tadpole squinted. "Yeah," he agreed. "Me either. Well, I don't think it's like that. You remember when you and I got baptized at that revival when I was seven? Remember?"

Teddy nodded. It had been his third or fourth time to get dunked.

"Remember how they told us we'd change, that we'd be new, that we'd be born again?" Tadpole asked.

"I also remember how hacked we were when nothing happened," said Teddy. "Shucks, lied to again. Too bad."

Tadpole snickered.

"They should have dunked us both a few more times," said Teddy. "And held me under."

"This time, it's real," said Tad. "God loves me, Teddy Bear. He's listening to me and showing me that He's the only One you and I can depend on. How do you think you and I found each other? He sent us here. He loves us, T.B.! Now, I understand. And I want other people to have what I've got."

Teddy squinted at the nine-year-old. Tad seemed to have matured five years in six days.

"I gave my life to Jesus Sunday night," said the fourth grader, his voice high. He winced at his brother. "And this time, I gave all of me. I was baptized in the river and this time, I was filled with the Holy Spirit." He grinned proudly.

His brother winced. "You know..." Teddy paused, thoughtfully. "That doesn't make a whole lot of sense, Tadpole."

"You believe in Jesus, doncha?" asked Tad, anxiously.

Teddy stared out at the river. "You know, I've been wondering about that for years," he said. "And about a month ago, I started talking to Him again, like I used to when I was a little guy your age, back when I lived with my grandmother in New Mexico. This time, I told Him that if He wanted me to understand what I was supposed to do, He was going to have to send somebody to explain it to me."

Tadpole's eyes twinkled in excitement. "Yeah? Would you believe that I've been worrying about you all week? I couldn't think of anything else—like whether you were maybe gonna get killed without me being able to talk to you. Today, I've been praying like crazy that you'd come up here, 'cuz, Bear, I want you to be in heaven if something happens. I want to spend all of eternity with my crazy brother. Maybe they'll let us two be warrior angels." He grinned, then squinted seriously. "But mostly I had to talk to you 'cuz you don't believe in no preachers except Leroy. You don't trust hardly any adults. And you suspect all kids who act goody-good."

"Like you."

"I'm not goody-good."

"I know."

Tadpole grinned. "You believe in Jesus?" he asked again.

"Of course," said Teddy, surprised by the loudness of his own voice. "I have ever since I was little. I just don't understand why everybody disagrees about every little thing. My Uncle Willem hates Pentecostals. The Charismatics say you have to watch out for the Evangelicals and the Assemblies of God say the Charismatics and Evangelicals don't have anything they haven't had for a hundred years. The Baptists won't have anything to do with any of them. Plus, the Church of Christ people are really fine folks, but they hate all the other guys and say none of them are following the Bible."

Tad smiled. "Do you want Jesus to be the Lord of your life?"

In irritation, Teddy squinted at his brother. "What do you mean by that?"

"The Bible says the demons in hell believe and tremble. The difference in them and Christians is that we ask Jesus to use us in whatever way we can be used. I've given my whole life to Him. I am His. To live is Christ and to die is gain."

Teddy winced at the boy. "What am I going to do this time? What do I have to change? Do I need to get soaked again?"

"God wants everything—your cussing when you get mad, your *Playboys* you've got under the mattress, all the dirty parts in your novel. Then, when you've given Him everything, you'll begin to see what has to change. And it'll be totally up to you."

"Right," said Teddy, staring out at the river. "Let's say I do all this, what's going to be expected of me? I'm no preacher. I'm going to be a newspaper reporter."

"Jesus died for newspaper reporters," said Tadpole. "Jesus suffered and died for newspaper reporters, because He loves them, too."

Teddy stared at the river.

"Ask Jesus to come in if you want Him in," whispered Tad. "Do it, Bear. But only if it's what you want."

Teddy closed one eye and tracked a bat crossing the river in the darkness.

He closed both eyes. And he became grave. "Jesus," he said in the stillness. "You've been really important in my life before. I ask You to come into my whole heart and life and be important to me again."

Tadpole whooped.

Teddy sat back, grinning, feeling light-headed and greatly at peace.

In Tadpole's cabin, Teddy unrolled his sleeping bag onto the floor beside his brother's bunk. The other bunks were full of church kids Teddy didn't know. Jay slammed open the door and stared at Teddy.

"What's this I hear?" he rasped accusingly.

"Huh?" said Teddy, grinning weakly.

Jay glared at Tadpole. "Yo, Tad," he said, "Keep it up and nobody around here will be sane." Then he disappeared into the night.

✐   ✐   ✐

The East Tulsa church bus pulled up beside the cafeteria. Grinning, Teddy waved at Phoebe, the beautiful girl who filled his dreams.

As the church bus door opened, she leaped down the steps, glancing back at the large man at the steering wheel. "Daddy," she called, "this is Teddy."

A dark, burly man set the parking brake, checked the light switches, then pulled the bus' key out of the ignition and turned his attention to the nervous boy.

"So," said the man, "how old are you?"

"Fifteen," answered Teddy, his voice embarrassingly high. Phoebe giggled. "Fifteen," he repeated, his voice low. "Sir."

"Mmmmm," said his girlfriend's father. "Why do you live at the boys' ranch?"

Uncomfortably, Teddy glanced at Phoebe. "My mom ran off on me when I was 10," he answered.

Phoebe's dad stared at him. "Do you play football?"

Teddy grinned. "Yes sir," he said. "I'm a defensive guard on the junior varsity team. And I'm the place kicker."

Later, as Teddy and Phoebe sat alone on their flat boulder beside the river, "Do you believe in prophecy?" she asked.

"Huh?"

"Do you believe God talks to humans and tells them stuff?"

"Sure. I guess. He did it in the Bible all the time."

"Well, this is what the Lord put in my heart while I was praying for you this morning. Wanna hear it?"

Teddy grinned.

"Teddy, you are here on Earth for a mighty purpose that you do not even suspect. You will be the leader of millions of people. You are the son of kings. You will be a leader of the final battle."

Incredulously, Teddy stared at her.

"I used to dream something like that all the time."

"Really?" she asked. "Wow."

"Yeah," said Teddy. "Some Aztec guy usually tells me I am going to lead the rebellion. Against what I don't know. Us southern boys, though, tend to side with the Rebels."

"You never told me about that," whispered Phoebe. "That's scary. You're an important person, Teddy Bear. You're going to be a world leader. But I think you're going to be tested. You're going to have to choose."

"Right," snickered the boy.

⟢   ⟢   ⟢

"I'm going to marry Phoebe," Teddy wrote in his notebook. *"I haven't told her, but I think she knows. We're so much alike. And she knows me, inside. She feels the stuff I feel. She doesn't care about old things that don't matter."*

He paused. *"Rusty O'Neill shot himself two nights ago. That's about all I know about it. His dad had come to get him. They didn't act too happy—neither one of them. Rusty told me that his dad used to...well, do stuff that I'm not going to write here. His dad was an alcoholic, he said.*

"The last time I saw Rus, I was wearing a pair of Clive's penny loafers that his mother sent him. They were too big for him and I was still very clothes conscious. I was trying to figure how to con Clive out of those shoes.

"The ranch choir was singing at a youth rally in Broken Arrow, Oklahoma, sponsored by the churches in the Tulsa area.

"I saw Rus in the audience, and then he came up afterwards, but we didn't say hardly anything because I was with Phoebe. It was weird. But then from the back of the church, he waved at me as if he had been very glad to see me. I waved back.

"I think I was too preoccupied with how I looked that day because I knew Phoebe's mom was really worried about her and me—that's what Phoebe's best friend, Cindy Kirby, said. Did I look rebellious enough that their youth minister would see I hadn't given in, but good enough that her mom would think I was okay? Did I look cute enough that all the girls from

the Broken Arrow church would want to talk to me about summer camp?

"Before we went home, my house mom told me that the preacher's wife from Rus's church had said he had just come so he could see me and Tadpole—who wasn't there.

"Phoebe and I went out to look for him and saw him in the back of his preacher's station wagon, so I waved and grinned and he scrambled up to the back seat window and I think we said something. He was all grins and admiration. I was nice and acted like I enjoyed seeing him again.

"I can catch little remembrances. I can remember that his mother was funny whenever she came to visit at the ranch. She hardly ever came to see him, though. She had real straight, long hair and sad eyes. She liked me. She made sculpture: busts and heads. People said she was an alcoholic, too, like Rus's dad.

"The preacher's wife called this morning to tell Leroy, then asked to talk to my house mom, so she would tell Tadpole and me. She said Rusty had been to church, all dressed up, just the Sunday before.

"She said he had shot himself at home and by the time an ambulance was called, Rusty was dead.

"I'm not going to tell Tadpole. He doesn't need to know about stuff like this yet. I don't know what made Rusty do it, but Tad doesn't need to be thinking about stuff like that."

"What I don't get is why Rus's dad couldn't have stopped it.

"What's wrong with these people?

"Where was his mother?"

His eyes suddenly moist, Teddy was thinking of his own mother, the daughter of the well-known missionary widow Madeline Behre in Botswana, Africa.

Her name was Trixie.

Trixie.

Teddy trembled as he remembered.
He clenched his pencil.
Trixie.

     ✐   ✐   ✐

Trixie Behre had escaped the tedium of her mother's mission compound to a private school in Switzerland at age fifteen. She didn't even last a semester, but ran away. She hitchhiked through Italy and Austria, first staying with increasingly alarmed missionary friends. Then she took up with a rock band on a USO tour in Germany, then sought out her Aunt Maud, a semi-retired magazine writer living in the Netherlands.

At age seventeen, Trixie tried Hare Krishna, spending two months in airports selling incense. Then, she turned up in a Madrid hospital with hepatitis. She was pregnant, too.

She talked glibly of having an abortion, then seemed to forget her condition, taking up with an American photographer called "Missouri" who was in the hospital for drug problems. She confided to Aunt Maud that she thought having a child would calm Missouri down.

Trixie went into labor in December while she, Maud and Missouri were tracking down an underground Yugoslav artists' show near Slovenj Gradec. They dashed for a hospital in Austria—twenty miles away.

They didn't make it. Teddy was born in an ancient church in Everndorf, Austria. Auntie, Missouri, Trixie and the newborn returned to Holland, where after three weeks of motherhood, Trixie took off without explanation after Missouri accepted an assignment in India.

She called from Frankfurt, weeping that she had met a really nice twenty-two-year-old Polish writer whose wife and kids lived back in Wroclaw. Teddy's grandmother came up from

Africa to get the baby. She christened him Theophilus—"Friend of God."

Teddy spent his first year at a bush clinic in Botswana, doted on by mission nurses.

But his grandmother's health deteriorated. She had suffered from tuberculosis early in her missionary years and had even spent two years in a Mozambique tuberculosis sanatorium.

When Teddy was four, her health forced her to return home to the United States.

She threw herself into completing half-written books, speaking at religious conventions and appearing on religious television talk shows. Still, she kept up with her longtime task as the mission secretary.

And—to everyone's amazement—took up her old diversion of long-distance bicycle riding.

For hours on end, five-year-old Teddy would sit buckled into a plastic seat on the back of his grandmother's beloved ten-speed Peugeot that she called "Peggy," belting out church choruses as she pedaled around town.

One afternoon, the kindergartener pushed his thick glasses up on his nose and, beside his grandmother, he watched in silence as a rattlesnake lost its anger, uncoiled and slithered away.

"He was just scared," she whispered.

On Saturdays Teddy and his grandmother ate pancakes with Santa Fe Bicycling Society members who recounted rides in New Zealand and Mexico and Oklahoma and Spain and Iowa. Frequently, Mrs. Behre would interject bicycling adventures that had happened while she was a little girl in the Netherlands or tales of how she had biked between African bush mission stations in Botswana, where she had been a missionary for thirty-two years with Teddy's late grandfather.

It did not escape little Teddy that the bike club members patiently endured her evangelistic efforts or that she seemed so oblivious to their discomfort.

Teddy got his own twelve-speed when he turned eight. By the time he was nine, he had become an enthusiastic, if easily-winded, bicycle hiker.

Bicycles would be with him from then on. As a nine-year-old, he found the release of pedaling so hard that nothing else matters, of riding one-hundred-fifty miles in one day over unfamiliar terrain, of passing personal limits and proving to oneself the impossible.

Of just riding until everything else fades into unimportance.

Shortly after Teddy's ninth birthday, his grandmother's old heart condition flared, diabetes and arthritis worsened and she developed emphysema. Her bike riding dropped off.

Briefly, she and the fourth grader moved to the dry air of Arizona, but she felt useless and told her adult children that she wanted to die among her friends, near her church and with her beloved Santa Fe Bicycle Club.

In his grandmother's last six months, Teddy matured beyond his years, taking care of her bottled oxygen, fixing simple meals, helping make her comfortable.

But deep hurts and resentments remained. Teddy endured church and squirmed during his grandmother's unending sales pitches about religion.

She spent most of the time on the living room sofa, scrawling personal messages on mimeographed newsletters that detailed the work back in Africa. Although bedfast, she raised money for a new hospital wing, a new chapel and three church buildings out in the bush.

And she had Teddy read aloud to her *Hans Brinker and the Silver Skates, Tom Sawyer, A Mid-Summer Night's Dream,* the

Narnia Chronicles, the Wizard of Oz, the Scarlet Pimpernel, the Hobbit. When she told him Bible stories, she tried to ignore how his young eyes averted nervously, his interest gone, his mind elsewhere. Fervently, she prayed for him and told him details of her fifteen-year break with the traditional church of her youth.

But as long as he could remember he'd heard it all before: One day in the bush near Bulawayo, Zimbabwe, she'd happened onto a native revival. Unschooled Africans were praising God in what she recognized as old-timey American Pentecostal Holy Rollerism. She set to work at showing them their doctrinal flaws. They countered with stories of miracles and healings. She showed them their Scriptural error. Lovingly, they convinced her of hers.

Church leaders at home in the United States and Holland were at first alarmed at her vivid claims of natives rising from the dead; of believers praying over water for communion and it turning to wine; of being bitten by a red cobra, immediately going into prayer with native pastors and suffering no ill effects.

She co-authored two books detailing this spontaneous movement in the bush, the joy, sincerity and faith of the Africans. Some old friends called it witchcraft. Her husband quietly attributed it to menopause.

Most contributors forgave what they saw as only a bit of excess. For years, the Behres' had been one of the most success-ful missionary efforts in southern Africa.

As Teddy neared his tenth birthday, her mimeographed notes from New Mexico became more brief. Her only son, Teddy's Uncle Will, who preached at a tiny church in nearby Los Cerrillos, became increasingly irritated with her affiliations with wild-eyed people and oddball churches. He refused to help with the mailings.

Ladies at a Full Gospel Holiness church in Five Points had to take on the task typing the newsletter, running the mimeograph, stuffing envelopes and taking everything to the post office.

Then one night, Mrs. Behre died.

She had known she was going to die. Everyone does when the time comes. And sure enough, that evening as Teddy had come in and checked her oxygen, she had grasped his hand tightly.

"I love you very much, Theophilus," she had rasped softly.

The boy looked at her strangely. "I know," he answered, his voice unexpectedly hoarse. Their eyes held for a long time. Then, nervously, he pushed his glasses up on his nose.

"You make me so proud," she whispered. "You are such a fine young man. You're going to be so magnificent in everything you do."

The fifth grader's eyes were filling with tears. The old woman smiled. Gently, "I think it's about time for me to go be with your Grandpa," she said. "But don't get upset. You're going to be just fine."

Teddy nodded. She gripped her grandson's hand and closed her eyes.

She awoke in the night and was pleased that the boy had disappeared off to his own room. "Heavenly Father," she whispered, "protect that boy. Now he's truly in Your hands. There's nothing else I can do."

And she was filled with a great peace. She knew her little Teddy Bear would be watched over.

Sometime that night she found herself walking in a great, but not particularly troubling, darkness. She was strolling toward and watching, as if merely curious—a great, white light in the distance. Then, she began to realize how easy it had become to walk, a perfectly delightful feeling after so many years of arthritic pain.

She recognized the figure standing in the light. It was Theodore, her husband. "Darling!" she called, running to him and embracing him.

He was so different and yet the same—but that didn't trouble her, for she, too, was no longer a decrepit old woman. In an incredible swirl of heavenly delight, she found herself surrounded by her own beloved mother, her grandmother and a best friend from grammar school and a funny old Botswanan witch she had won to Christianity in her first years in Africa.

There was a time of judgment, and she passed through it very quickly. Instead of a stern, white-bearded God glowering down at her from a towering throne, however, she found herself embraced by the presence of a great, mighty, longtime Friend. In great reverence, she knelt as He welcomed her warmly.

He had been her Friend for sixty years. Hours and hours she had knelt in His presence in early morning darknesses, in sunny childhood mornings...and in lonely retirement's long afternoons. Now, she beheld Him as He truly was and it was beyond human words.

So great was His delight with her! And hers with Him! And at the same time, she knew with great joy that she was greatly blessed to be so welcomed. Many were not—and their judgment was a terrible thing. Damnation without hope of parole.

For all eternity.

Now as she stood amid a vast choir, her voice was strong and the praises glorious. She closed her eyes and felt indescribable joy. So much was completely resolved. So many friends were here. Such wonderful times. The mighty praises of the redeemed reverberated off of the...walls? Did this great place have walls?

She did not know. There was so much to experience. If she had ever known happiness on earth, it certainly did not compare with this. Such mighty peace and fulfillment. And rest.

It was at the funeral that Teddy met his mom for the first time.

Trixie was old for her twenty-eight years, bony, chain-smoking, wearing a flamboyant wide-brimmed hat. She kept leering at her son, then, she would look away.

He'd heard too many warnings about her to just rush up and embrace her, although he longed to. On one hand, there were all sorts of things that he needed to tell her. He wanted to say he really liked her even though nobody else did and that he forgave her totally—that everything was okay.

But on the other hand, he'd been told she was a little crazy. And she looked it. So, he just smiled shyly.

Uncle Will took his hand and told Trixie and her unintroduced boyfriend that this was Teddy, that he would be fine, not to worry, that he would be coming to live in Los Cerrillos, that adoption proceedings had already begun.

Teddy looked up in surprise—pushing his glasses up on his greasy nose.

Trixie nodded curtly and walked into the church.

Teddy broke away from Uncle Will and plopped down beside her in a pew up at the front. He tried whispering to her, but she acted like he wasn't there, dabbing at her eyes with a filthy handkerchief, staring ahead and ignoring the hundreds of eyes that she imagined were fixed on this little drama as abandoned waif tried to make up to mysterious, heartless mother.

The service was long, emotional and festive. Although the Behre clan was staunchly traditional, Grandma had made it plain that her funeral was to be conducted by Charismatics. Pentecostals. Holiness people. People who praised God loudly with raised hands, who spoke aloud in prophecy and "messages from the Lord," who sang spontaneous songs and offered healings, who thanked God in all circumstances—including funerals.

As Uncle Will stared at his feet and flipped through a hymnal, a forty-seven-voice choir from one of Grandma's favorite churches belted out "Oh, Happy Day," then her personal theme song, Martin Luther's "A Mighty Fortress Is Our God."

Members of the news media watched, amused but respectful. The old lady had been well known and a number of prominent figures were attending the service. The first speaker—a former adviser to U.S. presidents turned street evangelist and the subject of two made-for-TV movies—told of his personal battle when his wife had fought against cancer during their work with Los Angeles street gangs and of how Mrs. Behre had come to him years before, wanting to speak to West Coast churches about the revival in Africa.

Then a religious talk show host from Virginia rambled on in a subdued voice about his long discussions with Mrs. Behre about obscure Bible prophecies. He recounted an incident where a guest had asked her if the Tribulation in the Book of Revelation would occur before or after the Rapture—that is, whether all Christians would be caught up into heaven before the calamities at the end of the world.

"Only an American could ask such a question," had declared Teddy's grandmother. "What does it matter? Our task is to take the Word to the world, not to waste time pondering whether our lazy, easy existence will be inconvenienced by His second coming."

The other two speakers had been flown in from Indonesia and Surinam.

The dark-skinned Indonesian exhorted the congregation into loud singing and made everyone march around the inside of the church, praising God for giving the world a "true servant" and rejoicing that she had been permitted to stay on Earth sixty-eight years, "even though heaven has been less beautiful all the time that she remained among us."

"Now, she's won!" he shouted in his thick accent. "She has run the good race, she has smashed Satan's nose over and over in the good fight! The angels are singing and she is right there in the midst of them, no longer burdened with an old lady's strained voice, no longer in pain, never again to be afflicted by age, but victorious, TRIUMPHANT, and taking residence in a great mansion of her very own in a beautiful city with gates like pearls, streets of gold and radiating with the very presence of God!"

The last speaker, an old schoolmate who had spent his life translating the Bible into jungle dialects, fumbled for words and began to cry. The congregation stirred with emotion. The TV and newspaper people fumbled, uneasy.

"My dear, sweet Madeline," the old man whispered. "You're home."

As Teddy sat next to his inattentive mother, glancing at the still form of his beloved grandmother in her coffin, he knew that Grandma was not truly gone. But in his humanness, he could not begin to understand what had become of her.

After his grandmother's funeral, Trixie came to the house—which Uncle Willem had already put up for sale. The excited Teddy showed his mother his rock collection and his straight-A report cards. He read her some stories he'd written at school about his turtle and about his grandmother's bicycle, "Peggy."

"Why Peggy?" asked Trixie as she examined the ten-speed out on the back porch.

"Because it's a Peugeot," said Teddy, softly, stroking its handlebars. His eyes began to mist.

"Oh."

Then, laughing as he insisted they go for a ride, Trixie fumbled with the handlebar brakes and the pedals' toe-clips. Teddy retrieved his bike off the front lawn.

And he took his mother on a tour of their neighborhood. As darkness fell, he showed her the ruins of a hotel where Theodore Roosevelt and Mark Twain had once stayed.

Mother and son came into the house arm-in-arm, Trixie announcing that they were going to Albuquerque to spend the next day at an amusement park. Whooping, Teddy charged outside.

Out by her boyfriend's microbus, Trixie shook hands with various gawking neighbors and crammed Teddy inside.

She swore aloud as they pulled out. She fumbled for a cigarette. "Well, Teddy, we'll show them they can't break up a great act like you and me."

Teddy leaned forward against the back of her seat, not daring to believe what he thought she was saying.

"What do you mean?" he whispered.

"My brother says he's going to adopt you," she snapped. "He said this is my chance to tell you goodbye. Can you believe that?"

She exhaled a long stream of smoke.

Teddy sat back in his seat. Gene began talking about how they were going to be rich from winning television game shows.

"Is Uncle Will gonna adopt me?" asked Teddy.

"No, you're going with me!" exclaimed his mother.

Teddy jumped up and hugged her. He began crying—and so did she.

Back in his seat, he began to get excited about the possibilities. But he was nervous. He wasn't sure what he'd gotten himself into. He hadn't packed anything. He hadn't brought his bicycle. That night, they slept in the bus, Teddy up front, Trixie and Gene in the back. Teddy observed that he hadn't brought any pajamas.

"Sleep in the buff," suggested Trixie. "It'll put hair on your chest."

"Naked?" exclaimed Teddy, giggling. He stripped down to his underwear—and euphoric—charged outside, yelling at his mother to watch him be a frog. Disappointed, he stood atop an old anthill as she ignored him.

From back in the van, "Put your clothes on, you little nudist," she snapped. "You look like a monkey."

He woke in the night, alarmed that he couldn't hear his grandmother's heavy breathing on the respirator. Then he remembered and peered around in the darkness. In the back, Gene and Trixie were whispering. She giggled.

"Can I sleep with you guys?" Teddy asked suddenly, his high voice sharp in the stillness.

There was an awkward silence, then: "NO!" boomed Trixie's voice, unnaturally hoarse. "Go jogging or something. Take a cold shower."

She laughed, then whispered.

"You better behave yourself, boy!" warned Gene. "You want me to come up there and beat your tail?"

"No," answered Teddy.

"Then, go to sleep. And quit being a little pest."

Near Flagstaff, Trixie dozed off while she was driving and almost wrecked the van. She dropped her cigarette and the bus's filthy shag carpet began to smoulder, filling the vehicle with acrid fumes.

Bellowing, Gene ordered her to stop and began beating out the fire with her purse. She protested, began screeching and swearing, trying to wrestle the purse away from him as the van swung into the middle lane, then off into the grass of the right-of-way as the fire spread.

Astonished, Teddy watched the two scream, gouge and pull hair. Gene punched her in the mouth and kicked her in the stomach, then found himself covered with a howling, punching ten-year-old. Trixie bellowed, pushing Teddy aside and began biting Gene's hand. He slugged her, then yelled, her fingernails raking his neck.

With smoke billowing out of the windows, Trixie stopped on the median. A trucker stopped and with a little extinguisher put out the sputtering fire, then got mad when Gene accused him of trying to come on romantically to Trixie.

There was a scream and Trixie was on top of Gene again. The trucker shook his head at Teddy as the two scratched, punched and bit.

"I don't think she needs any help, kid," chuckled the man as Trixie gained the upper hand and—sitting on Gene's chest—swore in his face. The trucker drove off, Teddy watching with disappointment. He would have preferred to go with the man.

Humiliated and furious, Gene leaped into the van and left the cursing mother and her son standing in the weeds of the interstate. Trixie screamed toward the heavens.

Teddy began to shiver. In his hands, he held his broken glasses—snapped at the nosepiece. Without them, the world was a blur.

Trixie shouted to the wind that they'd "show him." She flagged down a motor home and the two hitched a ride to Salt Lake City. A kindly retired couple listened sympathetically as Trixie told of being newly widowed and how she and "Junior" were on their way to her parents' farm in Canada.

The husband and wife dropped them off at a Salt Lake City motel, paying for their room and giving Trixie $100. She thanked them profusely, even started crying. A confused Teddy went inside and watched TV.

His grandmother had hated television. He'd never gotten to watch much—and it fascinated him.

From a vending machine, he bought a roll of adhesive tape and patched his glasses back together—with a stupid-looking mass of adhesive tape sitting on the bridge of his nose.

That night, Trixie didn't come back to the room and after all the TV channels went off the air, Teddy began to panic. Every time a car drove up, he jumped up and went to the window.

Around 3 a.m., he woke up the manager and told him that something terrible had happened, that Trixie had said she'd be right back. The man called the police.

For three hours, Teddy drove around with two joking patrolmen, getting more and more scared. Then, a call came over the radio.

She'd turned up.

Everything was okay, exulted the third grader, wondering why the two policemen looked at each other and laughed knowingly.

They took him to the bus station where a disheveled, sullen Trixie was waiting with a vice detective who bought mother and son tickets on the next bus—which happened to be going to Denver.

The man tweaked Teddy's cheek and told him never to come back to Salt Lake City. On the bus, Trixie refused to talk about it.

Leaving Teddy in a filthy Denver hotel room, Trixie disappeared again for three days.

The first night, he thought he was going to starve to death. He began praying, like his grandmother had done the times that she was short of money and the cupboards were bare. He wanted to go back to Los Cerrillos. With Trixie, nothing made any sense.

And in the night, he began having the dream that would become so familiar:

Teddy—atop the great Aztec Pyramid of the Sun—sat down on a ceremonial pedestal. "Why did you waste your time here, Dad?" His young, high voice was strident with emotion.

There was an icy silence. Then, "I have known you across the ages," whispered the old man Quetzalcoatl. "You brought me the great hope that gave my life its only joy, Teddy, my son. You are the only one who can follow and protect my Aztecs and my Toltecs and my beloved Kachijils."

The old man held his son's shoulder and slowly, deliberately, raised one arm. The night sky turned scarlet, illuminating the proud, robed figure. Thunder rolled from the heavens.

"I am Teotl Ixca," he whispered, his high, old voice somehow filling the ceremonial plazas and promenades. "Quehecut in quih vi, in puic ramal zaquil al, zaquil quahol."

You are the sun and moon of mankind.

Lightning flashed across the sky. Gold dust fluttered down over the hushed multitude. Great flocks of squawking chickens appeared in the midst.

"Ca tzih ta ch'uxoc," called the old man: Our word and command be fulfilled.

"Don't you know who you are?" he whispered, turning to Teddy.

Early in the wee morning hours of the third day, Trixie showed up driving an enormous convertible and took Teddy to an all-night McDonalds. There, she told him to order anything he wanted.

After three shakes, a Happy Meal, an extra order of fries, half an apple turn-over, a fish sandwich with mustard on it and a box of McDonaldland cookies, Teddy got sick and threw up all over himself.

Trixie began ranting, acted like she was going to call the health department, threatened to sue the store, then accepted fifty dollars from the whining night manager and shoveled the still-nauseous, moaning Teddy into the car.

"We're going to Chicago," she announced.

Twice Teddy vomited again in the back seat. Trixie began swearing at him, then put down the convertible top—which improved the smell considerably. She told him to use his shirt to clean things up, that vomiting was disgusting and that he'd better not ever do it again around her.

"I know you're not sick," she yelled. "You're just trying to get back at me. Well, it won't work, so you can just quit. It may have worked on my mother, but it won't on me."

Teddy wailed, said he was going to die of pneumonia if she didn't put the roof back up, then demanded to know why she wasn't taking him to a doctor with the $50 like she'd told the night manager she would.

Trixie was silent, then started laughing and taunting him: "Just who do you think is boss, anyway?" she asked repeatedly.

Teddy began planning to jump out of the car the first time she stopped. Instead, he curled up on the unsoiled side and fell asleep.

When he awoke, they were in Rock Springs, Wyoming. Trixie told him she was sorry, that she had only borrowed the car for a few days from a guy she'd met and that they were going to have to live on the McDonalds $50 until she got a job.

Then, she asked him if he could throw up on purpose.

Beside the road, they practiced without result.

At a Kentucky Fried Chicken, they bought a whole barrel of Original Recipe. Teddy chomped through six pieces and three Dr. Peppers, but was unable to vomit—just belch loudly. The two got quite a kick out of it.

Then, for no apparent reason, Trixie began to get sore again.

In Cheyenne, they decided they'd better save their money and just camp out in a large park they found near a highway interchange.

Then Trixie carefully explained that she might be gone several days. Leaving Teddy with the car, she jumped on a city bus and was gone.

The first afternoon, Teddy ate all the chicken that was left. Then, after the car was ticketed three times by a meter maid who began asking him nosy questions, he started staying under an old bandstand, which was cooler anyway.

That evening, he investigated a nearby shopping mall and began rationalizing which was better—to starve to death or get caught stealing something to eat from one of the shops.

One health food store was giving out free samples, but after Teddy's fourth visit, the teen-age girl told him he'd have to come back with his parents before he could have anymore.

It got cold that night and Teddy began praying that the mosquitoes would go away, that he could get warm...that God would do something to get him back to Uncle Willem's house.

The next morning, he loitered inside one of the truck stops' restaurants until the cashier threw him out. Discouraged, he stuck around the parking lot. Then, a waitress came out, looked around for him and told him to come back inside.

While he wolfed down a hamburger, he answered all the questions of the eight waitresses, the fry cook, the Iranian dishwashers and a skeptical parade of truckers.

Teddy told them all about his grandmother's funeral and getting thrown out of Salt Lake City, then getting the car in Denver.

"Where is your mother now?" asked the doubtful-looking cashier.

"I don't know. She went downtown to look for a job, I think, three days ago. She told me that she was going to turn some tricks and be right back."

Nearby truck drivers roared. One of the waitresses tousled his hair. He grinned blankly with no idea what he'd said that was so funny. He began to suspect that "turn some tricks" was dirty when the drivers began repeating it for everybody who hadn't heard.

"I bet you don't have nobody in the world," said the fry cook. "Just on your own in the great big gear-jammin' highway of life."

The waitresses got quiet at such a poetic thought. One of them sniffled.

"I'll tell you what I think," snapped the cashier. "I bet his folks are outside watchin' from a beat-up pickup. This kid's too slick. He's bummed meals before. Some people teach their young to do it, you know?"

"There's nobody watchin' outside," protested Teddy. "I didn't bum no meal from you. You gave it to me."

"I ain't givin' you nothin', you little midget," trumpeted the cashier. "If you don't have the money to pay for what you just ate, you're gonna have to wash every dish and pan that we've got in the back or I'll call the juvenile authorities on you."

Teddy crammed the rest of the hamburger in his mouth, then asked where the dishes were.

Everybody cheered. The cashier told him to get out.

Embarrassed, feeling somewhat degraded, little Teddy moped under the bandstand. He really wanted to go back to Uncle Willem's house now.

That afternoon, he returned to find four police cars around the car. A wrecker was getting ready to tow it away. Teddy ducked down into some high weeds, glad he'd eaten all the chicken.

That night, he went back to the truck stop, intending to offer to wash the dishes for real. Instead, the cashier ordered him another hamburger and began grilling him as to who he really was and where he really came from.

As the night busboys gathered around and customers stared, he started crying and told about running off when Trixie had seemed so nice and getting left behind by Gene and how he wanted to go home to New Mexico.

"Well, Sweetheart," said the cashier, "let's call up this Uncle Will of yours right now and get you home. You're too nice a little boy to be out here like this."

At the pay phone, she dialed the number Teddy gave. Aunt Minnie accepted the collect charges.

"Ma'am," said the cashier, while everybody at the counter listened. "I've got a little boy here who really wants to come home. Can you tell us where to send him? We've got truckers here from all over and any one of them can drop him off without no trouble."

Everybody nodded, smiling around at each other. There was a good feeling in the air. Somebody said they ought to call the TV news.

"Sure, I'll hold on," said the cashier. Then, she put her hand on the mouthpiece. "She's gone to get your uncle." She waited. "Hello, sir? My name is Melba Newcastle and I'm calling from the MacKay Truck Haven in Cheyenne, Wyoming, and I've got a lonely little boy here who is sorrier than heck that he run off with that no-good mother of his and wants to come home and be your adopted son like you-all planned."

Truckers and waitresses applauded.

Teddy sniffled. He was going home.

"I see," said the cashier. She nodded. "Well —" She listened. "Well, I don't know about that," she said. "He's all by his lonesome. He's begged two meals from us already. He's too nice of a little boy to be out like this. He tried to get a job here a'washin' dishes."

She listened. "Well, that's the strangest attitude I've ever heard in my life," she said, her voice becoming huffy. "He's your responsibility, mister, not mine."

She listened. "You look here," she said. "The boy says you're a preacher, but you don't sound like one to me. I don't think you have the backbone to tell this sweet little boy here what you've just said to me. Here, I'm going to put him on the line."

His heart in his throat, Teddy took the phone. Something was wrong. Maybe they'd gotten the wrong number.

"Uncle Will?" he asked. He pushed his glasses up on his nose. "I'm sorry. I want to come home. I want to come home bad."

There was silence on the other end.

"Theophilus," said a stern voice on the other end. "You shouldn't blame yourself. I'm not saying you can't come home. But, your mother has accepted responsibility for you and she's going to have to be the one to get you out of this. Go tell her that you want her to bring you home and that she'll have to sign the papers that give us custody. We'll adopt you like we planned, Teddy, but we'll not have my sister disrupting your and our lives from now on. Do you understand me?"

"I don't know where she is," said Teddy, sniffling.

"Well, go to the police. They will find her and send you home."

"I can't," sobbed Teddy. "I don't know where she is. She left. She keeps going away and not coming back."

There was silence.

"Teddy, your mother has decided that she wants to be responsible for you. That was her decision and you willingly went off with her. We'll take you in, but first your mother must sign over complete custody and agreed to stay away from you."

"I won't ever run off again," sobbed Teddy.

"I know you won't. Teddy, try to understand: For most of my life, I have let my sister get away without bearing her responsibilities. This time, you and I are going to teach her a lesson. If she wants to be responsible for you, then that's what she's going to have to do."

"I don't even know where she is," wailed Teddy. "I WANNA COME HOME RIGHT NOW!"

The mood had darkened in the restaurant. Truckers began murmuring. Teddy leaned his face to the wall, tears dripping off of his nose.

"Teddy, for your good, this is how it has to be," said Uncle Will. "You're too young to understand and I know it seems as if I'm being awfully mean, but I'm not. This is for your own good. You mother is just going to have to sign you over to us so that she can never kidnap you again."

Teddy heaved.

"Give me a call when you've gone to the police and you've talked over things with your mother," said his uncle.

"I don't know where she is," cried Teddy.

"You don't have to. Call the police and let them take care of you until they can locate her."

"Okay," sniffled Teddy.

"Theophilus," said Uncle Will. "Do you see just what sort of person your mother really is? Do you see why we have to do this?"

"Yes," sobbed the boy, although he didn't understand at all. "Goodbye."

"Teddy —" said his uncle.

Little Teddy hung up. Taking off his glasses, he leaned against the wall and wept.

A waitress gently held him as the cashier called the police. Then, an angry trucker called a radio station talk show and related a rather garbled version of what had happened.

The talk show host called up Will. After two callers told him off on the air, the minister hung up.

A newspaper photographer showed up about the same time that the police did. A sobbing Teddy and the furious waitresses and truckers retold his story eight or ten times.

The photographer posed a photo of Teddy holding up a truck stop cereal bowl in the classic *Oliver Twist* pose, then followed him all the way to the "Rainbow House," a half-way house for abused and abandoned children. A bored reporter met them there, but the police decided the boy had talked to enough civilians. There was a yelling match and multiple phone calls, then the reporter was permitted a short interview. Teddy became frustrated when the man couldn't get it through his head that Trixie hadn't dumped him at the truck stop. The reporter's eyes seemed to glaze as the ten-year-old detailed about Denver and Salt Lake City and Flagstaff.

"Well, thanks for talking to me, Terry," the man said as he left.

"Teddy!" exclaimed the boy.

Among the other kids, Teddy was a celebrity, at least until the police and truck drivers and waitresses all went away.

That night, some of the bigger boys caught him in the shower and crammed a burning salve up his buttocks. They laughed as he pleaded with them to leave him alone.

He told a volunteer on them and was moved to the room for littler kids.

His poignant photo was on the front page of the Cheyenne afternoon newspaper the next day with a nice caption about the unidentified minor who was abandoned at a truck stop and given refuge at the "Rainbow House," a United Fund agency. *"Thanks to you, it's working,"* ended the caption, noting that the city's annual United Fund drive was only $230,000 from the year's goal.

Teddy got into three fights the first day, winning against all but one bigger boy.

That night, an unsmiling matron watched him as he took another shower and made him wash between his toes, then made him soap down his hair with a foul-smelling disinfectant—which got him crying.

Then, she made him put on Donald Duck sleepers that were too little before escorting him into the safety of the nursery.

Melba came to visit him twice the next week, bringing him books and cards from the truckers and waitresses. Concerned, she listened as he told of all his fighting. "I don't think this is a very nice place," concluded Teddy.

"How would you like to come live with me?" Melba asked softly as he leaned back in her lap in the TV room.

"YEAH!" he exclaimed, distracted by a *Beverly Hillbillies* rerun. He twisted around and hugged Melba's neck, keeping one eye on the TV. Grannie Clampett had lost her glasses and was trying to talk to a seal that she thought was one of Ellie May's boyfriends.

"Do you think I could be a very good mommy?" Melba was asking. She began crying suddenly, holding little Teddy close. "Teddy, I can't have children. You and me, we could have something really special. You're smart, just like I was. Can you be real good?"

Enthusiastically, Teddy nodded. Grannie was trying to talk to the seal. He giggled as the seal barked. "With a cough like that, you got no business swimming!" Grannie was declaring.

Melba hugged Teddy. "We're gonna be happy, you and me," she whispered, conspiratorially. "We're gonna blow this joint."

Teddy nodded, smiling, pretending not to watch as Melba wiped her eyes. She rocked him, rubbing his back. On the TV, Grannie was trying to talk to an otter that she thought was Ellie's beau's little brother. "They ain't much fer conversation," she declared, "but they shore kin SWIM!" Teddy laughed.

Melba sat down on his bunk. She held a big stuffed bear. "Here," she said, softly, a little distantly.

"THANKS!" exclaimed Teddy. Warily, he reached up and hugged her neck.

The cashier seemed nervous about something. She didn't hug him back as tightly as usual.

"I hate it here," declared Teddy, his voice high. "Can I start being your boy today? You promised."

Melba pulled his arms from around her neck. Alarmed, Teddy struggled into her lap, knowing it was all off. Somehow, he'd known all along. He tried to hug her, but she removed his arms. "I wanna go with you," he wailed.

"You HUSH!" she ordered. Then, softly, "I'd take you in a minute." Gently, she brushed his blond curls. She stood.

"I want you to listen to me. Here's why you can't be my boy. I'm not qualified, even if I had gone through their proper channels. Plus, you are unadoptable. They say you've got a real mother, that lousy Trixie you talk about. Right now, she's missing. And if she ever turns up and signs a release, then, you've got all sorts of family in New Mexico which has claim on you. Do you understand me, boy? You belong to them."

Teddy nodded.

"I'd take you home with me in a minute," said Melba. She stood, then brushed his face. "But with all their fancy rules, they're gonna get you on welfare and everything before this is over with. I wish I could do something about it, but I can't."

And then, she was gone.

Three weeks later, Teddy was sent to the Southern Wyoming Children's Diagnostic Center outside of Cheyenne. It looked like a school campus, except for the high, barbed-wire-topped, chain-link fence. Teddy was assigned to a cottage where fourteen other boys lived with a twenty-two-year-old resident counselor and his nineteen-year-old wife, a fat, grouchy girl who watched television most of the time. Teddy immediately took a dislike to her. She only watched soap operas, which were too dull for the third grader's tastes. The counselor, named Irv, took down all of Teddy's information in a monotone. He gave Teddy a clipping of his front-page picture with the cereal bowl.

That afternoon, Teddy went to a class with teen-age boys who were making dowel rods from pieces of wood on an enormous wood-working lathe.

When he went back to his room, he found that most of the stuff that Melba had brought him from the truck stop had been stolen.

Irv said there was nothing he could do about it, but that if Teddy recognized any of his stuff in other people's rooms, he could try to claim them. He added that it wasn't legal for him or Teddy to search the other rooms.

Weeping, Teddy demanded to know how to get a search warrant. Irv told him to shut up and forget it—that he hadn't had any of the stuff long enough for it to really be his anyway, that making a big deal would just cause problems.

Teddy sulked in his room, then went into the recreation room and watched "General Hospital," "Days of Our Lives" and an old rerun of "Dark Shadows." The latter wasn't half bad, all about a neurotic vampire.

His roommate was a stuttering eleven-year-old named Justus, who thought it was funny to pee on the wall of the bathroom and who, at night, had screaming nightmares. He claimed he had been in dirty movies.

The second day he was there, Teddy got into a big fight and won, which only meant he had to fight more older kids.

He found to his surprise that winning seemed to make him a hero among the few other kids his age. And he began to learn how, as a left-hander, he was a natural fighter. Nobody seemed to know how to defend against him.

Mornings, he and the other sixth graders—which included some boys as old as seventeen—were taught by a retired seismologist named Mrs. Daugherty. Afternoons, he went to wood shop where they made more dowels.

Apparently, the school had a contract to sell the wooden rods.

Teddy had been there ten days when a substitute teacher was sent to wood shop when the regular teacher got sick.

While the substitute attempted to call the roll, a kid named Johnny Kerguelen started acting mentally retarded and kept volunteering to help out. To everyone's entertainment, he lurched around the room, dropping things, talking in a slur and trying to assist.

The substitute fell for every bit of it. So, when Teddy jumped up and suddenly announced that it was time for him to carry Johnny's books so Kerguelen could go to his "special...you know" class, the teacher let both boys leave.

There were whoops behind them as Teddy and Johnny ducked away. They spent the whole afternoon hiding behind the water tower. There, Teddy learned how to smoke cigarettes.

Both boys were lying on the rim behind the water tower, enjoying the warm sun, when Kerguelen began to wax forth with advice, thick in profanity that impressed Teddy. He had no idea what most of it meant. But he really liked the mean sound of it.

"What's a jaydee?" Teddy asked, feeling tough with a ci-garette bobbing on his lip. His eyes watered from the smoke.

In a stream of rich obscenities, Johnny drawled that a J.D. was what Teddy was. A juvenile delinquent. From anyone else, the filthy explanation would have been extraordinarily offen-sive. But, the lonely Teddy sensed a growing bonding with the kid.

"I'm not a juvenile delinquent," protested Teddy, pushing his glasses up on his nose.

Johnny scoffed. And he drove home a point: if Teddy wasn't a delinquent, then why was he at the center? Good kids got to go to foster homes.

Teddy was too naive to articulate the lessons in reformatory etiquette he was learning: that in order to have friends, he had to fit in; that to fit in, he had to act meaner than weaklings who tried to be cruel to him and he had to be invisible to the bullies who could be truly vicious. He had to quit using big words and good English. He had to work on his drawl and learn how to swear creatively. He had to quit putting everybody so much on guard by appearing so eager, so clever, so bright, so sharp. He had to play dull, tough and stupid.

It wasn't hard.

In fact, it was fun.

He tried a third cigarette.

Johnny told him not to worry about inhaling for a while.

But Teddy tried it anyway and after a head-spinning cough-ing bout, began to get the hang of it. The menthol made him feel goofy. He liked it.

That evening, he and Johnny were called up in front of the cafeteria and given swats with a thick, taped-up paddle for their truancy from wood shop.

But everybody knew how they had done it and they were celebrities. Teddy—proudly carrying a pack of Johnny's cigarettes in his front shirt pocket—gritted his teeth and didn't cry as the paddle slammed into his buttocks, stinging through his jeans. And he discovered that not crying over licks made him a "man."

After dinner, Kerguelen's friends, people Teddy didn't even know, asked to borrow cigarettes from him. Johnny nodded his approval. And that night, the other twelve boys in Teddy's cottage sneaked into his room and wanted to know if he and Johnny had really sneaked off to a whorehouse.

Teddy played it straight—even though he had only an inkling of what a whorehouse was—and insisted that they'd had a good time, but that Johnny had told him not to talk about it.

Everybody laughed, knowing he was lying.

Then, somebody got Justus started telling all about his dirty movie days. As the boy described a violent motorcycle gang, a pale ten-year-old with the dull look of the semi-retarded nudged Teddy for a cigarette. Justus gave Teddy a big grin and asked for one, then lit up nonchalantly while the other boys grinned.

"I don't like smokin', but, you're my frien'," Justus told his roommate. Teddy laughed.

"Tell Pooh-Bear what you did that time with that dog," ordered a sullen kid who wore one earring.

What Justus claimed he did in a low-budget movie with a puppy was more than Teddy could fathom. But, he tried not to let on.

Late that night after everybody had told all the dirty jokes they could think of and Teddy'd told the only two he knew, which weren't very dirty, they left.

In the empty room, Justus went morose and set fire to all of Kerguelen's matches, then got all excited, trying to keep the fire going in the metal trash can. He burned his notebook, Teddy's spiral, then started tearing out pages of his books.

Teddy pushed open all the windows and hugged his pillow in the smoky darkness. The other boys had talked derisively about a kid in another cottage who was gay. Teddy knew what that was...he thought. Johnny had told him some details. It all sounded unbelievable.

In the darkness, Teddy longed to be home with his grandmother.

Justus finally lost interest in the fire and went to bed. And that night, Teddy dreamed about leering one-eyed women and murderous motorcycle gangs and being forced to do things for grinding movie cameras....

✐   ✐   ✐

"Is this your boy?" had asked the Wyoming judge.

Trixie, her hair bright red and messier than usual, peered at Teddy in false surprise.

"Oh, my baby," she howled. "My sweet baby. How you've grown!"

They drove away from the courthouse with a man Trixie called Dobson.

"Well, I didn't have any choice," Teddy's mother exploded in the front seat. "It was either take him with us or six months for solicitation."

The man growled something Teddy couldn't hear.

"Well, he's my little boy and I can do with him whatever I want," she snapped.

Teddy huddled in the back.

"You shut up!" yelled the man, staring at him in the rear-view mirror.

"I didn't say anything," retorted the boy, pushing new glasses up on his nose.

The car screeched to a stop and the man was over the seat, shaking Teddy by his collar.

"Don't you ever sass me," he roared, slapping Teddy and breaking his glasses. "Do you hear?"

Trixie stared at the stunned boy and shook her head reprovingly. Dobson started up the car again as the crying Teddy gathered up the pieces of his glasses. He could barely see anything without them.

That night, they stayed in a motel, skipping out on the bill at 3 a.m.

Teddy learned quickly that Dobson was vicious, to keep out of his reach—to attempt to be invisible.

With his glasses newly patched together with adhesive tape, the three headed for California.

Excited, Teddy ran down to the Great Salt Lake and jumped in. He splashed alone, spraying the bad-tasting water and playing submarine. Ignoring him, Dobson and Trixie kissed on a dirty tablecloth.

Teddy whispered to himself, made motor noises and pretended he was a shark. He waded far out into the shallow lake.

"You shut up out there," bellowed Dobson, his voice carrying across the water. "You want me to beat your butt?"

Teddy played silently.

At Pilot Peak, Nevada, he played in the car while Trixie and Dobson went to the casino. They came out after Teddy had fallen asleep, Trixie screeching, Dobson being physically carried by five large men. He was livid with rage and shouted threats. At the car, twice he turned as if to go back in, challenging them to come back and fight him.

It was still dark when Teddy was awakened again by Dobson stopping the car in the blackness of the desert and demanding to know what he thought was so funny.

"Nothin'," whispered Teddy, not even able to remember if he'd been dreaming.

"I'll teach you to talk back to me, you little sissy," whispered the man, yanking him over the seat.

"You better listen to Dobson, hear?" yelled Trixie.

Dobson shoved Teddy ahead of him, then ceremoniously removed his belt. "You'll never sass anybody again," he snarled, curling the belt into a whip.

The boy lay in the sandy dirt and cried. Dobson yanked him up and shook him once more. "You quit that cryin'," he growled, seemingly concerned. Then, he hugged Teddy tight.

Teddy hung limp, swallowing blood from his lip.

By the car, Trixie began lecturing Teddy, her voice wavering in the desert wind.

✏️   ✏️   ✏️

Dobson owned a cabin on Lake Tahoe. He and Trixie settled in, working the casinos on the Nevada side. Teddy had chores—chopping firewood, running the vacuum cleaner, doing the laundry. The two times that he forgot to get the clothes out of the dryer before Dobson's ruffled casino shirts became wrinkled, he was beaten severely.

Once when he broke a axe handle, Dobson whalloped him with the back of his hand until Teddy lost consciousness as Dobson yelled that he should take care of things that weren't his. Another time, Dobson became furious when Teddy acted disinterested in learning how to change the oil in the car and belted the boy around until his cheeks bled.

Mostly, Teddy stayed in the cabin and watched a lot of TV. His favorite were reruns: *I Love Lucy, Andy Griffith, The Addams Family, Twilight Zone, Leave It to Beaver, ADAM-12,* and *Perry Mason.* He soon knew all the old *Star Trek* adventures and could imitate Alfred Hitchcock perfectly.

Growing ever more silent, he tried to do his chores when Trixie and Dobson were gone. Repeatedly, however, he miscalculated and took the full brunt of the man's unpredictable fury. He learned that when Dobson was determined to discipline him, it was best to immediately admit guilt and take the punishment without trying to offer excuses. When Dobson had decided he needed to be hit, nothing was going to help except humble submission.

The one consolation was that Dobson apparently had an idea of a certain toughness he wanted to see in Teddy.

The boy strove to achieve the image.

And he got wily.

He began to realize that Dobson really liked him a lot and softened up considerably when Teddy called him "Dad." Dobson liked pretending he was Teddy's father whenever they went into town.

Dobson had alcoholic tendencies and thought it manly of Teddy to down shots of whatever he was drinking and get a little crazy with him.

He thought it was hilarious to sit on the lake, the two of them downing a six-pack of beer, lifting toasts to people who looked irritated at drinking by someone as young as Teddy.

When Dobson was rampaging drunk, he would give Teddy money and cried if the boy would stand on the kitchen table and sing "Amazing Grace."

One of Teddy's most startling discoveries was that Dobson craved being invited to go along on the boy's explorations of the mountainside, of being shown deer-frequented salt licks, fresh water springs, quiet fishing banks and one particular bluff where you could see into the showers of an abandoned Girl Scout summer camp.

Dobson taught him how to drive, showed him how to shoot skeet and how to fish for trout at a little-known brook where the boy caught a twelve-pound cutthroat trout that the two decided to let go.

And Teddy began to work on the car with him. Teddy tried to be like Dobson and began pretending the man really was his dad.

Then, Dobson went away. Alone, Teddy explored the lake and mountains by himself. At first, he was a little lonely. But Dobson hadn't been much of a playmate and—as Henry David Thoreau once observed: "I never found the companion that was so companionable as solitude."

Teddy took to sleeping out under the pines, swimming in the lake whenever he pleased, making friends with campers and scavenging the sometimes extraordinary discards left behind in trash dumpsters and litter barrels.

Sometimes he told smiling blue-haired women that his mother ran a soup kitchen for bums. That always got a reaction—and occasionally a donation.

And he began having his dream again:

Standing atop the great Aztec Pyramid of the Sun, he frowned solemnly, his head held high. In front of him, from a couch, an old man received the vast crowd's adoration. He turned weakly to Teddy. "Well, Teddy," the old man rasped with an aged cynicism in his voice. "You came."

Teddy stared over the mass of Indians below. They, too, had seen Teddy's sudden arrival—and stirred with excitement.

"Don't you know who you are?" the old man rasped.

Silently, he awoke and stared at the twilight sky.

In mid-April, he went into town and tried to enroll himself in school, but upon walking in the door realized immediately that it was a mistake. Self-consciously, he fidgeted in a chair in the office as kids his age out in the hall giggled and pointed at his grubby clothes, his blond mass of matted curls and his patched-together glasses.

Feeling conspicuous that his jacket in the warm room had begun to reek of bourbon, sweat and wood smoke, he had to admit he didn't know his address, then balked at telling the suspicious receptionist where he'd attended school before.

For the next few weeks, he started spending a lot of time in the city library, reading, sitting in the comfortable chairs in the back—away from the picture windows—devouring the science fiction works of Robert Heinlein, Madeline L'Engle and Andre Norton, the Thornton Burgess animal series and such diverse books as *The People of the Deer* by Farley Mowat, *A Street in Marrakech* by Elizabeth Fernea and Sterling North's *Rascal.*

William Golden's *Lord of the Flies,* captivated him totally. For a week, he ran around naked on a secluded cove on the lake, hiding from boaters, spying on campers, pretending he was the hero, Ralph.

Then Dobson came back.

"You are going to make one hell of a drinking partner," Dobson bellowed as they took turns shooting his shotgun at the power lines and passing back and forth a bottle of gin that Trixie had stolen from work.

She knew that keeping Dobson drunk was a key to peaceful living.

But Teddy started liking the sensation, too.

Before long, he was drinking anything that he could find. In the campgrounds, he'd sneak down to tents in the night and empty out their ice coolers of six packs. Sometimes he'd poke around in garbage cans and find half-emptied wine bottles.

It was in July or August that Ted began realizing that he was doing things when he was drunk that he couldn't remember afterwards. One morning, he bolted awake in the back of a furious camper's parked car, a spilled ice cooler open beside him, empty beer cans tossed around the back seat.

Sitting morosely in the park rangers' office, not only did he have no recollection of crawling in the back seat, but could not remember drinking the beers.

"What is this?" asked a ranger who was his friend, a 40-ish supervisor named Melinda Dunlap. In her office, she turned the pages of the notebook he had been carrying.

Ashamed, Teddy peered: "*WhEN he Hits you gRIn and dont lIt him No becase yOU can keep It from huRtIng becase he ThInk you LIke It,*" read one note. Although drunkenly scrawled, it was unmistakably in the ten-year-old's handwriting.

"*WhEN you doIng stuFF You want TO dO you are showIng thIm that YOU lIke It and thy can't even do It. You dont care when thy act lIke thy dont lIke you.*"

"I guess I was drinking," grinned the boy.

Melinda stared at him silently.

"Teddy, I don't think we'd be doing you any favor not turning you in. You tell your dad that you've got to start going to school or I'm going to have to report you," she said.

She read over the notebook, her brow knitted with concern.

"I've always said a kid belongs with his folks. No matter how bad they are, you're better off," she said. "However, you are approaching the extreme."

Guiltily, Ted shrugged and tried to grin.

He told Dobson what she'd said and the man responded with rather colorful obscenities. Teddy giggled. And that was the end of it.

Then summer passed, autumn turned cold and the first snow came. Dobson lost his job as a blackjack dealer and started staying drunk and sinking into violent depressions. He would belt Trixie or Teddy for no reason at all, accusing them of talking about him behind his back. Or he would load his shotguns and level them out the window, then on the mother and son.

Teddy spent his eleventh birthday alone in an old shack where he had a roaring fire going in a broken pot-bellied stove. He climbed the tallest tree in Desolation Valley, pounded his chest and pretended he was a gorilla. Closing his eyes, he shivered and listened to his voice echoing through the canyons.

Then, prowling around the campgrounds, he ran into some old buddies, mountain climbers from Spain and Lebanon with whom he'd spent almost three weeks that summer. They'd paid him to show them good fishing spots and secluded swimming beaches.

When he informed them that it was his birthday, they whooped and acted crazy, breaking out a bottle of brandy. He swallowed the little sip they poured into the bottom of a cup for him, then grabbed the bottle and began swigging mouthfuls. His friends gawked—alarmed, but amused.

Alarmed at how badly he was dressed for winter, they took him into town and outfitted him with fancy climbing boots, a new pair of jeans, long underwear, two thick, blue plaid flannel shirts—and a brand-new pair of glasses. One of the boys dug in the back of the van and gave Teddy a faded goose-down parka, a pair of old ski mittens and a knit cap with ear flaps that had "Innsbruck" woven into it.

Stunned, Teddy yanked on the cap and declared that he had been born in Austria, which they all pooh-poohed until he indignantly began spouting details and town names.

Around the campfire, they didn't say anything as he piggishly guzzled their beer. They taught him to sing "Happy Birthday" in Lebanese.

And late that evening, Teddy hopefully asked if they would take him with them. Dramatically, he told them about Dobson's frequent beatings.

Nobody laughed.

They began debating the issue among themselves in French, Spanish and Lebanese. One of the girls began crying and stomped around the campfire, apparently arguing his case and refusing all rebuttal. She hugged him and made what sounded like an eloquent plea.

Nervously, another girl, Rachael, explained in English—for Teddy's benefit, apparently—that they could not, that they would be arrested for kidnapping, that without a passport Teddy could not go on with them to Spain, and that not even a crazy mother was going to give up such a nice boy as Teddy to a group of "old hippies."

Teddy disputed that, saying that Trixie wanted to get rid of him, that she complained all the time about being saddled with a kid.

The oldest man in the group—a man named Dov—noted that even so, Teddy would need a passport and that would take weeks and that one of them would have to accept guardianship over him and that would have to be done through the courts.

Then, one of the big, blond climbers, a half-Lebanese half-Dane named Riiser, proposed that they go to Alaska and spend the winter in the Brooks Range. Teddy wouldn't need a passport to go to Alaska. That was vetoed. The Brooks would have to be done some spring, not during the winter.

The debate continued, but Teddy knew he wasn't going anywhere. Nevertheless, their caring was extraordinary. Somebody got out a guitar.

Later that night, one of the men, Orlando, took Teddy for a walk and told Teddy of growing up as an orphan in Barcelona, Spain.

"I made it," he said, seriously. "You will, too. Use your head. You do not let bad kids lead you astray. Never forget to say your prayers and—" he pointed to his eye, "— Ojo! Ojo! Watch! Watch out for yourself. You are the only one who will."

Teddy slept curled up next to Orlando, the campfire flickering, his heart troubled, but his mind resolute. Deep in the night, the man cuddled up to him, awakening him and talking nonsense. Not at all alarmed, Teddy listened and realized that his friend was talking in his sleep. Tenderly, Orlando held him, patting him on the back, whispering assurances to him in Spanish.

Teddy closed his eyes and pretended that Orlando was his dad. And he dreamed:

Teddy—atop the great Aztec Pyramid of the Sun—sat down on a ceremonial pedestal. "Why did you waste your time here, Dad?" His young, high voice was strident with emotion. "Why can't we change it? I'll go back and we'll do stuff again and pick somewhere better. I'll stay and we'll do great stuff together."

"I am Teotl Ixca," he whispered, his high, old voice somehow filling the ceremonial plazas and promenades. "Don't you know who you are?" he rasped.

"What?" demanded Teddy.

"Your temptation is far, far greater than mine, Teddy! You are the fulfillment of the great prophecies. You will be the mighty one who leads the final battle."

✐   ✐   ✐

Teddy wandered back to Dobson's cabin several days later. Trixie had her arm in a cast. Her face was bruised. She took

Teddy out to the highway and they hitched a ride to Illinois, where they stayed a few weeks before heading for Detroit, then Texas.

Teddy would not see Dobson or Orlando again.

"How old are you?" asked the Corpus Christi, Texas, hotel manager. "Sixteen?"

"Yeah," slurred the eleven-year-old, leaning on the counter. "No, I'm fourteen."

"You look more like twelve," cooed the olive-skinned man with permanent circles under his eyes.

"Yeah?" exclaimed the boy.

"Does your mother know you drink?"

"Does yours?"

"I don't like kids drinking," said the man, his voice oily. "And you've stayed drunk ever since you started coming around here. Where do you live?"

"I get drunk all the time," bragged Teddy. "But I'm not really drunk now."

"How old are you, really?"

"Fifteen."

"Where do you live, kid? Where's your father?"

"He's a big movie star and rock singer. He owns a whole airline company.'"

The man laughed.

So did Teddy, leaning on the counter, wondering how easy it would be to stick his hand in the cash drawer.

"You're Trixie's boy, aren't you?" asked the man. "I had gotten the idea you were just a little boy."

Teddy grinned proudly. Donaciano made him an offer. He could bus tables in the hotel restaurant in exchange for meals—whatever Greg, the eccentric chef, had extra—and for whatever tips he could hustle. But, if the police or health inspectors came around, Teddy had to beat it out the back door. If he got caught, he had to say he was Donaciano's son so they wouldn't all get into child labor law trouble.

"If the cops come in, you don't want to say too much," oozed Donaciano, smiling, the bags under his eyes darkening. "If you know what I mean."

And thus Teddy grew a little chubby on prime rib, chocolate mousse, cherries jubilee and Greg's Chinese specialties: moo goo gai pan, sweet and sour, Szechuan pork, Peking duck, cashew chicken.

Not only did Teddy eat whatever the temperamental chef served up, but also sampled any interesting leftovers on plates he carried back into the kitchen. And if he was sneaky enough, he could finish off whatever drinks that were left.

After getting caught stealing waitresses' tips a couple of times, he learned how to cheerfully, unobtrusively re-fill water glasses, keep an eye on butter plates and whisk away emptied plates with such a flair that when customers spotted the curly-haired kid sitting on his stool by the cashier, they often flipped him a quarter or slipped him a half-dollar.

When income was slow, he took to palming the waitresses' quarters and an occasional dollar bill while cleaning off tables, being sure to leave enough that the girls weren't suspicious.

Trixie "worked the bar," where Teddy was allowed in only to carry in clean glasses and where he knew better than to give her more than just a knowing wink.

He heard all about the other bar "hostesses." Most were just as weird as Trixie. Cornelia thought the Mafia was after her, since she'd been the secretary at a door-to-door pots and pans company headquarters, which she said was controlled by organized crime.

Puni, a half-Chinese girl from Guam had about twenty cats in her room, all named "Puppy."

Nicole wore her hair in elaborate corn rows woven with bells, pieces of ivory, beads and broken glass. She told customers she was from Gabon, Africa. The bartender told Teddy it was more like Winston-Salem, North Carolina.

The boy became fond of most of the restaurant waitresses: Betty, a divorcee who also waited tables at the Holiday Inn; Frances, chain-smoking and nervous, who had an ugly nineteen-year-old daughter who worked weekends; Georgia, who also worked as an artists' model at the junior college; Annabelle, a smooth, flirting thirty-year-old with three kids Teddy's age, whom she never allowed him to meet. Teddy—who told all the women he was fourteen—had too smart of a mouth, she told Paul, the dishwasher.

In Corpus Christi, eleven-year-old Teddy enrolled in school for the first time since Wyoming. Seven weeks into the spring semester, Trixie took him down and promised the officials that she would try to find his records, bluffing him into the seventh grade.

Walking to school the first day, he got in a fight with Lucky, a short thirteen-year-old in the sixth grade, who—like the other kids who lived around the hotel—thought Teddy was fourteen and had flunked a lot.

Neither boy won the fight. It ended with them laughing and deciding to be friends. They arrived at school with their clothes torn, their hair messed and their arms around each other.

How come he was just a seventh grader? "I missed a lot of school. Actually, I'm lucky they don't put me back with the third graders," explained Teddy, laughing, truthfully.

Lucky lived in one of the condos behind the hotel. And he smoked menthol cigarettes.

"Man, you really get off on these things," Teddy observed the first time that Teddy bummed one. Lucky watched the big boy inhale. "Do you ever really get off, you know, on stuff?"

Teddy thought he meant marijuana, which he admitted he'd done at "this state school for delinquents, you know, in Wyoming." He didn't tell that pot had had no effect on him. But Lucky did hashish. After school, Teddy tried it for the first time. The brown resin had an incredible effect that Teddy liked much more than getting drunk. Lucky and fifteen or twenty other kids who lived in the neighborhood, it turned out, were a gang. Their eyes puffy, their minds happily oozing along in peaceful contempt, they were the Confederate Army. Lucky was General Robert E. Lee.

Getting high with them was like nothing Teddy had ever known. Like a small army, they would attack small parks, laughing, climbing trees, splashing in ornamental fountains, hooting, disrupting baseball games, stealing balls from little kids.

Their heads buzzing, they went looking for Union Army maggots: elderly ladies feeding pigeons, old men shuffling to the grocery store, kids with lunch money.

They showed Teddy how to play "Sherman Marching Through Georgia." Fifteen to twenty strong, they swarmed onto a sidewalk, grabbing sacks out of peoples' arms, yanking purses off of arms, ripping watches off of arms, necklaces from necks, wallets out of pockets. Laughing, cheering, taunting, they kicked shins, stomped feet and fled.

Hooting hilariously, they ran, knowing they were indomitable. Sure, people gave chase. The boys with loot sprinted away while the others milled, laughing, asking inane questions, threatening to call police, tripping, swarming, yelling, trembling in "epileptic fits."

It was fun. But the third time that Teddy came to work high, Donaciano kicked him out, then fired Trixie.

Without any luggage, they boarded a bus and went to Padre Island.

On Padre Island, Trixie had to entertain her customers out of her and Teddy's motel room. She lectured him on the evils of drugs, ordering him to stay sober.

He assured her he would. But he didn't get high anymore, since he didn't know anybody on Padre Island.

He knew ways he could make some money. He'd discovered that people would pay for little boys in the same way that they would pay for Trixie. Donaciano had sounded him out on that idea and Lucky had bragged that he did it for as much as $500.

Doing it sounded exciting the way Donaciano described it. But Teddy didn't think it was for him. It was difficult to explain why. It was just that doing it didn't sound like something he wanted to do.

One warm night late that summer, sitting on the dirty sand of the beach, Teddy was reading an old *Reader's Digest* he had taken out of the bus station.

It had a checklist on alcoholism.

Yes, he and Trixie frequently got so drunk that he couldn't remember what they'd talked about or what movie they'd been watching on TV.

No, he didn't prefer being drunk. But, he preferred her drunk—she was an awful lot more sociable when she was loaded. No, he had no trouble having fun when he wasn't drunk. He was becoming a good surfer, using a board he had stolen from a vacationing kid from Tennessee who had been stupid enough to let him borrow it.

No, he couldn't drink just one or two, there was no point in that: he liked getting very drunk. He liked getting totally smashed.

Yes, he liked drinking by himself.

He went on down the list, added up his points and dug a trench in the sand with his toe.

He was an alcoholic, according to the survey.

"God," prayed Teddy, suddenly, surprising even himself. Nervously, he continued digging with his toe. "My mother's a thief and a whore. We're both liars and we cheat people and steal stuff."

He stared out at the surf.

He didn't know why he'd started praying.

He sniffled.

"How come You're so mean to me? Other kids have their own rooms and horses and mothers who like them and fathers who take them to football practice."

He wiped a tear off his cheek.

"My mother is crazy. And I'm a drunk and a doper."

The ocean roared.

Why hadn't God let him grow up in Los Cerrillos at his Uncle Willem's house? By now, Teddy could have been a Boy Scout. Tears began running down his face.

"Quit it. Please," he whispered. "I didn't do nothing to You."

He hunched down on the sand and began seeing himself on the telephone, talking with Uncle Will, asking him to come get him—and crying and talking to Aunt Minnie and hearing Janny yell that they'd been praying for him all the time.

Teddy dug in his pocket. He had enough coins to reach the operator and call collect.

He jogged back toward the motel carport where there was a pay phone.

But, he considered, what if Uncle Will wouldn't accept the call? What if he still said Trixie had to sign the papers?

Teddy trembled.

He began to practice what he would say. He repeated it over and over.

They'd have to let him come. He was their nephew. It would work out.

But maybe, he thought, he ought to practice some more what he wanted to say. He'd get it all worked out. And he wouldn't lie. He'd think it all out so he wouldn't get carried away and tell Uncle Will a bunch of crazy stuff.

He put the money back in his pocket.

That night, lying awake in the empty motel room, he had even a better idea. He would hitchhike back to New Mexico. He'd surprise them.

He'd just knock on the door and everybody would be so happy to see him that they wouldn't know what to say. *Yeah.*

However, in the early morning darkness, Trixie woke him and together they pushed their rental car down the beach motel driveway.

"Having car trouble?" called the manager through the stillness. He held a rifle.

"Go!" whispered Trixie, swearing under her breath. "Go!"

Teddy pushed his shoulder into the rear fender. The car slowly picked up speed.

"You there!" yelled the manager. "Stop right there."

"Let's git!" exulted Trixie, pulling open the driver's door. Teddy yanked open the passenger door and dived in.

Trixie fumbled with the key.

The car slogged to a stop.

Trixie spat, suddenly cursing in fury.

"I've got a gun," shouted the motel owner, running down beside the car in his bathrobe.

"Should I call the police?" screeched his wife up on a balcony.

"I already have," he yelled, holding the rifle on the two.

"My goodness!" drawled Trixie in her southern best. "The little ol' battery is deader than a doornail and Teddy here, he's the mechanic in our family when Duke—that's what I call my husband—isn't around! Now, Theodore really has learned a lot about cars from his father! Duke runs a Ford dealership right outside of Jackson! And Theodore says to me, he says, 'Mommy, I think we can get that car started.' But, I told him not to worry about it, that we would get some of you men to show us what to do in the morning or where to find a garage! But bless his little heart, he couldn't sleep! And he come to me a'cryin' and in the middle of the night and he says 'Mommy, when are you going to let me be a man? I know how to fix that car!'

"Well, what is a mother to say? He is so very much like his father—"

The motel owner—who wasn't swallowing any of it—yelled back at his wife on the stairs to call the police again. He leveled the rifle at Trixie's head. "You ain't running out on your bill!" he yelled. "No way."

"Well," said Trixie, "let's see here! Y'all take American Express?" she fished in her purse and pulled out a man's wallet.

Teddy slumped down in his seat.

       ✐   ✐   ✐

At the jail, Trixie had started shrieking it was all a mistake, that she was Maybelle McMichaels and that there was going to be big trouble.

Teddy could tell that everybody knew she was lying. He didn't know why she bothered.

"Be a man, Theodore Benjamin Harrison McMichaels," she had wept, dabbing his face with a flimsy handkerchief. "And take care of your dear, dear self.

"Don't let anything happen to you. Remember the Bible story of *Daniel and the Lions' Den* and trust in the Lord that He will protect you in your time of dire need and humiliation.

"If they mistreat or abuse you, just refuse to eat, honey. Scream and yell and let them know what your daddy is going to do to them. I tremble at the very thought of Duke busting in here and cleaning out this house of iniquity!"

Teddy was placed in a foster home. The McPhersons had a thing about kids, enthused the social worker, pulling into the driveway. "You're really going to like them," she said. "And they've got two eighth graders about your age."

Ted had told the police he was fourteen.

The house was old, the lawn sparse. A boy with thick glasses charged across the big porch, chasing a little Indian kid.

Both stared as the social worker and Teddy came up to the door. "You our new bruvvah?" asked the kid with glasses. He was taller than Teddy and had an awkward gait, as if he had muscular dystrophy.

"Hey, Robbie!" greeted the social worker, tapping at the door again. "This here's Teddy Bear. He's the one I told you about. He's your age."

"Awwww WIGHT!" exclaimed the vacant-eyed kid, wiping a snotty nose with the too-long sleeves of his jeans jacket. He grinned. "You gonna get my ol' bunk."

The door swung open and a disheveled woman holding a black six-year-old by the collar smiled apologetically.

"Come on in, Dawn," she said. She knelt with the six-year-old. "Dumont, what did I say I would do if you didn't mind me? What did I say?"

The kid tried to squirm out of her firm grip. "You say he be stan' in corner."

"That's right. Now, what do you have to do?"

"Him haffa stan' in corner."

"Why?"

The kid squirmed, grinning at Teddy. The social worker nudged him. The two wandered into what once had been a dining room. It was lined with double bunks.

Toys were everywhere.

"The McPhersons are really nice people," said the social worker. "You're gonna really like them."

Teddy looked doubtful.

Mrs. McPherson came in and gave Teddy the one empty bunk. She didn't act at all surprised that he had no luggage. Joe McPherson was a distant man who sat in front of the television and sipped beer. He didn't talk to the kids and Teddy was cautioned by Robbie to leave him alone.

"Les' go play!" enthused the kid, who volunteered that he was in special education. Teddy was perplexed. He didn't act retarded, just...odd.

In a parking lot across from the house, Robbie and Teddy tried to join a soccer game. The other kids, some from the McPherson household, bellowed their refusal to have Robbie on their team. Finally, a team captained by intense fourteen-year-old Edward agreed to take Robbie if they got Teddy, too.

The first time Teddy stole the ball, he passed it back to the wildly cheering Robbie, who immediately panicked, fumbled and kicked blindly, knocking the ball out of bounds.

"Never, never pass to Robert," intoned Edward while the ball was being retrieved. "He's..." The boy waved circles around his ear. "Nutso. He's got a damaged brain."

Teddy squinted over at the kid. His arms and legs strangely awkward, Robbie was yelling for somebody to pass him the ball. Somehow, it hadn't registered on him that he'd kicked it into the next county.

"Are you our new brother?" asked Edward. "You that Teddy guy?"

Ted nodded.

"My name's Teddy, too," said Edward. His intense eyes seemed to bug in irritation. "An' don't you ever call me that. I'll strangle you. You understand me? I hate it."

Teddy nodded.

There were ten foster kids besides Teddy in the McPherson household. Edward was the oldest and took his responsibilities very seriously. Robbie was next. Then, there were four eleven-year-olds: Teddy; quiet, almost-sullen James, who was half-blood Sioux Indian and from Montana; goofy clown Chris, a bright-eyed kid who slept in the bunk below Teddy; and Dare, a black kid with Oriental eyes and hair that was only curly, not kinky. Then, there was five-year-old Andy, who everybody liked, who the first night quietly crawled into Teddy's lap and went to sleep while the TV droned on. There was Dumont, a dark, wiry black six-year-old who spoke in a thick garble. He had a baby brother, Jubal, who toddled around and had a thing about shedding his diaper.

Teddy would spend the summer as Teddy McPherson. In September, he was enrolled in the ninth grade, since he had told everybody he was fourteen.

It pleased Ted that he fitted into junior high. He was as big as many of the smaller ninth graders. He could read as well as anybody. He thought wood shop was a blast. However, in English, history, geography and alegebra, he was in over his head. He'd never done much multiplication or division.

It was to Chris that Teddy shared the secret that he wasn't really fourteen, but eleven. Chris thought it was hilarious and told Edward, who immediately told Mrs. McPherson. The next day, they all had to go to school and get Teddy out of the ninth grade and into the sixth.

The neighborhood World War II army retreated along a dry creek bed. Giving out a yell, Edward dropped to one knee and with an imaginary musket picked off an unseen German sniper.

"How come you're not in my new class?" asked Teddy, beside Chris. "I thought there was only one sixth grade."

Chris grimaced, spinning and shooting imaginary Germans.

"Are you in special ed?" asked Teddy. "Like Robbie?"

"No!"

"Did you flunk?"

"I'm in first."

"First? You're in first grade?"

Chris made a face, then pulled the pin out of an imaginary hand grenade, tossing it over his shoulder. Edward was urging everybody to retreat faster down the creek bed.

"My mom and I was carnies," said Chris, a proud note in his voice. "See, we were always traveling with the fair and carnivals and stuff and I didn't get to go to school."

"That's why you can't read!" exclaimed Teddy. "I thought you were just dumb."

Chris gave him a very dirty look. "I hear you can't even add two plus two," he shot.

"Oh, yeah?" guffawed Teddy. "It's four."

The creek turned. A large pipe gaped open. "Them Yanks'll never figure out where we went if we go into this secret tunnel!" yelled Edward. "Come on!"

"We're not supposed to!" exclaimed Robbie.

"What's two hundred and eighty-seven plus four million and fifty thousand?" asked Chris.

"It's dark!" protested somebody else. "And it stinks."

"I don't know," said Teddy. "But you don't either."

"Come on!" yelled Edward, his eyes bugging out. "Mah name's Majah Francis Marion, but folks calls me the Swamp Fox. I welcomes y'uns to the Louisians biyous and offah you the protection of my secret tunnels. Now, if you will follow me!"

The Army trailed reluctantly, Chris in the rear. "Hey," said Teddy. "I read real good. I'll teach you, huh? Want to?"

"I hate reading."

"It's easy. I'll show you. You teach me numbers and I'll teach you words."

Chris looked very skeptical.

"You know your alphabet?" asked Teddy.

Chris nodded.

"Let's hear it."

Softly, Chris sang the alphabet song.

"See, you're smart," said Teddy. "Okay. What sound does 'A' make?"

Sloshing through the Galveston storm sewer, Chris got his first phonics lesson. Robbie dropped back and joined in. His inability to remember letters' sounds encouraged Chris considerably.

"I should be in third," confessed Teddy. "Maybe if I go back to third, they'll let you come up."

Chris looked hopeful.

"Umm," mumbled the Swamp Fox. In front of him, there was no more tunnel—just dark, wet, stagnant air. "Y'all hold up!"

Carefully, Edward inched forward. He felt around the edge and—leaning all the way out—touched down at about two and a half feet. He crawled out and stood up.

"Fohwad, men," he drawled, brushing himself off.

"I'm not goin' no farther," exclaimed a neighbor kid. "It's dark in here."

"Come on," pleaded Edward, his voice high.

"Where are we going?" demanded Robbie.

"We're lost," growled James.

"Ah assure you that we is somewheh neah Paris," said the Swamp Fox. "Or London. Let's go!"

"We're staying right here," said a kid in front of Teddy and Chris.

"Who cares what you do?" yelled Teddy, shoving past him. "Come on, Swamp Fox! Let's go get some Germans." Chris whooped and followed.

The other kids whimpered and scooted along behind them.

Twenty minutes later, the pipe opened out into the evening sky, twenty feet out over the ocean.

The Swamp Fox peered out.

"Uh, we're at the gulf," he said, unsteadily. "We can't get out this way."

Teddy pushed up to the front. He stared at the dirty water.

"We can all swim," he reminded. Every Friday, the McPhersons went into a YMCA in Houston, where all the boys took swimming lessons and played water polo with their foster mom.

The Swamp Fox stuck his head back out the pipe.

"Let us then make this an amphibious assault," he said. "Hold your muskets and powder over your head."

He crouched in the pipe's opening. Sea gulls screamed.

"LaFayette, we are here!" Edward yelled, leaping. Robbie followed.

James surfaced 50 feet away. Behind him, a dog-paddling Dare sputtered and fought toward the bank.

Beside Teddy in the pipe, Chris took a breath and reluctantly tumbled into the water. On the beach, Edward stifled a yell as Robbie went under.

Alone in the pipe, Teddy crouched.

Chris bobbed to the surface, gasped for breath and began kicking toward the splashing, hooting Robbie.

✐   ✐   ✐

Trixie got out of jail in October and amid much weeping, retrieved her son. The two stayed at Leo House, a church-run halfway house for abused wives. Then, she disappeared again. No one ever told Teddy why he couldn't go back to the McPhersons. He would not see them again.

Glassy-eyed, he sat quietly in the car as a welfare worker told him what a good place the Anchor of Hope Christian Children's Home was.

"This is...Theophilus?" asked a smiling woman.

Teddy wavered hesitantly.

"I'm Mr. Mays and this is my wife," said a man. His wife continued smiling. The man held his hand out to Teddy. "Well, did you bring anything with you?"

Teddy lifted his dirty knapsack. Nervously, he pushed his glasses up on his nose.

✐   ✐   ✐

"Hey," said Chuck, his chubby roommate.

Teddy looked up from his math book.

"You smoke?" whispered Chuck, his eyes guarded, his face blank.

Teddy squinted and glanced around. "Do you?" he shot back, his voice low.

"Kind of," said Chuck mysteriously. "Come on."

Teddy followed the fat boy around in back of the chicken houses and down a ravine, around the side of a hill and out of sight of the rest of the ranch.

Down by a little stream, four other boys were sitting on boulders.

"Hey," greeted one named Marcus. Teddy had given him a wide berth since hearing that he'd killed his stepfather. The fifteen-year-old had ice-cold blue eyes and never smiled.

The other boys appeared to be smoking cigars.

Expertly, Chuck examined a wild vine hanging from one of the trees. He broke off a few lengths, then dug in his jeans pocket for a match and lit it on the zipper of his fly.

Expertly, he lit up his "cigarette," then gave it to Teddy. Experimentally, he drew on it and coughed. It tasted like burning garbage.

"What is this?" he asked.

"Grapevine. What do you think?"

"Not too bad," lied Teddy, inhaling again and feeling his eyes water.

It would turn out that real cigarettes were extremely scarce. Smokers had to bribe the goody-goody kids of the choir to smuggle packs back from weekend trips.

"You ever done it with a girl?" asked a boy named Reggie. He peered at Teddy. "You know?"

"What?" exclaimed Teddy incredulously.

"We know a girl who wants to do it with you. She thinks you're cute," said Chuck. "I've done it to her, kind of. Want to?"

Teddy glanced around at the blank, staring faces.

"You're crazy," he said, crossing his arms.

✐　　　✐　　　✐

At the Anchor of Hope, anyone caught with cigarettes had to eat them—one cigarette a day until they were gone.

"Whose are these?" asked Mays one evening. The cottage's TV room became deathly silent. Everybody looked up.

Mays held an entire pack of menthols. Hungrily, Teddy stared at them.

"Teddy Behre, are these yours?"

In silent horror, Ted looked into the man's grim face.

"Nossir," he whispered.

"They were found tucked up under the dining room table where you sit. If they're not yours, then whose are they?"

Teddy suspected they were Reggie's or Chuck's. "Mine, sir," he lied, hanging his head. If he didn't take the blame quickly, everybody might be punished.

"Outside," commanded the man, softly but terribly.

Mr. Mays put his hands in his pockets and strolled ahead on a cattle path. Solemnly, Teddy followed, shuffling his feet and kicking up dust. The trail cut up a hill, through a woods and out across a field where several sick-looking horses were grazing.

Mr. Mays stopped on the edge of the woods and examined a sapling. He bent down and pulled it up.

"Ever chew on sassafras, T.B.?" he asked in a strangely detached voice. Teddy accepted the root and sniffed it. It smelled like root beer. He followed the man down another wooded hill into a ravine. "Do you know the penalty for possessing these cancer-causing coffin-nails?"

Teddy nodded, keeping up with the man's pace.

"Do you think that because you are new, you are exempt?"

"When I was at this school in Wyoming," said Teddy, his voice high, "they let us smoke all we wanted. Nobody cared. Plus, my dad smokes. I just wanted to be like him."

"T.B., I'm an old schoolmate of your Uncle Will. I happen to know you've never had a father."

Teddy didn't say anything.

"Your uncle and I had a long talk and you're going to be staying with us for some time. Your mother's signed a release."

Startled, Teddy looked up in disbelief. And for reasons he didn't understand, his eyes filled with tears.

"T.B., you were warned concerning smoking. Now, I have to punish you."

Teddy sniffled and didn't say anything. Now even his own mother didn't want him.

"Do you realize it's your fault that I have to discipline you?" Teddy nodded at the ground. He trembled. Mays took out his pocket knife and began cutting a small branch off of a willow tree sapling.

"I won't do nothing again," croaked Teddy urgently. "I'm sorry. I promise."

"I certainly hope so. I only want to have to whip you once." Teddy shook in agony. Trixie hadn't even said goodbye. He sniffled as the man slowly cut the leaves off of the branch and trimmed it to about a three-foot length.

"T.B., I'm going to give you a good switching. It's the best way I know to let you see that I mean business."

Ted trembled. "I don't want to get whipped," he said. Unexpected tears rolled down his cheeks.

"Pull down your pants," said Mays.

Teddy hesitated, frowning. Mays moved forward and Teddy quickly undid his belt buckle and let his jeans fall around his ankles. He began sobbing uncontrollably.

"Please don't whip me," he cried. "I won't do it again."

"Grab your ankles," advised Mays. "If you twist around, it'll hurt all over. If you hold still, it'll just hurt on your behind."

Teddy sobbed and grabbed his ankles.

"This is going to hurt me as much as you, T.B.," intoned the man. And with that, he set to lashing Ted across the buttocks. The boy howled—a little more than was necessary.

"I really want to enjoy the years I'm going to be your housefather," said Mr. Mays, between strokes. "I can tell you are an exceptional boy. I'm going to give you 50, T.B., because I really want you to remember what I say."

When he was through, Teddy fell over in the grass and rocks and didn't move. He hadn't twisted around after the first ten. He had held his ankles and stood still. Now, he felt like he was on fire.

Mays' licks had been steady, determined and emotionless. Dobson's whippings usually had been in anger. But afterwards, Dobson often had been filled with shame and had held the crying boy close and talked softly, gently to him, promising to buy him things or go places with him.

"Now, it's all over, T.B.," said Mr. Mays. "Nobody's seen or heard you cry. We don't ever have to think or talk about it again. You made a mistake and you've been punished. Now, you can start all over again. I want you to be a leader in our family."

Ted stood up. He pulled up his pants and gingerly snapped them.

"Jesus," said Mr. Mays. He was kneeling down beside Teddy. "Help T.B. He hurts so much inside that he doesn't know what to do or say. Help me if I punished him severely or in anger."

Teddy sniffled. Mr. Mays was still beside him. He put his arm on the boy's shoulder. Teddy sniffled, then: "I believe in Jesus," he blubbered.

"Good. That's good, T.B."

"I pray and God listens," said Teddy. "I'm here and my mom hates me because I disobeyed God."

"My, my. What makes you say that?"

Teddy told him all about Trixie and not calling Uncle Willem the time that he had felt God wanted him to.

Then, tearfully, he told about life with Dobson and getting arrested, about Wyoming and smoking hashish in Corpus Christi. And regretting it immediately, he told Mays about Marcus.

The man was silent.

"What grade are you, Teddy?" he asked after a minute or so.

"Fifth," said Teddy. "Well, not really. I was in third when I quit. Then, I was in the eighth, but I shouldn't have been and they made me go back, you know."

"You're just in the fifth? How old are you? You're about thirteen, aren't you?"

Teddy hung his head. "I'm only eleven," he said. "I'm just real big. I'm a mountain climber and fishin' guide."

"I figured you for at least twelve."

"Some people think I'm fourteen." Then, impulsively, he looked up. "Do you mind if I call you 'Dad'?"

"Please do," said Mr. Mays. "That's what you're supposed to call me. I'm your housefather and spiritual leader."

Teddy grinned and hugged him.

But he was aware that the skinny man hesitated and didn't hug him back.

         ✐   ✐   ✐

"T.B.," called Mays, walking out of the administration building. The late Texas winter had hit. Teddy, who was three days away from turning twelve, was playing football on the snow-flecked, brown lawn with some junior high school boys. He was wearing a couple of sweaters under a jacket donated from a nearby church.

"Come here," called the man.

Teddy, Chuck and Reggie charged over and peered at a notebook the man held.

"Why?" asked Reggie.

"I just want to talk to T.B.," said Mr. Mays. "You go on."

Reluctantly, Reggie and Chuck charged back into the football game.

"Who helped you write this?" asked Mays.

"What?" asked Teddy.

"This," said Mays, holding up Teddy's notebook.

"What were you in trouble for?" grinned Reggie.

"Nothing," said Teddy. "He just wanted to know if I wrote something. I guess Mrs. Dawson didn't think I'd done it."

"Did you?" asked Reggie.

"Sure."

"What is it?" asked Chuck.

"A book."

"A book? It looks awful short," scoffed Reggie.

"I'm not finished."

"I never knew anybody who wrote a book," marveled Chuck. "What's it about?"

"This guy who can move around in space and time and be wherever he wants to be. Want to hear some of it?"

"No," said Reggie.

"I do. Wow." Chuck sat down on the cold sidewalk. Impatiently, Reggie sat down, too.

Teddy plopped down and began flipping pages.

"Okay," he said. *Wolf—standing atop the great Pyramid of the Sun—frowned solemnly, his head held high. In front of him, from a couch atop the pyramid, an old man received the vast crowd's adoration. He turned weakly and looked in surprise at the boy* "Well," *the old man rasped.* "You came."

"Who's the old man?" asked Reggie.

"Just shut up and listen," ordered Chuck. "Go ahead."

Wolf glanced almost disdainfully at the Indians. "Why did you waste your time here, Dad?" *His young, high voice was strident with emotion.* "You're gonna be exiled—given to the Evil One for what you have done here...and you hate him as much as he hates you!"

"Don't call Lucifer the Evil One," rasped Quetzalcoatl. *"He and I have made our peace. He recognizes what I am. I will continue to have great power."*

"No!" exclaimed Wolf, crying suddenly. *"You can't! You're not like that!"*

"I require my freedom," whispered Quetzalcoatl.

"It's not freedom!" screamed Wolf.

"Don't you know who you are?" rasped the old man

"What's this about?" interrupted Reggie again.

"Shut up!" bellowed Chuck.

Teddy sighed and frowned at Reggie, who grimaced, then jumped up and walked off.

"Your grandma wrote books, didn't she?" asked Mr. Mays. Teddy was helping him nail new "facer board" trim on the eaves of one of the cottages.

"Yessir," said Teddy. "And she was on TV, too. All the time."

"I don't believe she understood what she was writing about," said Mays. "These people tend to be unbalanced, emotional people who work themselves up into hysteria and call it religion. Have you ever seen anybody healed?"

"Sure," said Teddy.

"You're very young," Mays had said. "When you're older, you'll realize what really happened. It was all in those peoples' heads."

"You ever huffed toulie?" asked Chuck, his voice strangely distant. It was after lights-out.

Teddy sat up. "What?"

"You ever been high?"

"Oh. Yeah, sure. All the time. One time I read this article? It said I was an alcoholic."

"Yeah? Where'd you detox?"

"Huh?"

"Where'd you go through detoxification? All alcoholics have to detox. "

"What's detox?"

"Where'd you go to get sober?"

"Nowhere. I was in a foster home where they locked up the beer when they caught me stealing it. I was drunk the night before I came there, though." The latter was a lie.

"You ever had DTs?"

"What's that?"

"Where you shake real bad and hurt and see stuff that really isn't there, like purple elephants?"

"No way."

"You weren't no alcoholic."

"You ever take pills?" asked Teddy.

"No."

"I did. Once, I took some pills once that these campers gave me. I got real crazy and couldn't sleep for two days. It was speed. I got really scared. And I've done grass and hash. And one time, I may have done opium. Me and Trixie smoked some stuff some john gave her. And it put us to sleep and we dreamed all sorts of stuff. It was just reefer, but I think it had opium or maybe heroin on it."

"Don't do it no more," ordered Chuck.

Teddy looked over at him, surprised.

"I was huffing toulie one time and I saw the earth pass before my eyes," said Chuck. "I saw how it is all going to end. I seen the final battle, too, like in your book."

In the dark, Teddy sat up on one elbow and peered at him.

"I seen the purest music," said Chuck softly, "not really, but in my mind. I looked up in the sky and could imagine, you know what I mean? It was there, but it wasn't."

"How do you huff toulie?"

"I ain't telling you. You would do it, you junkie," Chuck leaned back. "It's bad. You get a definite buzzing and your head is vibrating and you get a rhythm and you get these neat little rushes and if something really...like my friend said, it's like tuning in on the crickets."

Chuck made cricket sounds and laughed wistfully. "It's really bad. It's different than anything I've ever done. And you don't come down for a long time. It's not as good at first, but it lasts, like I was going to play a record and I got out the record and forgot what song I was going to hear."

Teddy squinted at him.

"But it will really screw up your head—do permanent damage, too. No kidding. It will fry your brain. My sister come home and says 'I'll kill you, if you've been huffing, I'm gonna kill you.' She said, 'let me smell your breath. See, she had done it and she knew how bad it can get and she really started getting on my head about it. And I was so stoned she scared the, well, I didn't go to sleep that night, so afraid that I wouldn't wake up. See, when you're huffing, if somebody puts something in your head, you believe it."

Teddy didn't say anything.

"And don't you do it," said Chuck. "Huffing stuff burns up your brain, so I don't want you doing it. I got good friends who can't even remember my name. There's this kid who was like you named Cliff. He was my friend, but now he's like retarded. He's twenty years old, but he just rides his bike around in front of Wal-Mart."

"Let's do it," urged Teddy. "It sounds great."

"No way, Teddy," said the older boy, very seriously. "I ain't never met nobody like you."

He was silent for a moment. Teddy sat up, the depth of Chuck's concern sinking in.

"You ain't like the rest of us, Teddy," said Chuck. "You're gonna be somebody. When you first came here, I thought you were fifteen, I really did. And you're only twelve.

"And now, you go and write something like this book. Man, Teddy, you mess up your head and it's going to be a terrible tragedy. You would be robbing the world. It would be like Beethoven's mother having an abortion before he could be born. You're gonna be famous. And I'm gonna tell people I knew you."

Teddy smiled in the dark.

"So promise me," said Chuck. "You promise me you won't get high ever again."

"I promise," said Teddy, softly. A chill went through his body. He stared seriously at his roomie.

"You better mean it."

Teddy grinned. He shrugged.

Teddy was helping dig post holes when a bicyclist rode by on the road. Then, six rode past. Within two hours, hundreds had passed, old men, middle-aged women, teen-aged girls, kids with their parents.

"Where is your *bicycle?*" yelled a man at the working boys. Mr. Mays didn't even look up.

"I don't have one," yelled Teddy. "Where are you going?"

"Oklahoma," called somebody else.

A woman paused and took a picture of the youngsters. Teddy slid down the bank and walked over to her. She rode a beautiful blue and gold twelve-speed. Gently, Teddy touched the padded handlebars.

"Why are you racing?" he asked. "You raising money for something?"

"Racing is for idiots," said the woman, lowering her sunglasses. "This is the annual Great Tour Across Oklahoma."

"Huh?" asked Teddy. "We're in Texas."

"Well, we're very careful not to take this bicycling too seriously. So this year, we're not going to do any riding in Oklahoma."

"What?" asked Teddy, grinning.

"We're riding from Houston to the Oklahoma border. There's the most incredible south wind you've ever seen. It's pushing us 90 miles a day without any sweat. This is the most fun I've had since I was a girl."

"Wow," said Teddy.

He climbed back up on the bank.

"They're bicycling to Oklahoma," he said.

Mrs. Mays nodded tersely.

"I've never seen a bigger waste of energy or time," he said. "The paper said there were going to be 3,000 of them go by here. Can you believe that? It's absurd."

"It looks like fun."

The other boys peered at the stream of riders.

Nobody said anything.

That July, Teddy was permitted to leave the Anchor of Hope and return to Los Cerrillos.

        ✐   ✐   ✐

"Well," said Uncle Will, "where's your luggage?"

Teddy held up his filthy blue knapsack, which had a couple of t-shirts, ten notebooks and a wall plaque that Chuck had secretly made him that read *"Lo, though I walk through the valley of the shadow of death, I fear no evil, because I'm the meanest muthah in the valley."*

Will motioned for him to get in the car.

Teddy's uncle said almost nothing for the next twelve hours. The whole family ran out to greet the exhausted twelve-year-old when he and his weary Uncle Will pulled up into the driveway.

"Teddy Bear!" yelled his cousin Janny, "Come on, I'll show you my—I mean OUR room. You're going to stay with me."

"You want to play football?" asked Hans, who now was in junior high.

"No," declined Teddy. "You still got any horses?"

"Sure," interjected Janny, putting his hand on Teddy's shoulder, determined not to let any of his big brothers usurp his responsibility over the new arrival. "Come on."

Actually, the family had one pony.

And about twenty new sheep.

Out in the barn, "Damn," said Teddy. "What do you want sheep for?"

"You cussed!" exclaimed Janny, genuinely shocked. "Wow. Dad'll bust your butt."

Embarrassed, Teddy bit his lip and resolved to watch his mouth. Everybody at Anchor of Hope cussed when the adults weren't around.

Janny took Teddy up to the loft in the barn and proudly showed him a private place hollowed out in the hay bales. It had a cot, two bales arranged to look like chairs and a bookshelf made out of concrete blocks and boards.

Teddy picked out a book called *Closer Than My Shadow: The Holy Spirit and Your Child.* Teddy remembered it from his grandmother's library.

"What do you have this for?" asked Teddy.

"I don't know," said Janny. "My grandmother gave it to me back when I was little. My dad has thrown it away twice, but I always find it. I keep it up here. Want to see the cows?"

Teddy squinted at him, as if for the first time realizing that his grandmother was Janny's grandmother.

"Do you remember her?" Teddy asked, his voice suddenly hoarse. He put the book down and sat on the cot.

"Sure." Janny sprawled out on a hay bale. He stared at Teddy, something obviously on his mind: "Do you really not know who your dad is?" he asked, his voice filled with curiosity.

Teddy grimaced as if in pain. But he withheld the usual lie about Dobson being his dad.

"I don't see how your mom wouldn't know," said Janny. "I mean, they had to be married, didn't they—unless she was just doing it with all sorts of guys."

Ignoring the comment, Teddy picked out another book: *Gypsy Moth Circles the World,* by Sir Francis Chichester.

"What's this about?" he guffawed. "A moth?"

Janny peered at the title. "It's about an old man who sailed around the world in a sailboat all by himself."

"Yeah?" asked Teddy. He flipped it open and began reading.

His first night, he woke up shouting in fright. His uncle, aunt and various older cousins rushed into the room as a startled Janny picked himself up off of the floor—where he'd fallen out of the lower bunk in surprise.

"What's going on?" asked Uncle Will.

Teddy whimpered.

Aunt Minnie climbed up the ladder to the top bunk and put a hand on Teddy's head, then his stomach.

The boy shook.

"I was dreaming that I had to go to this party when Trixie and I were in Chicago where these rich people paid her to let them spray-paint me all over silver and walk around naked at their party. But I got really sick and seeing things that weren't really there ..."

"You girls get back to bed," said Uncle Will.

His wife began stroking the twelve-year-old's hair.

"I thought demons and snakes and dragons were after me an'—an' —" Teddy started shaking all over. "The demons started calling me names," he blubbered, "and I had to be rushed to this hospital and the police got really mad at Trixie. That rich guy had to pay them a whole lot of money and then he put us on a bus and gave her $500 to keep her mouth shut about everything."

"That's nothing to cry about," mused Janny. "Who's Trixie?"

"Let's all go back to sleep," said Aunt Minnie. "And don't you think about any of that anymore. Everything's going to be all right."

"How come they wanted you to be at a party like that?" asked Janny.

The older boys laughed.

"Go to sleep," ordered their father.

"Uncle Willem," said Teddy, sitting up. "How come you made me go to that place in Wyoming? I wanted to come here. I wanted to come real bad."

Aunt Minnie looked away.

"It just wasn't possible right then," said Teddy's uncle.

The room was silent.

"Teddy Bear," whispered Aunt Minnie, "you're here now and everything's going to be just fine from now on."

Teddy came home from his first day at Los Cerrillos Christian Academy humiliated. Worse than in his worst fears, they'd put him in the second grade. Classes at the Anchor of Hope hadn't been graded, so Teddy hadn't realized just how far behind he'd fallen.

After Aunt Minnie had a talk with the principal, the school let him go to speech, music, gym, art and reading with seventh graders his age. But, it was back with the little kids for arithmetic, spelling, social studies and penmanship.

Even after he went to the barber and got his curls trimmed to what Uncle Will considered a properly masculine haircut, he continued to be a hit with the ninth grade girls, much to Janny and Hans's chagrin.

It's hard to go wrong with a name like Teddy Behre.

Afternoons, Teddy taught Janny how to cuss and smoke cigarettes and Janny taught him how to fish with a cane pole for largemouth bass and how to set and check coyote traps. They herded the sheep and skinned rattlesnakes. They thought up dirty jokes. They explored arroyos, bummed swigs of whiskey from ranch hands at the big nearby spreads and found pieces of Indian pottery in the canyon.

And Teddy began to amaze everybody with his determination to catch up with his school work.

Some nights, he and Janny and Hans slept up in the hay loft and talked about running off.

But Teddy knew they wouldn't.

"Where'd you get this?" demanded Uncle Will, holding up a marijuana cigarette.

"I never saw it before in my life," lied twelve-year-old Teddy, turning bright scarlet.

"Hans?" thundered the minister.

In horror, Janny stared at his big brother.

"It's mine, it's mine," interjected Teddy suddenly. "They wanted to know what it's like to get off. I thought they ought to know."

"Get OFF?" roared Uncle Will, raising an open hand.

Teddy winced, assuming he was about to be whalloped. He gripped his eyes shut and shielded his head with his arms. Several times, he felt the blow coming and, wincing, twisted away.

But no hand fell.

He opened his eyes.

Terrified, Janny stared at him. Hans whimpered.

"Teddy," whispered his uncle, ashen-faced. "Oh, Father God, in what hell has this boy lived?" The minister shook with emotion. Teddy was enveloped in big hammy arms, hugged tight. And in the preacher's embrace the twelve-year-old started to cry.

"Whatcha writin'?" asked Janny

Teddy looked up from his bunk, covered with loose pages.

"At the ranch, I started this, uh, project."

Janny peered at the pages. "It's that book you talked about."

Self-consciously, Teddy fumbled with the pages. He'd forgotten telling his cousin about it. He usually didn't bring it up.

"Read some," ordered Janny. "You got any that has me in it?"

"Kind of," hedged Teddy.

"Read it."

"Okay," said Teddy, self-consciously shuffling pages.

Suddenly, "Don't you ever wish you could go live with your dad?" asked Janny.

Teddy looked startled. He pushed his glasses up on his nose. "Huh?" he managed.

"Doncha? Just a little?"

"Which—my real dad?" asked Teddy. "Or Dobson?"

"Your real dad."

Teddy frowned. "When I was little, Grandma told me that if I ever met him, I'd recognize him. So, I used to look for him everywhere I went."

"Did you ever see him?"

"I don't know. I bet he'll show up maybe at my high school graduation or my wedding or something. You know."

Janny stared at him. He grinned sympathetically.

One afternoon, Teddy found his grandmother's old bike "Peggy" in the barn and spent the rest of the week cleaning it up. It was almost too small for his long legs.

His first spin on it, he left Jan and his shiny dirt bike behind and rode down the highway and past the water tower. He poked around tumbled-down downtown Los Cerrillos, unexpected emotions flooding him. Tears on his cheeks, he remembered the road vividly. He turned the corner and kept going until he got to the ghost town of Madrid four miles away.

All afternoon, he poked around familiar places, stopping at deserted houses, roadside parks and a hot spring his grandmother had found once when he was maybe five.

Alone, he cried for the woman who had loved him and cared for him, the warm, saintly woman who was such an embarrassment to her fundamentalist family.

Teddy was in trouble when he found his way home after dark. Uncle Will was out in the car trying to find him.

Teddy had to promise not to do it again.

Every week, he helped his aunt go out and check on the town's elderly shut-ins. Between stops, she talked about Jesus a lot and kept telling him that he needed to get saved.

He finally told her that he had accepted Jesus back when he was six. But, he hadn't been baptized, noted his aunt.

"I got saved," he said, "you know?"

"No," she said, embarrassed. "Were you baptized in water? Did you get immersed, under the water?"

"Yeah, at the Anchor of Hope," he said.

"Was it for the remission of your sins?"

"I don't know."

"Then, you're not saved," she said. "The Bible says that Satan's demons believe in God and tremble. But that doesn't make them Christians. Ye must be born of the water for the remission of your sins."

"Oh," said Teddy.

That Sunday, he went up in front of the church and Uncle Will dunked him under in the big baptistry behind the pulpit. Everybody acted very proud of him, except Hans and Janny. At school, they talked a lot about the time they had gotten caught with the marijuana. Hans liked to make it sound like they'd gotten high lots of times.

In gym, the older boys asked Teddy about drugs he'd never heard of. He didn't let on, since it seemed to mean a lot to Hans. Sometimes, he told about drugs he had seen people doing—or that he'd read about.

What really had him concerned was how Janny started going around acting stoned. None of the Behre boys were doing any drugs, but Hans and Janny seemed determined to make it look like they were.

Not Teddy. He was a bikie.

Whenever Uncle Will gave begrudging permission, Teddy rode his bike off to nearby towns—sometimes all the way to Santa Fe, thirty-five miles away.

And the boy continued worrying about Trixie showing up or his being accused of doing something and getting sent away. He vowed to behave himself.

"I'm very proud of the way you've overcome your problems," said Uncle Will one day while Janny was running the tractor and Hans and Teddy and the three older boys were loading hay bales. "I can see that as you're older you've begun to understand that some things that you were taught just aren't so."

Teddy tried to grin.

"What really makes me furious about these Pentecostals who got their claws into your grandmother is how they like to act like they've got some sort of monopoly on holiness," said Will. Teddy sat down on the tractor fender. "They all go to church, get all worked up, then go home and drink beer and run around on their wives.

"We used to have a real problem with them coming into our church and trying to get things stirred up. I just run them off."

That summer, Teddy got a paper route—which he quickly built up to one hundred thirty seven customers on a twenty-two-mile daily bicycle route.

He found solitude in the quiet rural roads. Zipping along in the pre-dawn darkness, he could outrun any dogs or out-dodge any high schoolers in pickups who tried to chase him.

He made friends with many of the people on his route and spent Saturdays collecting—talking with the lonely septuagenarian widows who took a personal pride in the sharp youngster who everyone knew had jumped in one year from second grade to fifth and wanted so badly to be allowed to try seventh grade in the fall with everybody else his age.

His favorite customers were Mrs. Julian and Mrs. Cuminsky.

Mrs. Julian always talked about patriotism, her husband who had been a merchant seaman and of years she had lived in Jamaica. She started giving him piano lessons—although she could no longer play because of her arthritis. He took to it immediately—with Aunt Minnie's encouragement, but to Hans and Jan's alarm. Teddy's favorite pieces were some of the easy Bach *Well-Tempered Clavier* exercises. By fall, he was tackling Rachmaninoff's *Prelude in C Sharp Minor*.

Janny liked to mimic Mrs. Julian's coaching, which could be heard all over town: "Louder! Teddy Behre! Feel the power! No, No! On your fingertips! Softly there! Pick up your hand! Now, *fortisimo!* Louder! I can't even hearah you—" all while Teddy was pounding, making the knickknacks on the top of the piano dance, "—Louder! Mr. Rachmaninoff was angry, Teddy Behre! Louder! Play him! No, no, go back! Here, I will show youah!"

Mrs. Julian would greet him with new finds from garage sales: Gershwin, Liszt, Schubert records. They argued about Stravinsky, which he called goofy and she maintained was divine.

For long hours Mrs. Cuminsky would tell him of how once Los Cerrillos had been a thriving town. Her favorite TV show was "Professional Wrestling" and she would not abide the thought that it was all fake. Her hero was "Cowboy Bill McGirk," the good-guy who every week destroyed various Arabs, Russians and Turks.

When she had to go to the hospital with breast cancer, Teddy worried about her and prayed for her daily. He spent two nights sitting with her when she was in intensive care and the family asked the church to help watch her twenty-four hours a day.

She recovered.

            📎   📎   📎

"Hi," said Teddy, plopping into the metal chair beside Santa Fe juvenile probation officer Gene Ortega's squadroom desk.

The detective pecked at his typewriter.

"Hey, Little Bear," said the half-Navajo, scowling at a hand-written report, then at the typewriter. "How's the bicyclist?"

"That corporal thinks you're my dad," grinned Teddy.

Ortega laughed heartily.

"Well, it's possible," he mused. "What was your mom's name again?" He chuckled.

Teddy scowled. "I got a dad," he lied, muttering darkly.

"You never told me."

"He's busy," growled Teddy. He glanced around at the room. Four officers sat in one corner by a candy machine and yelled at a baseball game on TV.

"What does he do?"

"I don't know."

Ortega nodded, dropping the subject. "You coming to Scouts tonight?" he asked. The detective was a troop adviser for the kids interested in police work.

"Naw," said Teddy. "My uncle won't bring me and he doesn't like me biking around after dark. He doesn't like Scouts, either. He told me I ought to be doing more stuff at church before I take on something like that."

Ortega nodded impassively, but Teddy could tell he was offended. "I ought to be glad he lets you go to the bike club. You gonna be at the meeting Thursday?" Ortega was the touring chairman of the Santa Fe Bicycling Society.

"Sure," said Teddy. He paused. "No, I can't. But I get to go with you guys next month to the Grand Canyon. And I'm bringing my cousin Jan. He's almost like my brother."

"It must be tough living with a preacher," said Ortega.

"Naw," said Teddy. He pretended to read the papers on the detective's desk.

Ortega plunked savagely at the typewriter. He hunted for the "k" key, then jammed it.

Teddy grinned. "Well, I gotta go see some guys," he said.

Ortega looked up. "What are you up to?" he asked, warily.

"I'm gonna help the bike racers this afternoon practice for the time trials."

Ortega leaned back. "You keeping up with summer school?"

"Yes, Mother," grinned Teddy. "See you."

Ortega waved and resumed pecking. "Hey," he yelled, not looking up. Teddy paused in the doorway.

"Get rid of those cigarettes," barked the detective.

"Yes, Mother," called Teddy, grinning. Ortega knew he had no cigarettes.

For three miles they straggled out, safety flags flapping in the wind, 200 bicyclists of the fourth annual "On the Brink" bicycle rendezvous at the Grand Canyon.

At the back, Teddy irritatedly coached Janny along.

"You promised me that we wouldn't have to keep up," spat the younger boy.

Teddy nodded impassively. He stopped. Janny halted immediately and jumped off his bike.

"Come on, you pansy," said Teddy. "We'll miss the sunset at the point."

"Big buzz," scoffed Janny, picking up a red and bronze piece of sandstone. He hurled it out over the side of the canyon. "Come on," he said. "Race you."

"No," said Teddy. "Come on. Quit bein' a baby."

But Janny was gone.

"You pansy!" yelled Teddy. "Come back here."

"I found a path," called Janny. "And a cave!"

Interested, Teddy reluctantly went to look. The path was a rock shelf on the side of the canyon wall. The cave was layers of limestone slab overhanging a hollow where rocky soil had washed away.

Janny squatted defiantly in the shelter. He grinned at Teddy, then belched loudly.

Teddy carefully made his way down, pausing and absorbing the setting sun bathing the canyon in hazy golds, scarlets and purples.

"Hey," Janny yelled. "Look!"

Down several hundred feet was an enormous plant with a towering flower stalk.

"It's a century plant," said Teddy. "It only blooms every 100 years and then it dies."

"Our class already had that in science, dummy," jabbed Janny. "Let's go."

Hanging onto trees and bushes, the two raced down the steep caynon slope. After several minutes, Janny stood on a two-foot ledge.

"Come on, pansy," he taunted.

And then he dropped out of sight.

"Quit playin' around," yelled Teddy.

"Teddy Bear!" Janny yelled, his voice farther away than it should have been.

"Where are you?" called Teddy.

"Help me!" blubbered Janny.

Teddy slipped and almost fell, unable to keep a footing in the path's loose rocks. A shower of pebbles fell over the edge.

"Yahhhh! Quit it! Help me, Bear!"

Carefully, Teddy peered. Then, he saw. At the bottom of a steep slope, a crying Janny clutched a gnarled mesquite bush and a stubby cactus. Gingerly, he held up a needle-bristling arm, then slipped and had to grab again at the spiny column. One foot stuck out into space. Beyond was nothing.

"Get me outa here!" he pleaded.

"Come on," yelled Teddy. He dared not venture onto the steep slope. "Just climb back up. Get your foot up."

Janny began blubbering.

"Hey," said Teddy, his concern building. "I'm kidding. I'll get you out."

Janny screamed. Teddy could see that he was bleeding. As Teddy debated whether to go get help, "I'm gonna fall, Bear!" Janny wailed. "I'm gonna fall."

"Hang on. Hang on tight." Teddy yanked off his jacket. But it wasn't long enough to reach his cousin. He kicked off his boots and yanked off his jeans. Shivering, he knotted a jacket sleeve to a pants leg.

"See if you can grab this!" he yelled hurling the makeshift lifeline down to Janny.

"Hey, you're in your underwear," yelled his cousin, suddenly trying to joke, his voice fighting panic. "Hey, girls!"

Teddy stared, scared by the terror in Jan's eyes. The younger suddenly slipped and cried out.

"Grab my pants leg," yelled Teddy.

But the end was too far away by ten feet. Teddy anchored one knee around a pine tree and leaned out. Janny reached out and tried to grab.

"Okay!" cheered Teddy, trying to sound calm. "Try again! When you grab it, get it real good and I'll pull you up."

"I can't!"

"Dang it, do it!"

Janny swung one leg up and tried to hook his ankle around the cactus. Then, he reached out and snatched the pants leg. Teddy's jacket tore away under the sudden weight as the mesquite roots crumbled away. Janny grabbed at the cactus, screamed, then was gone.

There was no echoing yell.

A crow glided overhead.

"Jan!" yelled Teddy.

"Janny!"

Yanking his pants back on, the twelve-year-old peered.

"Janny!"

Rangers said Jan had died instantly upon impact, 700 feet down.

Ortega called the Behres in Los Cerrillos. And he had to also tell them that after helping recover Janny's body, Teddy had disappeared.

Alone, the young hitchhiker sat against the passenger door as the insurance salesman bought himself a hamburger in Flagstaff.

"Here," said the man, climbing back into the car. He handed Teddy a milk shake and cheeseburger. "I know you're hungry."

Teddy wolfed down the food.

"Where you headed?" asked the man.

"Los Angeles," lied Teddy. "To live with my dad."

"I live in Los Angeles," said the man. "What part of town is he in?"

"Disneyland," blurted Teddy, who knew nothing about Los Angeles.

"That's Anaheim," laughed the man. "You beter not let the chamber of commerce hear you calling them L.A."

Teddy didn't laugh. "Hey," he said, suddenly. "Thanks a lot." And he was out of the car.

"Kid!" yelled the man.

Twelve years old and convinced he'd killed his cousin, Teddy had nowhere to go. This time, he didn't even have crazy Trixie.

For two days, he hid beneath an underpass in Flagstaff, keeping out of sight of kids his age on bicycles and a crew of road workers.

The third evening, he waited until after dark and began walking, thumbing and watching out for the police that he imagined were searching for him. His head down, he tried to look unthreatening, likeable and worthy of a ride. After what seemed hours, a too-talkative truck driver picked him up and took him all the way to Texas, telling him his life story and about all the operations he'd had on his liver.

In El Paso, certain that the authorities would be watching for him, Teddy decided to head down into Mexico, just across the river from the truck stop. But he lost his nerve upon spotting an array of multi-uniformed Mexican officials standing around on the Ciudad Juarez side of the busy pedestrian bridge. So, he loitered on the span, just across the border, but just short of the port of entry.

He ignored ragged Mexican kids his age who tried to summon him taxis, sell him souvenirs or give him sales pitches on girls and nightclubs. Morosely, he peered through the chain-link fence at a soccer game on the sand bar below.

When it began to get dark, he headed back and realized with sudden panic that he was going to have to go through American immigration. Nervously, he approached the rundown turnstiles, certain that arrest was imminent.

"Where you from, son?" asked a grey-shirted man taking I.D. cards from Mexicans.

"California, uh, I mean Albuquerque." Teddy's voice was too-high and suddenly shaky. Certain he was betraying his self-consciousness, "New Mexico," he croaked, his voice low.

"Where in Albuquerque?" asked the man.

"Near Five Points."

"How long were you in Mexico?" asked the man, eying him strangely.

"I lived there 'most all my life," said Teddy, gritting his teeth in mid-sentence as he realized the guy had asked "Mexico," not "New Mexico." He grinned sheepishly. "I lived in New Mexico almost all my life. I didn't go across to Mexico. I just stood on the bridge."

"Wanted to see what it looked like, huh?" asked the man.

"Yeah," said the twelve-year-old softly, grinning up at the man.

"Go in there," said the man, motioning him through the turnstile and continuing to take I.D.s from the Mexicans crowding the walkway. Reluctantly, Teddy sauntered into a big room. The immigration officer waved to a woman who motioned for Teddy to come to her counter.

"Empty your pockets," she said.

"Why?" he exclaimed.

"Just put everything in this tray," she said.

Unhappily, he pulled out forty-seven cents in change, a tattered Arkansas map that he had swiped from the trucker and his wallet, which contained $8, his *Albuquerque Daily World* paperboy identification and school pictures of Janny, Hans and various girls from school.

"Is that it?" asked the woman.

"Yes ma'am."

She eyed him suspiciously.

"Do you smoke marijuana?" she asked.

"Huh? No. *Never.*"

"Where are your parents?"

"I live with my uncle and aunt," he said, thinking fast. "They're at church. I got bored and just walked up on the bridge to see what Mexico looks like. I didn't go all the way across. They won't let kids go without their parents, will they?"

The woman studied him.

"Okay," she said. "Get out of here."

Hurriedly, he repacked his pockets. Walking quickly across the parking lot, he grinned at a friendly-looking elderly couple in a camper. Behind rolled-up windows, the woman looked alarmed and said something to her husband, who quickly started the engine. Staring at him, they pulled away, the woman continuing to glance back at him anxiously as she reported to her husband. Teddy grimaced, his head down, as he could hear her locking her door.

On the nearby interstate, he held out his thumb and almost immediately was picked up by a man in a new Chevrolet station wagon. All the way out of town, the 40-ish guy pumped him for information about sexual experiences.

The twelve-year-old finally told a few lies and the man seemed disappointed, then got extremely evasive when Teddy conversationally asked where he was going and if he'd been on the road long. Teddy slumped down against the door as they headed across the desert. The guy put on an ancient Redd Foxx eight-track party tape of dirty jokes. Teddy didn't understand most of them, but laughed with the driver at the punchlines. Teddy didn't like the man, but riding with him beat thumbing.

The twelve-year-old rode with him to Tucumcari, New Mexico, where in the wee morning hours, the man announced he was getting a motel room. He didn't invite Teddy to come along—which was just as well, because the boy wouldn't have gone.

The twelve-year-old spent the next several hours unsuccessfully trying to hitch another ride, then attempted to nap under a bridge—but couldn't sleep due to the cold.

Around 5 a.m., a van stopped on the right-of-way on the other side of the four-lane. Waving enthusiastically, Teddy slogged across the muddy median and jumped in. The college-agers were smoking marijuana and although he didn't particularly want to get high, he was dead tired and appreciated anybody sharing anything with him. And so, he got more stoned than ever before in his life and laughed and sang and acted crazy and fell asleep. When he woke up, they were camped at a roadside rest stop near Eads, Colorado.

He would have liked to go on with them, but the driver—for no apparent reason—accused Teddy of coming on to his wife. Teddy took off on foot.

He regretted it immediately. The prairie wind was bitterly cold and he had no jacket. Plus, the people in the van had had several bags of potato chips. He desperately wished he was still high.

He walked for miles, turning and looking as harmless as possible at approaching cars, before a woman trucker stopped and took him all the way to a truck stop outside of Palo Duro, Texas, near Amarillo. She couldn't take him any further, she said, since she was getting near her terminal and she wasn't supposed to have riders.

For several days and nights, he rode with strangers, making up lies about himself and a sick dad in Houston, Dallas or wherever he thought they were going. Due to his size, he was able to make people believe he was fifteen or 16. He got a job busing tables and washing dishes at a truck stop outside of Austin where he was befriended by a chain-smoking lady named Babs. She had an office of sorts in a booth in the truckers' part of the restaurant and reminded him a lot of Melba.

He told her he was 16. She owned three motor homes and an Airstream trailer parked out back and told him she "coordinated" a dating service. It wasn't hard to figure out that she was a madam.

She didn't ask him any questions about himself, but around 1 a.m.—at the end of his shift—asked him if he'd like to stay with her, that she needed "a man around the house." It sounded great. For a week, he slept on a threadbare velveteen sofa in her trailer and was adopted by her girls. They all thought he was cute and called him "Pooh," the name he had told the restaurant manager.

One early morning when business was dead, a girl he had talked with a lot named Betti asked him to help her fix a stopped up sink in one of the motor homes. After he unclogged it with a plunger, she asked if he'd like to help her finish off a bottle of burgundy that she was afraid was going to spoil in her little refrigerator.

Then, "Pooh, you're such a sweet little guy," she said softly, gently. "I want to show you just what a big little man you are. I can make you very happy."

Politely, he declined.

He took off that morning with a trucker going to Dallas. Teddy spent a week sleeping in an old landfill not far from where John F. Kennedy was assassinated, according to a Vietnam veteran he helped pick up aluminum beer cans. In cardboard and tin lean-to shacks, quite a community of down-and-outs lived in the landfill—old women who pushed around everything they owned in grocery carts, winos who were always hitting him up for change that he didn't have. A guy who called himself "Doc" went on and on about how they all looked after each other. But Teddy knew it was really everybody for himself.

For a week, Teddy hung around a soup kitchen run by an Episcopal church. He drove around in an old U.S. Mail truck with volunteers and a very hyper woman named Charlotte, begging blemished and rejected produce at farmers' markets and grocery warehouses.

Since he was almost as big as any man, he frequently had to prove he was a fighter to keep from getting shaken down for a jacket he had stolen from a laundromat. He headed back to Austin, hoping to find Babs again. But he ended up in Lubbock, Texas, where he got free meals by working at the "Soul's Harbor" rescue mission for alcoholics and out-of-work oilfield workers. He told the old preacher who ran it that he was fifteen and looking for his father.

It would be wrong to say that life on his own for the twelve-year-old was placid. But he was big for his age and able to fight. His voice was low. His muscles were those of a New Mexico farm boy and cross-country bicyclist.

There was an easy-going cooperation among those who haunted the bus depots, who slept in alleys and condemned buildings, who caught rides on freight trains. However, there was always a self-centeredness, a distrust and a depression—a pervasive atmosphere of failure, futility and despair. For a kid, there was the constant fear of people who acted nice, but invariably would proposition him for sexual acts. He decided to try to find an aunt who he knew lived in Detroit.

Sleeping under bridges in Oklahoma, staying in empty buildings in Kansas, he would dream: *"I found him!" would yell a familiar voice. Through a fog, Teddy would see Hans and Janny standing over him.*

Conspiratorially, the two would whisper that they'd brought some cigarettes. And Teddy felt Aunt Minnie hugging him, the girls saying that his calf missed him, the older guys saying they needed a third baseman. In the darkness, Teddy muffled his cries. The calf would lick his face. Janny would whoop about something.

"Lord God, restore Your little boy to his health," his grandmother would pray in the darkness. She knelt beside him, one hand on his shoulder. Other people laid hands on his forehead, his chest. "Father, heal him of the hurts and heartaches." And on and on they would continue into the wee hours. "Oh, Father, we thank You and we know that by Your stripes we are healed, for it says so in your Holy Scriptures," would yell a preacher friend of his grandmother's. "And I stand on Your promises and believe as I know that this little boy believes."

Teen-aged girls would whisper and brush his hair with their fingers. Teddy would smile, falling back asleep as everyone shouted praises to God and danced deliriously around him.

And Teddy felt the deep peace of being greatly loved. And he would sit up and hug his grandmother—but nobody would be there.

And Teddy's heart would be suddenly empty. He would look about him and know that he was sleeping in a culvert in Lee's Summit, Missouri, or an old barn outside of Kansas City.

For an entire week, he slept in a deserted top floor salon of Kansas City's old Union Station train terminal. Twice he scrounged good food from trash dumpsters behind the posh hotels across from the cavernous old train station. He hung around a World War I memorial park during the day, then split after he only narrowly missed getting picked up in a surprise police sweep as officers rousted winos, runaways, bums and crazies. Apparently, they were looking for an escaped con who had walked away from a nearby pre-release center.

After he was robbed of a small backpack he had stolen from a sixteen-year-old runaway who'd picked a fight with him, he headed for Detroit in earnest. It would take him weeks.

✐   ✐   ✐

Shivering in the October wind, he shook back matted blond curls and gently knocked on the screen door of his aunt's house.

Teddy's cousin Barry answered the door. Aloofly, the teenager stared at Teddy and called to his mother.

"Yes?" she asked.

"Auntie Liz?" the freezing Teddy asked from the steps.

"Yes?" she repeated, opening the screen and eying him suspiciously.

"I bet you don't know who I am," Teddy said, shivering, trying to grin, shaking his greasy hair out of his face.

"You must be one of Willem's boys," she said, cautiously.

"No, I'm Theophilus, Trixie's boy. Theresa's boy." In horror, Aunt Liz peered behind him. "She's not with you, is she?"

"No, ma'am. I don't know where she is. She took off. May I please come inside? I'm freezing to death."

"Of course."

At a kitchen table, she served him milk and cold biscuits—the first things he'd eaten in two days. She didn't seem to notice that he wolfed them down ravenously. And she didn't offer anything else.

She wanted to know all about Theresa—Trixie. She shook her head knowingly as Teddy said he hadn't heard anything from her in a long time.

"I thought you were living with Will," she said.

"No," said Teddy, as absently as he could. His tattered shoes and too-big socks were beginning to thaw. He could tell that they were beginning to smell. He peeled off the dingy windbreaker he'd begged at a Goodwill store.

"You were living there when his youngest boy was killed, weren't you?"

Teddy nodded, feeling ever more self-conscious at how dirty he was. He could even smell himself.

That night, he slept on a couch in Barry's room. Barry stayed distant, informing him which towel to use, reluctantly obeying his mother by giving Teddy clean clothes.

Ted became increasingly uncomfortable as his aunt told him bluntly she was not very sure what to do with him. "We've never had a runaway come here," she said, pointedly. "But, I can't very well just send you back out into the cold."

That night, Teddy found a book—James Clavell's *King Rat*—and read it while Barry and his mother sang and played the piano downstairs. Once, he ventured down, thinking he would offer to play Rachmaninoff or Bach, but decided against it. His aunt and his cousin were having a great time and made no move to include him.

He went back up to his couch, wondering where Aunt Liz's husband was.

Barry came up just before midnight, stripped naked and began parading back and forth to the restroom—brushing his teeth, combing his hair, gargling.

Uncomfortably, Teddy concentrated on his book. Barry picked out several more old t-shirts and some worn-out jeans and tossed them on the couch.

Teddy stayed two weeks, but began feeling like a parasite. Barry remained aloof, except for liking to walk around naked. His mother seemed to think it was charming.

Teddy borrowed a knapsack Barry used for a school gym sack and left one morning before dawn, hitching a ride with a trucker going to Alexandria, Louisiana.

He thought maybe he should visit the Anchor of Hope. It would be good to see Chuck. Meals continued to be infrequent and warm places to sleep rare. In Shreveport, he was beaten up and almost raped by a nineteen-year-old transient he'd been hitchhiking with. He got away by claiming to have the AIDS virus.

✐   ✐   ✐

Teddy turned thirteen—becoming a teenager—in Paris, Texas, riding on the side of a railroad tank car. As usual, he kept his birthday to himself. Two transients he had made friends with thought he was a small seventeen.

Even when he made friends, he learned to stay on his guard—remembering Shreveport—and stayed ready in a flash to present an unexpected snarling, bristling front and to be able to spring away into the darkness.

He rode the train to Rochester, Minnesota, where the weather grew bitingly cold. In Minneapolis, starving, alone and hungry in his soul, he was walking along the bank of mid-town Lake Hiawatha, watching some rather obvious homosexuals laughing with each other and trying to hold hands as they cross-country skied.

He was nervous—he had stolen a parka from a restaurant coat rack and some clean clothes out of a laundromat. With his fingers he was combing out the tangled mess of his golden curls when a car pulled up to the curb. An obviously agitated man swung open the door.

"Hi," greeted the man, smiling, friendly. He clutched a haughty-looking poodle. "How would you like to go to a party?"

"Huh?" exclaimed Teddy. Suddenly, "Pervert!" he yelled, laughing, kicking the door, yelling accusing obscenities.

The nearby skiing gays looked up in panic. The car squealed away as the laughing Teddy bellowed taunts. But as the homosexual couples slipped away, he grew depressed and lonely. He began wondering what it would have been like to go with the guy. He could get new clothes, stay in an apartment, even eat decent food. All he had to do was…Teddy grimaced.

He wasn't gay.

He didn't want to be.

And he didn't want to pretend.

It wasn't like he hadn't ever thought about being gay. An empty pit gnawing in the bottom of his stomach, he stretched himself up on his toes. And getting paid for doing gay stuff would be no worse than stealing clothes or digging through

filthy dumpsters. He was going to have to do something—he
was hungry.

And he had a right to live, he told himself. He just needed to
get some money. It would just be a way to make some cash. He
figured he could be really good at it...unless he had to do
disgusting stuff like Lucky had told him about—sicko, painful
stuff.

He stepped out onto the sidewalk and wondered how he was
supposed to let anybody know he was available. He knew there
was something about a bandana in a rear pocket or one ear ring.
But in which ear? It was supposed to be important. Lucky had
told him about that. One ear meant that you were a pickup. The
other ear meant that you were a motorcycle rider and liked
killing pickups.

Teddy just decided to swing his butt like Trixie used to do
when she was looking for a john.

"Hi there," said a dark man in a blue Lincoln as the power
window slowly slid down.

Just like he'd seen his mom do, Teddy grinned and leaned in.
He winked. "Hi," he oozed, his eyes unable to hold the man's
gaze. Determinedly, he giggled and tossed his hair back.

"Where are you staying?" monotoned the man.

"Nowhere," smiled Teddy.

"How old are you?"

"Sixteen," lied Teddy, rolling his eyes.

"Don't give me that. You're 18 if you're a day."

"Hey, you got me," said Teddy, grinning and catching on.
"Man, I'm legal."

"How much?"

"Three hundred."

The man didn't even look back. He just jammed the acceler-
ator and sped away. Teddy yelped, jumping clear in time.

He headed on down the sidewalk. He quit swinging his hips after he noticed a man and wife in the window of the Burger King staring at him, disgust in their eyes.

He looped the lake twice before "Young man," called a grey-haired man walking with a cane. "Young man." He gestured. Teddy walked over. The man squeezed his arm, too friendly. "Are you the sort of boy who might like to give an old gentleman company?"

Teddy eyed the old guy, his stomach writhing.

"I'm not cheap," he said, his voice high, quivering.

"Oh, no," said the old man.

Teddy stared at him uneasily. The old man was becoming nervous. *Ah, well,* decided Teddy, *having somewhere warm to spend the night would be worth it.*

"Sure," he said.

The old man put his arm around him and together they walked slowly down a side street. The man pinched him to feel of his arms, his chest. He began whispering an old Johnny Matthis song.

At the man's house, the old guy offered him a drink. In the cluttered bedroom, Teddy downed three scotch-and-waters before the numbness of intoxication hit. The old man whispered and helped him take off his shirt, then giggled and started talking about people Teddy didn't know. Teddy closed his eyes and tried to pretend he was somewhere else.

But instead, an incredible revulsion swept over him as the old man gently put his hand on Teddy's knee. Reeling, Ted reeled forward violently and vomited all over the old man.

Sputtering in embarrassment, Teddy leaped up and grabbed his shirt—and a wallet on the dresser. Pulling on his pants, Teddy grabbed a gold pen out of the man's jacket on the bedpost and threatened him darkly with violence if the police were called.

On the dark street, he laughed a little too hysterically. He flipped open the wallet. In it was $127, an American Express card, two Visa cards, a Diner's Club card and a driver's license. In awe, Teddy stared at the license. It wasn't the old man's. The photo was of a blond, curly-haired teen named Donald Ross Dundee.

The old man's lover? His son? Teddy didn't care—now he was rich. Whooping, he tossed the pen into the ditch.

He used the American Express card to buy a ticket to Lake Tahoe, then changed his mind and turned it in for the fare to New York City and pocketed the $58 difference. He had an uncle in the Bronx, but he didn't know where. He threw a late thirteenth birthday party for himself at the rundown Ambassador Hotel and made plans to travel around the world.

Then, he spotted the cops. The hotel manager pointed to him from the main desk and the uniformed policemen advanced.

Teddy dived into the kitchen.

He spotted what he knew would be his salvation. He bolted past a cook and leaped into a garbage chute.

Covered with spoiled hollandaise sauce, he fled down an alley into the night.

✐   ✐   ✐

"Boy," called the woman, a bent, scraggly-haired old hag lugging five shopping bags. "Boy!"

"Yes, ma'am," said Teddy, jumping up from the New York City park bench.

"You want to have a warm bed tonight?" whispered the crone.

Ted looked her over. This seemed more perverse than the guy in Minneapolis.

"No, no," croaked the old woman, smiling—flattered—apparently reading his mind. "You look like you'd like a job and it happens I've got one for somebody who wants a place to stay out of the cruel elements."

Teddy cleared his throat. There was something not quite on the level about her.

"Have you got a cigarette?" she asked.

"No," lied Teddy.

"Then, how about a little kiss?"

Teddy grinned at her.

But she was dead serious, her puckered lips already extended. Lightly, he kissed her.

She smiled.

"I liked that," she said, "Allen."

Incredibly, she had quite a nice apartment in mid-Manhattan. The building showed signs of neglect, but inside it was swept and neat.

At the elevator sat a chubby kid in a clean shirt and new tennis shoes.

"Who's he?" he demanded of the woman, his voice shrill.

"This is Allen. There's no reason for you to get upset, Harold," crooned the old woman.

Chubby "Harold" stared knowingly at Teddy. Ted didn't know what else to do but follow the woman. She gave him the keys to her apartment and carefully placed her battered shopping bags in a closet. Then, she hung up the four sweaters she was wearing, stuck her drooping straw hat on a peg and turned her full attention to Teddy.

"Allen," she said, "you don't have anywhere to go. You're not a New York boy. You're out of money and the police probably are looking for you because your relatives have offered a reward for information as to your whereabouts. A private detective is trying to find you to take you back to Texas or Oklahoma or Arizona or wherever you're from."

"Not likely," said Teddy. "Nobody in my family wants me."

She stared at him and nodded, pleased.

Ted looked over the cluttered apartment in awe. It was crowded with dark old antiques and faded rugs. Yellowed doilies sat under a crowded assortment of vases, World's Fair souvenirs, framed photographs and books.

"My relatives don't care where I am as long as it's far away from them," he said. "And I don't think the cops are looking for me. I just got into town."

The old lady smiled, pleased.

"Good," she said. "Then, I want you to meet some people."

Door to door, they went through the building, meeting old women who held themselves up with aluminum walkers, old men puffing pipes, a blind lady who felt of his face.

The bag lady's name was Sarah. She owned the building.

The chubby kid was the last person on the tour.

"Harold will fill you in as to your duties," said Sarah, turning to get on the elevator.

"What d'ya think?" asked the kid in a Wisconsin or Iowa accent. He looked about fifteen.

"I don't know. Why does she call me Allen?"

"Because she always calls one of us Harold and the other one Allen. I think she had sons named that once. The other Allen ran off yesterday. He couldn't stand it in this madhouse. Haven't you figured it out yet?"

Teddy shook his head.

"She's crazy like a fox," said Harold. "You and me, we take care of all these old people in this building. We're the watch dogs. It ain't too rough. We just run off bums and keep the graffiti painters out mostly. And we don't make no trouble for the Overlords. They're this gang. You're gonna have to join up, but they won't care if you don't ever do nothing with them. Oh, yeah, and we run lots of errands. Groceries, prescriptions. But, you gotta keep straight. Don't rip off nobody here. And the old lady will get rid of you in a minute if she ever sees you high or tokin'."

"Don't the cops ..." Teddy paused. "I mean, what do you do if the cops come?"

"They'll leave us alone," said Harold. "They know what's going on. You and me, we do their job for them."

"Wow," said Teddy.

And so, he settled in. Sarah got him enrolled in school, where he only got to go every other week, since he had to pull his twelve-hour shifts in the lobby. Apparently, everything had been worked out for years.

At school, they called him Allen and nobody asked any questions.

Teddy learned some things in New York the hard way. Putting a lock on his school locker was like hanging out a red flag. The lock and all the contents of the locker would be gone when he returned. Once when he got a lock that couldn't be picked, his locker was set afire.

One Saturday, Teddy found an old single-speed bicycle in the basement and rode it to a nearby Boys' Club, thinking it was too battered for anyone to steal.

The big thirteen-year-old was greeted by jeers. Backed up by what looked like gang members, a high school guy demanded to know why Teddy had stolen his bike.

When Teddy stuttered that he'd dug it out of the basement, the older boy shoved him off and threatened to kill him if he ever stole anything of his again. Then, he rode off to the cheers of his friends. When Teddy went home that evening, he found the bike, or pieces of it, wrapped around the telephone pole by the apartment building's alley entrance.

Harold told him it was a warning. Of just what, Teddy didn't know.

Across from the school was a garbage-strewn lot that Ted recognized as one of the famous drug parks he had heard so much about. There you could buy anything. But it wasn't anything like he had imagined. The center of the lot was always packed with pushers from the Caribbean, scary-looking Rastafarians with wild hair, playing their music at top volume. The north side was run by Puerto Ricans, the southwest corner by blacks. Dazed dopers tottered around the sidewalk, often falling down, sick. All around were homosexual and straight prostitutes and their pimps. Police cars would park in front of the school without a ripple of concern from the park.

The junior high school was straight out of every late-night New York blackboard jungle movie Teddy had ever seen. The building had been erected almost 100 years before, but apparently hadn't been maintained very seriously in the last thirty.

Teddy kept to himself and hoped to remain an outsider, but immediately had to fight bigger jerks who hustled smaller kids for lunch money and homework. Graffiti covered most of the walls. Only a few ancient light fixtures survived. Most of the lights were naked bulbs hanging from fraying cables.

The janitors and physical education teachers seemed to be the same eight or ten enormous, yammering Haitians, who stuck together and did nothing that Teddy could tell except tell the black girls filthy jokes.

Frequently, the coaches, janitors and boy squad leaders would lock themselves in the locker rooms while gym classes were supposed to be playing football or basketball. Loud cheers and clapping could be heard through the skylights. Teddy suspected they were gambling or watching venereal disease movies.

Teddy's English teacher wore up to a dozen plastic, fake-turquoise bracelets on each arm and six or seven nonworking watches, which she kept face down against her skin. Her favorite punishment was collecting everybody's notebooks, so she could spend the rest of the day going through love notes, private doodles and drawings. She didn't seem to mind at all that confiscating notebooks meant that homework had to be turned in late in other classes. Actually, a good excuse for incomplete science or music homework was that Miss Czorinzky had taken up notebooks that day.

The music teacher was prone to tirades on the evils of popular music. Her other favorite teaching plan was to pull a pop quiz of a test given at the first of the year that most of the class had flunked. Their continuing to fail seemed to incense her—proof that she was wasting herself on hopeless morons. More than half of the class was stoned, drunk or belonged in a special class.

The speech teacher was an alcoholic who usually turned the class over to a favorite student, then disappeared into his office. The student, a bespectacled boy who drew computer programs on the blackboard, pretended not to notice when most of the class piled out the windows. Those who remained did homework from other classes. One week when Teddy came back from his shift at the apartment house, the man had gone on extended sick leave and the room had become a chaotic study hall. Teddy was told the teachers' union had placed sanctions on the school, barring members from serving as substitute teachers there after a biology substitute had been raped.

In algebra, the teacher ignored about thirty troublemakers who held court in the back and gave his attention to the ten or so "ducks" who sat on the front rows. Teddy had sort of a love/hate relationship with the man, who seemed to delight in mocking Teddy's accent—frequently demanding that he read something aloud "in cowboy."

The oppression of the school took its toll. A Bolshevik anywhere else, Teddy was a "duck" there—an over achiever, a straight arrow. At Harold's suggestion, he took a karate class at the Boys' Club. There, he made friends with the teacher, named Denny, a former Episcopal priest who took extra time to teach Ted classic Okinawan katas—formal fighting exercises. He began taking Teddy with the squad to competitions in Newark.

Quickly, Teddy earned his green belt. Proudly, he practiced kicks and strikes in the hotel lobby, the old people watching respectfully. Sarah didn't seem to like Teddy's growing self-confidence. She told him twice that he'd have to quit karate in the spring.

But Denny moved away inexplicably. Before he left, he told Teddy he could start wearing a brown belt. But the boy knew the promotion was honorary—he hadn't earned the degree. He had won several trophies at tournaments. After Denny was gone, Teddy bought karate books with the lunch money Sarah gave him and tried to keep in shape.

And Teddy resumed what Janny had taken to calling "the great American novel" and what Teddy was now calling *Wild-Eyed Pentecost*. He had left the jumbled manuscript behind in Los Cerrillos. But he knew the story. Before, Chuck, then Janny, had listened to the story with excitement. Teddy had woven his tales, looking forward to the praise or criticism. But in New York, nobody seemed very impressed. Harold said the stories were "dumb." His English teacher, weird Miss Czorinzky, said he should concentrate his efforts on more useful studies. But working on *Wild-Eyed Pentecost* gave Teddy peace.

In October, Harold disappeared. He had been trying to get Teddy to go with him to live with a guy who needed people to help round up runaways to make kiddie-porn flicks.

"I had a friend who made those kind of movies," said Teddy, warily. "That stuff's too weird for me."

Harold swore his derision. "You don't have to be in 'em. He'll pay us $5 for every kid he can use."

"That's sick."

"Hey, we're doing them a favor. You want them to die out in the cold? He pays 'em. It's how I stayed alive last winter. At first, it was pretty gross, but everybody's high. It's fun after a while, it's so stupid. You learn to quit taking it seriously. You're makin' fun of the sickos who buy that stuff." Harold laughed, too nervously. "And sometimes, these rich guys come watch and if they like you, they'll take you home and be your sugar daddy. How would you like that? To have anything you want? You ever done cocaine? One of those guys let us all have all the coke we could do while we were working. I was buzzing."

He disappeared a couple of days later without taking any of his belongings. At school, the rumor was that he had been in on making a "snuff flick"—a film in which one or more of the child stars is actually murdered on camera.

Teddy knew to discount rumors. But Harold never showed up again. The story was that he had had a bit part in the film and that they had surprised him, knifing him while the camera rolled. Snuffer stars are never told they are the one who will go. Part of the attraction of the films is the genuine terror of the dying child.

With the coming of winter, Teddy got restless again. He wanted to head south. He wanted to sneak into Los Cerrillos and see Mrs. Cuminsky and Mrs. Julian.

He wrote Sarah and the new "Harold"—a kid from Illinois named Tony Gillette—a goodbye note and took off.

When he tried to buy a plane ticket, the agent began to get nervous as she fumbled with the American Express card Teddy produced.

"I'll have to verify this card, Mr. Dundee," she said, picking up a phone.

But Teddy was gone. Trembling, he stood outside and knew that his cards were no good anymore.

For the rest of the day, he rode the subway, poking around the Village, refusing repeated approaches by homosexual pimps who mistook him for a lonely new arrival. He spent several hours on the landing for the boat out to the Statue of Liberty, eating Good Humor bars. He paid some of his last cash to go to the top of the World Trade Center.

That night, he slept in a trash dumpster until the wee hours when he was almost catapulted into a garbage truck making its rounds.

He took to the subway, then thought about checking out a rescue mission he had heard about on Times Square for young boy prostitutes. Teddy found the mission without any trouble, but they were overcrowded, said the lady at the front desk.

She looked him over.

"How old are you?" she asked. "You can't be more than thirteen."

Startled, Teddy grinned at her. Nobody had correctly guessed his age in years.

He stayed there two days, helping out in the kitchen, making friends with the cooks. He had grown too accustomed to eating. Warily, he shunned the other kids at first, then began asking if any of them had known Harold. It was incredible how young some of the "chickens" were—some only eight or nine.

Then, he took off again.

For all its faults, New York had everything you could want in a town, except maybe human warmth. And you had to be careful. His fourth night away from the rescue mission, he was "captured" by the Satans, a street gang that was recruiting new members. He had thought they were just going to rob him. The swaggering, doped-up leader checked out Teddy's wallet, took all of the credit cards but one that he didn't see, then quizzed him.

Teddy told him darkly that he was on the run for having killed somebody. He fumbled with the Okinawan karate fist on his belt buckle. And before he knew what was happening, somebody was behind him. In the corner of his eye, Teddy saw the lead pipe crashing into his head.

With a beautiful rear kick, Teddy slammed the attacker into the wall, then, dropping into a classic movie stance, informed the gang leader that he was ready to die, but that he was going to take half the gang with him.

The leader smiled and asked if he wanted to be a Satan. That night as his initiation, Ted got to go with the gang to a liquor store and hold a gun while some of the others stole bottles and emptied the cash register. And into the early hours, Teddy got drunk for the first time in months, somewhere near the top of a half-finished, abandoned apartment complex that overlooked the vast concrete canyon of unending Manhattan.

Teddy impressed the gang leader with tales of his travels and his descriptions of working a crowd *a la* the "Sherman marching through Georgia" method.

Early that morning, after learning that he was going to get to have "Serve Satan" tattooed on his knuckles, he slipped away to a bus station and—holding his breath—bought a ticket to Lake Tahoe with his sole remaining credit card. He decided that this time, he would finally find Dobson.

Two days later in Wichita, Kansas, three policemen boarded the bus and arrested him. He put up a fight and had his head cracked open with a night stick.

Three weeks later, Leroy MacDonald came up and brought him to Ouachita Hills Boys' Ranch.

There he met Angie.

And Sluggo.

And finally got a brother.

And an interceding prayer warrior of a grandmother.

⊘ ⊘ ⊘

"So, you are my new grandson," chuckled the frail, blind woman in the Fayetteville, Arkansas, hospital bed.

Awkwardly, Teddy stood beside Mr. MacDonald and Tadpole—*and tried not to stare.*

"Mrs. Julian," he blurted.

"Teddy Behre?" whispered the woman, recognizing the voice. She grasped his hand and suddenly remembered where she had heard his strange name "Teddy Bear" before. Of course: *Teddy Behre—Madeline Behre's little grandson!*

Stunned, "Mrs. Julian," Teddy whispered disbelievingly.

The woman held the boy's hand and clutched toward his face. "Is it really my little Teddy Behre? Madeline's grandson? Is it really you? Are you Thaddeus' special friend that he talks about? Can it really be you?"

Excitedly, Teddy hugged her—almost too hard. But he was careful, for he'd also had an invalid grandmother. This was his piano teacher—Mrs. Julian—from his paper route back home in Los Cerrillos. "Tadpole is *your* grandson!" Teddy exclaimed. "Wow! Mrs. Julian!"

The old lady was crying. "Teddy Behre," she exclaimed. "You are such a special boy. I knew it the first time I ever saw you. I have wondered so many times what happened to you. Now, you are my Thaddeus' big brother. Well, well, well! Thaddeus, you have done a very good job in finding me a new grandson and a brother for yourself!"

Behind the boys, Leroy MacDonald watched the scene in amazement.

"How come I never knew you had a grandson?" blurted Teddy Bear. "Tadpole didn't live with you back home."

"Yes, he did," snapped the old woman. "You just don't remember. He was too little for you to notice."

Teddy sat down on the bed beside her. He squinted, trying to remember.

"How is your Aunt Minnie?" asked Mrs. Julian, patting Teddy's hand gently. "She was having trouble with her nerves after...after Jan died—Well, I don't guess you would know about that, would you? How is your piano? Are you practicing?"

"Not very much," admitted Teddy, shamefacedly.

"Play me something."

Teddy, Tadpole, Leroy and a nurse helped put the old woman into a wheelchair, then Leroy pushed her down the hallway with Tadpole chattering excitedly at her side, detailing everything that had happened that week since his last telephone call.

In the recreation room, Teddy awkwardly sat down at an old upright piano. He tested the pedals, then, carefully, majestically, began Rachmaninoff's magnificent *Prelude in C Sharp Minor.*

"Louder, Teddy!" chuckled Mrs. Julian. "Louder! Mr. Rachmaninoff was angry! Louder!"

Tadpole sat down on the floor—spellbound, not by the music, but by what he saw: his Teddy Bear and his grandmother were longtime friends. Good friends.

Leroy MacDonald held Mrs. Julian's hand and agreed softly as she commented on what amazing talent "little Teddy Behre" had. Actually, MacDonald was not a fan of the classics—and Teddy's playing seemed so much noise. *"What a shame,"* Mrs. Julian was whispering to him. *"I have heard such terrible things about that boy, but I always knew different. And now he's with*

*you people, Leroy. He is a very good boy. He and I used to talk
and talk and talk for hours. He was my paperboy and one of my
very best piano students. There is enormous good in that boy
if somebody will just help him let it come out. Madeline poured
her life into that boy. He is very, very special."*

MacDonald softly agreed.

"The doctor says that she can return to the retirement tower
soon," said Leroy in the boys' ranch van on the way home.
"We're going to have to figure out ways to get you two over there
more often. Tadpole, your grandmother is an extraordinary
woman. Did you know that she donated the land that the ranch
is on?"

The first grader leaned forward, shaking his head.

"She's blind," said Teddy, still stunned at seeing his old friend
so stricken.

"I'll bring you two out with me here to Fayetteville every time
I come out," said Leroy. "You really brightened up her day—her
year for that matter."

Tadpole leaned back. "You know my grandmother," the first
grader mused to Teddy. "Neat."

"She was on my paper route," Teddy grinned. "We were
buddies."

In her dark room, "Lord, what a day," whispered the old
woman. "Madeline Behre's grandson is my little Thaddeus's
Teddy Bear—the boy that I've heard him talk about so much of
the time. It was as if You planned it that way. Now, what is Your
purpose for these two, Father?

"I know that they are both very special. And You do, too,
Father. What do You have planned for these young men of ours?
Oh, I am filled with such excitement. My little Teddy Bear is
turning out all right after all—almost all grown up and he's the

one that is taking such good care of my dear little Thaddeus. Thank You, Lord. Thank You.

"O, but they are just little boys, Father. Guide them. Surround them with Your light. Give them courage to do and be that which is right! Thank You, Lord! Madeline's little Teddy Bear! You are such a great God!"

✎   ✎   ✎

"Happy birthday!" yelled Tadpole. In homemade hats, all twenty-four kids of Teddy's cottage crowded into their room. Their housefather, Mr. Gilliam, whirled a noisemaker. Dazed, still half-asleep, Teddy sat up.

Giggling, Phoebe from Tulsa pushed into the room with a chocolate birthday cake with sixteen candles. Kids from her church crowded in the hallway, holding birthday presents. Tad challenged Teddy to blow the candles out.

Teddy found himself blinking back tears.

Tadpole sensed it immediately and comfortingly put his arm around his waist. Phoebe's mother wiped away a tear as Teddy shook. The room got quiet. Embarrassedly, Teddy glanced at Tadpole, then mumbled something to Phoebe's mother.

"Why, that's nothing to be ashamed of," she gushed, hugging Tadpole. "Go ahead and tell everybody."

Teddy shook his head.

"He said *nobody* in his whole life ever gave him a birthday party before," Tadpole announced.

Teddy blushed scarlet. Jumping up and down, Tadpole whooped. Phoebe wiped away a tear.

✎   ✎   ✎

"So, my new grandson is sixteen. O Lord, be my light and shield," prayed Miriam Julian. "Whom shall that boy fear with You on his side? I am so proud of him.

"Father, You are so good to us. He and Thaddeus are like nothing I have ever seen. They even look like brothers. When they come up to see me, the nurses whispered about Teddy like they would a grown man.

"They think he is my grandson, too. Father, I don't correct them because I believe it has given that boy such an anchor—a place in this confusing world—to become part of our family.

"He was so proud to introduce me to that girl's mother. What a nice girl, too—not like that scatter-brained Angie that he was so taken with. Lord, give that boy wisdom. Don't let him think with his glands. Let him be guided by Your plan and wisdom.

"I am so proud of him, Lord," she prayed. "Protect him from temptation. He is such a fine boy—but so many go astray at his age. Give him peace and a purpose to his life.

"Send him the right girl. Perhaps it is this Phoebe. She is very gentle with him and they are so sweet together. But send him the right young woman to be his special joy and companion.

"But, Father, let his deepest desire be to delight in Your presence and to flow in Your desire for his life. Let him learn to trust You to set him on a high rock out of reach of all his enemies. Let him know the joy of singing Your praises.

"O listen to my prayer, Father! You have been his help in all his trials and hard times—and I know that You won't leave him now. You won't forsake that boy, O God of our salvation! Your psalms say that if my own father and mother should abandon me, You would welcome me and give me comfort—well, I claim that comfort and home for my Teddy Bear.

"You, alone, are his Father. Let him be at peace in that."

"This day, I am sixteen years of age," Teddy wrote in his notebook. "This day has actually passed as it is 1:30 in the morning. I had a surprise birthday party with Phoebe Jane's youth group and all the kids from our house. It was neat.

"This day I spent doing a report for school. And I just finished Leon Uris' *Mila 18*.

"I hope I will not cease in my endeavor for acceptance, my fight to excel and live up to my potential.

"Clive has been gone two weeks now. He promised he'd write. Tad really misses him. It gets weird at mail call. Tad gets up at the front, so if a letter comes. And then, when nothing does, he cries.

"I wish dumb ol' self-centered Clive realized how important he was to Tad. What a jerk. By the time he left, he wanted us to call him 'Andre.' What a little wimp.

"Tadpole undeniably is my very best friend. He's only a little snot, but he doesn't act like it.

"Phoebe is next, then Kenny Enderby, then Howie Moore and Duff. And, of course, there's Gene Ortega and Leroy MacDonald. I could go on and pick others I have known, liked and thrived with for a season, but I always travel on, so to speak.

"Sometimes, I don't know about my feelings for Tad. I'd kill myself if I thought I was going to hurt him. Okay, let's be absolutely frank. Are my feelings for him kind of weird? Looking at him when he's naked is no big deal to me. He's just a goofy kid. I'm not like those weirdoes who paid Trixie to have me walk around painted silver that time.

"I kind of think I really would like to have sex with Phoebe someday—particularly after that time we were kissing at the Passion Play—but it's the same thing. I really love her, so I'm not going to go messing things up by doing stuff. I'm going to marry her.

"I feel funny sometimes when Tad climbs into bed with me and rocks against me in his sleep. Him and Sluggo used to come up with sex stuff themselves, sometimes—Tad asking me why he got, you know, excited when he was riding the horses. I told him it was just something that happens to guys, that it doesn't mean nothing.

"One time when he was eight or nine, some kid at the Dixons' house told him that Sluggo would pull down his pants for a quarter. Turned out Sluggo would. I decided that the two of us would go talk to Leroy about it, but not give any names, just ask advice. Leroy took Sluggo on his knee and told him it wasn't a very good idea. Then, after Sluggo left, Leroy got really, really upset and wanted to know names. When I wouldn't rat, Leroy gives me a really funny look. He did his goofy smile and told me to have a 'man-to-man' talk with the kid who was getting Sluggo to do it.

"So, I did. I explained to the little punk that I would use him as a punching bag if I ever heard anybody saying he was hurting Sluggo or making fun.

"But, the point is—if Tad was to tell me he wanted to do some kind of weird thing that sombody in the sixth grade was talking about, I know I'd just talk about it with him, show him why he wouldn't want to do something like that.

"But, how come I like it when Tad wants me to hold his hand when we go places? I think he's getting too old for that.

"But I like it when I hug him and he's upset or frustrated and stuff. Sometimes when Sluggo used to get hyper, I'd hold him and he calmed right down, just like his teacher told me.

"It's the greatest thing in the world being Tadpole's brother. At first it was like I was his father or something. But it means a lot to Tad that I'll bust some bully's head or go talk to Leroy.

"I think I was less than understanding with Clive. He was always worried what other people would think. Sometimes I was really crummy to him. Who knows what kind of damage I did? Maybe that's why he dumped us like he did. I must have been a real jerk sometimes, but Clive was a twit.

"I really like the way that Tad tries to be like me. He walks like me. He combs his hair like me. Everybody really thinks we're brothers. I wish we really were. Maybe somehow the guy who was my dad also was his. That would sure be something.

"I don't know.

"This day is gone. I am sixteen. Now, I can drive a car.

"Perhaps I am a man today. Who can say?"

✐   ✐   ✐

That spring, Teddy graduated early from high school with the highest grades of anybody in his class of 331.

The day he graduated, the sixteen-year-old moved to the University of Arkansas dorms in Fayetteville so he could start summer school. That had been Leroy's idea. After all, Teddy was as big as any freshman. He kept his age to himself.

Phoebe was still an eleventh grader, but was already applying for scholarships so she could join him in two years.

One provision of moving to Fayetteville was that Teddy had to call Tadpole every evening at 6:30 p.m. and that twice a week he had to visit Mrs. Julian, who lived in the nursing home four blocks from the university.

Teddy dropped by almost daily at first, then less frequently.

Within a week of moving into the university dorm, he started drinking again. He hadn't planned to. He went to a party in the dorm lobby and there were several kegs of beer and everybody was helping themselves.

Sipping a beer, he started talking to a spacy-acting sopho-more named Caroline Haas. She kept gigging him in the ribs and laughing as she got drunker. Then, somebody handed Teddy a roach-clip. And just like it was the most natural thing he'd ever done, he took a toke and passed the burning stub of a marijuana cigarette on.

And he began to get extremely angry with himself.

He went and sat down on a couch, feeling like a jerk for drinking anything—and especially for taking a hit off of the marijuana.

"Hey, what's wrong with you?" whispered Caroline, sinking in beside him.

"Nothing."

"Awwwwwww, poor li'l baby-boo. Him don' feel good." She leaned against him, both hands rubbing his chest and back. He tensed, feeling the softness of her breasts on his shoulder and side.

And then, he realized that she had passed out.

In disgust, he stood up and went back to his room.

"I was a grand failure," he wrote in his journal a subsequent evening. "I wish I could say that tonight was the last time I'll ever go to one of those things.

"I, naturally, got carried away and drank too much again. I wasn't ever out of control. I remained coherent.

"But, I was no shining light. I hustled every ugly chick there, supposedly trying to score for my roommate, a pimple-faced jerk named Baird.

"I could have done excellently for myself. I'd feed 'em stupid lines and they'd go for it. Then, I'd say 'Hey, babe, wanna go somewhere quiet?' And they all wanted to. Then, I'd say 'Great! Hold on. Baird? Come here. This is Baird. Baird, she's ready to go with you.

"Two girls threw their drinks in my face. One wouldn't go with him and I had to tell her that I was a cop, looking for people with drugs.

"I suspect I'll find myself at such again. But I wish there were some nice people here, like at the ranch.

"It's really stupid, but I spent most of the day moping over last night's notable failure. I showed myself that I can't put myself into impossible circumstances without getting myself into trouble.

"I am strong enough to triumph over anything, but…maybe I better not try attacking windmills."

"Teddy," asked Tad one weekend as they walked across the University of Arkansas campus. "When are you going to tell me all about sex?"

"Huh?" guffawed Teddy.

"Hey, I already know all about it," said Tad, glancing around self-consciously, "but what's physically maturing?"

"*What?*"

"What is it? Mr. Gilliam said he'd explain everything to me when I started physically maturing."

"Uh." Teddy made a face as he pondered an answer.

Tad waited, grinning.

"Well," said Teddy. He hesitated.

"What happens first?" pushed Tad.

Nervously, Teddy eyed his little brother. He glanced at his watch. "You really don't know?"

Seriously, Tad shook his head.

"Well, uh, you start, uh, I think, gee—" Teddy cleared his throat. "It's different with everybody. Generally, I think, you suspect something's going on when you start getting, ah—" he stopped walking and squinted at the kid. "Ah, you start getting, well, they call it body hair, around —" He winced and wiggled his eyebrows Groucho Marx style. "Dee, ah poysonal oyguns."

Tad nodded. "I know what you mean," he said.

Teddy looked at him very seriously.

"I've got some," Tad announced.

Teddy stared at him in disbelief. The kid was only eleven—almost twelve. His voice was still high and tinny.

"Naw."

"See," said Tad. He peeled off his T-shirt and held up his underarm. Teddy squinted. He couldn't see a thing. Tad put his shirt back on. "I've got some more you-know-where, but I better not show you—not here."

Teddy blinked at the kid. "Holy cow," he said. He hadn't started until he was twelve. Or maybe he'd been eleven. He couldn't remember, except that he'd been earlier than anybody else his age.

Tad smiled, placidly.

"Well," said Teddy as solemnly as possible. "Everybody gets it."

Tad nodded.

"And it's no big deal," said Teddy. "It doesn't mean you don't get to be a kid anymore. It doesn't mean anything except you're gonna grow up a little bit faster in the next few years or so."

Tad nodded and didn't say anything.

"You can look at me and know it doesn't mean you have to start acting grown up," said Teddy.

"You're plenty grown up," said Tad. "Mr. MacDonald says you're sixteen going on 45."

"Ummm," growled the older boy.

"I've got three girlfriends," volunteered Tad. "One of them is in the eighth grade, but she really likes me a lot."

"Oh, yeah? You're gonna break their hearts."

"I know. I gotta pick one."

"Naw. Keep 'em anxious."

In the winter twilight, Mrs. Julian lay unmoving in a hospital bed. "Lord," she prayed silently. "Why would You hit me with a stroke?" Suddenly, she was crying.

A tall boy stood, concerned. "Hey," whispered Teddy. "It's okay. I'm here."

"O Lord," prayed Mrs. Julian. "Thank You for this dear boy." And she was crying again. "I plead with You to help me, Lord, for You alone are my Rock of safety. If You refuse to answer me, I might as well give up and die. Lord, if I could move, I would lift my hands up to Your heavens and implore Your help. But I cannot move. I cannot even speak."

This boy needs you, whispered the heavens.

"Lord, this is not fair." She was crying again. "I cannot bear this. I cannot speak. I cannot reach out and touch him. He does not know if I realize he is here or not. But I do. Lord, show this boy that I am so thankful for his concern."

Suddenly, she realized that Teddy was holding her hand. He was caressing her fingers gently. "Hey," he whispered. "Hey. It's okay. Hey. Don't cry."

She stared at him, desperation in her eyes.

"Listen," whispered Teddy—who had been at her bedside all night—"I know you're having a rough time. But I know something that these doctors and nurses don't get. I know you're still in there. They talk to you like you're an idiot or some little child. Well, I know that you're in there and that you can hear me."

A nurse walked into the room and he paused. After she left, he winked. "Grandma," he whispered. "You're a fighter. And the great God that you have served for 70 years is still there, slugging it out on your behalf. But you've got to do your part. Fight! Don't let go. Tadpole and me, we really need you. You are all we've got. We're orphans once you're gone."

He grinned and shrugged.

"Well, not exactly," he whispered. "Trixie is in Oregon, I think. And maybe someday my dad will turn up. I rather doubt it. I don't think Trixie really knows which guy it was. And Tadpole's mom is in Nashville or Memphis, wherever...but you're our family.

Miriam stared into his eyes.

"O Lord," she prayed. "What a remarkable boy. Well, Lord, if I can't talk to him, then at least I can talk to You about him. Just look at him.

"He's so torn between worlds. He doesn't know which one he wants to choose: Your Way or the pointless pursuits of human ambition. He wants to be a newspaper reporter. What folly! But it is his dream. Father, show him in such an unmistakable way that he cannot find peace unless he is serving You.

"Yes, Lord, I know that he can serve you and be a reporter. Of course. It would be a terrible if only ungodly men were filling the paper with agnostic sneerings. But, Father, let him hear with his ears and know in his heart that great is the Lord and greatly to be praised! You have shown me time and time again that You have a special job for him—and for our faithful Thaddeus. Father, I pray Teddy will remain unfulfilled until he submits himself to You and Your great design for him.

"You brought him here for a great purpose—many purposes, I believe. He has been my grandson's hero and rock of stability. He has given Thaddeus a manly toughness that just pleases me beyond measure. He took a little boy who was afraid of the dark and had been raised by a fussy old woman—me. And this young man has transformed my little boy into a fine eleven-year-old young man who is strong and decisive and unafraid to love.

"But I believe, Lord, that You have sent Teddy Bear to us for other reasons. There is a great destiny on his life, isn't there, Father? This boy is to be someone great in Your master plan. I understand that he is an excellent writer. Well, I believe that You have even more than that planned for him.

"Let it be, Father! Let him get to the business of Your plan for him! Show him Your way, Lord! Discipline him in truth and grace! You, alone, are his Father. You, alone, will have to be the one to set him on the right path."

Teddy gripped her hand, then gently laid it on her chest. "Hey," he whispered. "I gotta go to class. But I'm gonna go get Tadpole this afternoon. We'll be back."

Miriam was crying again as he left.

"Grandma," whispered Tad. The strapping boy sat down beside her. Silently, Miriam looked at his increasingly adolescent face and smiled inwardly.

He was a very handsome boy.

Behind him, a tired looking Teddy Bear leaned against the wall.

"Father," prayed Miriam silently. "Let that boy know he can go home. He has classes to attend. He doesn't have to sit here with me every hour. He's got to get some sleep."

Teddy closed his eyes and seemed to doze off—standing against the wall.

"Grandma," whispered Tad. "I wish you could come to the ranch. Something really great is happening." Ted gazed into her eyes, then grinned.

"Teddy's right," he exclaimed. "You're okay, aren't you? Those stupid nurses say that you probably can't hear us, that the stroke did all sorts of terrible stuff. But you're there! You're still with us! Praise God!"

And suddenly the boy was lying with his head on her chest, holding her tightly. "Oh, Grandma, don't die," he whispered. "Don't go. I don't know what I'd do."

Inwardly, Miriam smiled. "Father," she prayed. "What a marvelous job we've done with this boy—You, me and Teddy Bear. And Leroy, too, I suppose. Just look at him. This is a strong young man who knows what is right and is trying to do it. Look at his shoulders and arms. This boy knows hard work—and how strong it has made him! Look into those eyes! This boy knows compassion. And he is so intelligent. And talented! O Lord, what a marvel he is! This must be what young King David looked like!"

The boy sat up, studying her face.

"O Father," she prayed. "I am ready to come be with You— except for one thing. I want to see Your purpose in these boys' eyes, radiating from their hearts. I cannot die not knowing if we have been successful in instilling a hunger for You in their very being.

"Lord, give them that burning desire for You."

✎ ✎ ✎

That evening, Miriam Julian died in her sleep. The doctors said that she had never come out of the coma after her stroke.

Her boys knew differently.

"O Lord," she marvelled as she took her place in an incredible heavenly choir, surrounded by old friends. At her elbow was her beloved husband. "O Lord, You are beautiful. Blessed is the Lamb of God that was slain! My mansion is far more than any human mind could possibly anticipate. O Lord! Thank You! Thank You! Thank You!"

She swayed in complete freedom of movement, her eyes closed, the majesty of the presence of God overwhelming her. "O Father," she prayed. "Be with my boys."

And her eyes were opened.

And she saw them both. Who they were. What they would become. "O Thou Mighty Creator," she breathed, "What a wondrous Father You truly are. What an honor. You have allowed me to have a small part in such a ..." She blinked in astonishment. "Great plan."

In enormous joy, she began to sing.

Two days before Thanksgiving, Tad's mother called him from Memphis, Tennessee. And she wanted her little boy. The sixth grader was ecstatic, but not especially surprised. After all, he and his grandmother had been praying for it to happen.

Tadpole went to his mom. In December, Teddy turned 18 more alone than ever in his life. It was with considerable foreboding at Christmas that he went to visit. An enthusiastic Tad greeted him at the airport, his mother in tow. She was a large woman, very shy, but very outspoken. Teddy didn't pry for details as to where she'd been all this time.

"So, you're my son's brother," was the first thing she said. "He's gonna have apoplexy if you don't come come live with us."

It took all evening for Teddy to realize that she was nothing like Trixie and that she accepted him fully—no jealousy, no suspicions, no wary questions about this former juvenile delinquent who had filled her son's life.

From the moment the evangelistic Tad arrived, he had gone to work on her. She and Tad had joined a noisy Word of Faith

Holiness Church across from their apartment and attended loud fellowships in people's homes four nights a week.

Jeanne became the cook at a coffeehouse run by an ex-Satanist who took teams of teen-agers out to preach over megaphones along the downtown "strip" where kids from all the Memphis high schools sat on their car hoods and drank beer and got high into the wee morning hours.

The next semester at the University of Arkansas, Teddy worked three jobs—as a busboy at a restaurant, as the newscaster on the campus radio station and as a full-time correspondent for the Tulsa newspaper's Fayetteville bureau. The rest of the time, he went to school. He joked that he slept on weekends and Thursdays.

His head aching from lack of sleep and a 18-hour day, Teddy picked up a Bible and sat down in front of his portable television.

He flipped through the channels and settled on an ancient *Gunsmoke* re-run. But, his mind was still going 100 mph. He flipped over to an old movie, then back.

One reason he was keeping up with his work and school was his ability to shift into high—yet maintain efficiency. He thrived on the deadline pressures at the newspaper and the demands of being an honors student. Now, still hyper from an especially good assignment, charged with adrenalin and the power of his own craft, he stared at the TV and kept switching from *Gunsmoke* to the movie and back, keeping up with both.

He juggled his Bible on his knee and skimmed Second Thessalonians. He finished it, feeling a little empty—as if he hadn't gotten what he had intended.

He liked the apostle Paul's letters. He stared blindly at the climax of the movie. He had anticipated the ending plot twists thirty minutes before. He closed the Bible and shut his eyes. He knew he was still racing. He had to slow down, unwind—gear down. He had to relax. He flipped over to *Gunsmoke*, then got up.

He started to call Phoebe, then didn't. His phone bill had been astronomical last month. He still hadn't paid it. Plus, he knew she was seeing some guy who went to her church.

They'd both agreed that the other should date. And Teddy had. But the thought that Phoebe would go out with some other guy irritated Teddy. He flopped back on his bed.

He had an idea.

Slipping into gym shorts and tennis shoes, he watched the end of *Gunsmoke* while stretching his legs out and doing a little meditation.

Festus saved everybody, Matt grabbed a gun and shot four bad guys, Kitty cried and Teddy went for a short run.

Months before, he'd been running seven-eight minute miles, fifteen miles at a shot. But shin splints plagued him, so he'd given it up. He much preferred bicycling—but it took longer to burn off the calories, frustrations and craziness. With running, he could reduce himself to exhaustion in no time.

Not this tension-driven day. A half-mile out, the shins started aching. Pain wrapped the front of Teddy's lower legs—shooting into his tendons, jarring each step. Tiptoe running relieved it only for a few feet.

Panting, Teddy paused—almost unable to walk.

Slowly, he padded into a neighborhood convenience grocery and stared at the beer case.

And he had a better idea: a pint of Wild Turkey bourbon.

Yeah. He wasn't interested in getting drunk, but he knew the potent whiskey would put him into blissful unconsciousness.

He jogged into the liquor store next door. Barely outside, he opened the bottle and swigged down two gulps. Guilt enveloped him, but faded with three more swallows.

By the time he got back to his apartment, he'd discarded the emptied bottle. A warm glow, a blissful fog of forgetfulness, a stupor of non-responsibility engulfed him. In his room, he cheerily shucked every piece of his clothes and collapsed, naked, singing to himself. He covered his face with his pillow and checked out.

He slept several hours, but they seemed like only seconds when the insistent ringing of his telephone blasted through his unconsciousness.

He pulled himself up to his desk, burped loudly and answered it. His watch said 4:47 a.m.

"Teddy. Mom's been in a car wreck. Can you come out here?" The emotion-choked voice was Tadpole's.

Teddy struggled to focus at the wall. "What?" he yelled, trying to sound sober.

"Where have you been? I've been trying to call you for hours."

Teddy flicked on the desk lamp, then realized he was naked and that the curtains were open. He turned it off. "How did it happen?" he asked, slowly, hoping Tad would only think he was groggy.

"She had this wreck. Can you come to Memphis and help me? I don't know what I'm supposed to do about stuff."

His head throbbing from the incredibility of the words and the volume of unslept-off alcohol in his veins, Teddy slumped over the desk.

"I've got a job, Tadpole. I gotta go to school. I can't just take off. Don't you know people from your church and that coffee-house?"

"Mmmmm," mumbled Tad. There were hospital noises in the background. "I mean, I need my *brother* out here. It's different. She's kind of bad off and I gotta do stuff and I don't know how."

"How badly hurt is she?"

"She's gonna be okay, but she's real messed up. They've got all sorts of tubes in her. We're praying and claiming this whole hospital for the Lord. And I need you here."

Teddy sighed.

"Tadpole, that doesn't make a whole lot of sense."

The line was silent.

"Okay," said Teddy. "I'll be out there."

"All right! Hurry. They want somebody to sign papers and I can't. I don't know what any of them mean and I'm not old enough anyway. This one guy keeps telling me I need to call my dad. I finally just told him I've never had one, that my birth certificate says 'UNKNOWN' and he got real embarrassed, then real mad."

Teddy smirked. He knew the feeling.

"It's going to take me a few hours to get out there," he said. "I'll see you in a bit."

"Whew. Good."

Teddy hung up. He sank to his knees, his head on the warm carpet. Why of all nights had he picked this one to get drunk? "Father, be with Jeanne," he whispered. "Tad really needs her."

He sighed, his eyes aching, his head beginning to throb. And he prayed that it would all be some kind of mistake, that Tad would call back and say that it was the wrong person, that Jeanne was at work and somebody that looked like her had stolen her car.

"Please, God," he mumbled. But suddenly, his mind was clear and strangely at peace. He exhaled sharply in dulled surprise. He knew that Jeanne was dead.

He trembled.

And he knew she'd been taken at the kindest time possible—before she faltered. He shook in intensity. But he knew all was well with Jeanne.

"Father, why?" he whispered. "How can You do this to Tad?"

But, kneeling on the carpet, once again he was drunk and pithy mouthed and very, very tired.

He called the airport. He could catch a plane to Memphis by 7 a.m.

Teddy paid the cabbie and jogged into St. Anthony's Medical Center. Nurses—looking dazed—walked past, glancing awkwardly at him. The lobby was packed with people from Tad's church, the fellowships, the coffeehouse.

"Theophilus is here," cried out a woman whose name Teddy didn't remember as she hugged him. Her red hair, piled elaborately atop her head and sprayed wire-stiff, scratched his face. "Theophilus, Theophilus. She was so happy, so ready."

Teddy stared around him in alarm. Then it was true? Jeanne *was* dead?

Tad hugged him, then buried his face in his chest. People crowded around. Some were humming a chorus. Some reached out to touch them, whispering prayers. And all was quiet, submissive, peaceful, even joyful. Teddy hugged the sixth grader, then hoisted him up. Tad softly began to cry, his head on Teddy's shoulder. Ted stroked his curly blond hair.

"The last thing she said," exclaimed a man Teddy didn't know, "was 'I see Jesus, Thaddeus. He's calling to me. And there's Mom! The pain is gone. Thaddeus, love your brother. You're all he has.' And then, she sat up just a bit and...died."

Tad looped an arm around the man, hugging him and Teddy together. People were crying, praying, singing. Teddy put Tad down and was summoned away to listen to a doctor's explanation of what had to be done.

✐   ✐   ✐

"She's so lucky," said the sixth grader softly as he and Teddy packed up the apartment. "She's with Jesus. And I'm so lucky. I finally got to meet my mother, lead her to Jesus and be with her for the happiest four months in her life."

Teddy didn't say anything.

"I wish I could have gone with her," said Tad.

Teddy folded up a dress and dropped it in a box with other things to be given away. Tadpole had to vacate the apartment in three days or pay another month's rent, which he didn't have. Jeanne had had no insurance.

"I called MacDonald from the airport. He's going to let you go back to the ranch," said Teddy.

Tad's eyes welled with tears. Suddenly, growling playfully, he dropped into a low stance. Laughing, he rushed over Teddy in a whole-body headlock.

Stoically, Teddy didn't fight back. He didn't respond at all. He just stood, attempting to ignore the boy swarming over him. Under Tad's weight, he dropped to his knees, then, gently growling, brushed his brother off onto the rug.

Giggling and protesting, Tad rolled away. Jumping up, he rammed his head into his brother's shoulder, then clenched him in a bear hug.

Teddy didn't struggle. He didn't do anything. Tad let him go, then clenched him again. The sixth grader tried to ignore his brother's unresponsiveness, then—"Gimme a back rub," the eleven-year-old demanded.

"Don't you think you're getting too old for me to be giving you massages?"

Tad feinted a punch. Then, weaving in a low wrestling stance, "I'll never get too old for my brother to give me a back massage," he declared, his voice high.

"You can get too big for another guy to give you one," said Teddy. "I just did it when you were little so you'd go to sleep."

"Quit it," whispered Tad. He dropped to his knees and began to cry.

Awkwardly, Teddy stood over the boy. With his knee, he gently pushed Tad's head.

Violently, Tad grabbed his brother's leg and threw him backward. As Teddy toppled, Tad was on top of him. Angrily, the sixth grader jutted his chin into Teddy's nose. "Quit it," Tad hissed. He squinted knowingly at Teddy. "Mom was right. You're worried."

"Huh?" winced Teddy.

"You are scared to love anybody."

"That's stupid," denied Teddy. He leaned back against the wall and hugged his knees. "I love you. I love Phoebe Jane. That's stupid."

"No it's not," grinned Tad, chuckling. "Remember that first time you kissed me? I was in the first grade. You spent the next hour telling me you weren't a homo, that it was okay for a brother to kiss his brother.

"So?" said Teddy uncomfortably.

"Were you lying to me? Are you worried? Are you really a homosexual?"

"No," exclaimed Teddy, stunned at the accusation.

"You sure? You don't know, do you?" grinned Tad. "You're worried that maybe you are because you love me and you don't think you're supposed to love another guy." With the wisdom of a man decades older, the sixth grader reached out and took his brother's hand.

Teddy uncomfrotably started to pull away.

Then he didn't.

"You've had lots of chances to do pervert stuff with me," laughed Tad, clutching Teddy's hand in both hands. "When I was little, I maybe would have let you. I probably would have let you do it, because I thought anything you wanted to do was great. Leroy and me, we had talks about that. He was kind of concerned."

Teddy winced and didn't answer.

"But you didn't ever do nothing," said Tad. "Leroy, he told me how you got molested when you were little. And I knew that different things bothered you sometimes—like when I was little and us guys in my class were goosing each other."

Teddy frowned, then started to say something, but didn't.

"I know how you got those credit cards that got you sent to the ranch," said Tad. "Leroy told me. I know how kids out on the street have to do stuff to make money. They do it for money."

Teddy grimaced. The room was silent.

"Look, Bear, I know all your secrets. You've told me everything about everything ever since I was six. I've slept with you, T.B., since I was a first grader.

"Remember that time I got a tick on my testicle? I cried and cried when you said I had to go to our housemother—and you finally pulled it off for me. Dang, Teddy Bear, I know everything about you. You're my brother. I know that you're no pervert. *I know.* I know all the stuff you're scared about, too." Defiantly, Tadpole kissed Ted on the cheek. The sixth grader sat back, a combative expression on his face. "You gonna hit me for kissing you? Go ahead. But I'll bust your nose, turkey. You're my dang brother and I can kiss you if I like."

Silently Teddy snickered, then reached up and tousled Tadpole's hair.

There was such a toughness, a fierceness in the sixth grader's eyes. And love. This kid really did love him. And Teddy loved him.

Teddy knew he had put that toughness there. This kid had been an insecure little sissy when they had first met.

Jumping up, "I love you, Teddy Bear," Tad shouted, marching around the room. "*I love you! I love you! I love you!*" He plopped down in the floor and squinted at the older boy. "Mom was going to adopt you, so you and me could really be brothers."

"Yeah. She and I talked about it," said Teddy. "I told her no."

"Why?"

"Because she and I decided it wouldn't accomplish anything. I mean, I'm 18. I don't need to be adopted by anybody."

"You didn't want to be my real brother?"

"Just because we don't happen to have the same parents doesn't mean that we're not brothers," said Teddy. "You'll always be my brother no matter what."

Tad grinned. And deep within him, he knew that loving this kid had been the smartest thing he had ever done.

That evening, Teddy talked to Leroy, then told Tad they would try living in Fayetteville together, but that it wasn't going to be easy.

Ted explained that they would have to get an apartment, that they were going to have to take turns cooking and cleaning up the place and that they were probably going to stay flat broke all the time.

He kept repeating that it was going to be hard—and that Tadpole had to agree he wouldn't argue about it if one day Teddy just decided Tad had to go back to the ranch.

Enthusiastically, the sixth grader agreed.

Leroy MacDonald did the necessary paperwork and the 18-year-old became the boy's legal guardian. Teddy bought a ring.

He knew was ready for marriage — settling down with the two people he loved, Tadpole and beautiful Phoebe Jane.

✐   ✐   ✐

"What are you going to do about that boy?" asked Phoebe's dad as he passed Teddy the dinner caserole.

"What?"

"My daughter deserves a normal life. She doesn't deserve the sacrifice of being saddled with a little fatherless orphan—and to have to raise a little teenager who isn't her responsibility—or yours. It's time that you two thought very seriously about this problem you've got."

Teddy stood. "You have no right," he said softly.

"I have every right," bellered her dad. "I'm not going to have an adolescent bastard as my first grandchild. He will not be welcome in this home."

"I'm a bastard," said Teddy. "That's two of us."

Phoebe's dad stared at him.

Teddy turned and slammed the front door behind him.

Phoebe did not return his phone calls. She didn't respond to a long letter he wrote apologizing. He thought about her every single day. He hurt. He wondered. But he did not try to see her.

✐   ✐   ✐

Teddy crammed his last three years at the University of Arkansas into two by taking summer school, interim semester courses and getting credit for working for the Tulsa newspaper's Fayetteville bureau.

He did not see Phoebe again.

He adjusted to being a parent to a little brother who began growing like a weed, who worked at four paper routes, who mowed lawns and repaired bicycles.

And who passed out tracts.

Teddy couldn't help but be awed about the sixth, then seventh grader's attitude about evangelism. In the sixth grade, he was chosen to escort the seventh grade's homecoming attendant—and wore a bumper sticker on the back of his tuxedo that declared: *"My God's Not Dead—Sorry About Yours."*

The night Teddy graduated from college, Tad smuggled his junior high stage band in under the University of Arkansas bleachers in the middle of commencement. When—amid the 6,527 others getting degrees—Teddy's name was called, discordant trumpets suddenly blasted "The Impossible Dream." The band played raucously as Teddy walked up, took a bow and was handed his diploma.

The two moved to Albuquerque, where Teddy had gotten a job at the *Albuquerque Daily World.* Tad enrolled in the eighth grade under his real name, Thaddeus Grey, but got the teachers to list him on class rolls as Tad Behre.

Ted and Tad Behre. They looked alike, which pleased both boys. They had the same dark brown eyes, the same chunky, muscular build, the same sandy, curly hair.

"Bear!" exclaimed Tadpole one evening as Teddy plodded in the door, exhausted from a twelve-hour shift at the paper. "Ted, look at this!" The kid was waving a thick packet of papers sheathed in a torn envelope.

"Huh?" muttered Teddy. "What have you got?"

"At school, we had to do our geneologies. I did one on our name—Behre. We're related to all sorts of European royalty."

Teddy winced, but did not comment.

"Look at this," bubbled Tad. "Your grandfather is a direct descendent of the Bourbons. That means that you are related to the old kings of Spain and France! And look at this, your great-great-grandmother was the Baroness of Friesland in the Netherlands.

"Where did you get all this?"

"It's all on computer in Utah," exclaimed Tad. "It cost me $35. They've got this stuff on just about anybody. Bear, we're royalty. The Bourbons were related to everybody. Hey, maybe we're the long-lost Crown Princes of Bulgaria or something!"

"Right," deadpanned Teddy.

"I'm not kidding!" exclaimed Tad. "Look at this! We're related to the royal families of England, France, Germany and Russia. They all intermarried since they couldn't marry commoners. So, we're tied in with all of them."

"Us and twenty million other Americans," said Teddy. "Just being related doesn't mean much, kiddo. Some outfit in England always does a geneology of every new U.S. President and their families are always related to some British king or some other famous European horse thief. That hardly puts him in line to the throne."

"It might!" exclaimed Tad. "I'm going to write to all these people."

Teddy snickered. "Feel free."

After a year at the Albuquerque paper, Teddy began giving serious thought to accepting an offer to work at what once had been one of the country's best newspapers, the *Des Moines Sentinel*—in Iowa. One of the editors there had been a judge in the Associated Press contest in which Teddy entered a series he did on a seventeen-year-old convict killed at New Mexico State Penitentiary.

Just as the boys were about to move to Des Moines, that editor—now retired—called and told him a big newspaper chain had bought the paper and that it was going downhill quickly.

So, Teddy stayed in Albuquerque.

Then, Teddy's old probation officer Gene Ortega and the Santa Fe and Albuquerque bike clubs sold the newspaper on sponsoring a cross-New Mexico bike ride. Teddy volunteered to go along and write stories about it.

It was assumed the ride would be a one-time publicity stunt attracting maybe a dozen bike club members.

Instead, 7,500 riders—mostly novices—showed up.

In print, Teddy dubbed the thing "The World's Greatest Bicycle Ride," since it was sponsored by the *Albuquerque Daily World.*

The evangelistic Tad remained a kid who went to rock concerts only to stand outside and rail on a megaphone against what he considered satanic influences inside. The boy seemed to have unlimited energy. Immediately upon their arrival in Albuquerque he found a Christian coffeehouse and got on staff first as janitor, then, at fourteen, as assistant team coordinator.

He grew impatient with just being a kid. He wanted to be a missionary to—of all places—Israel. He expected the impossible from God and—whether he got it or not—constantly gave Him credit for everything good. Bad things didn't seem to happen to Tad—if you gauged his life by his conversation.

He had setbacks, but he didn't believe in talking about them. Such was "negative confession," he said. For months, he lectured Teddy constantly that God only wanted you to speak in positives.

Teddy pointed out that this wasn't practical for a journalist. A story about a tornado could hardly read: *"Most of Albuquerque's residents were miraculously spared from harm Tuesday while three were taken to a glorious rendezvous with the Lord Jesus Christ (at least, let's hope that's where they went) when one of nature's incredible wonders put on a spectacular (but not very tidy) display of might and power that is giving city planners a chance to completely rethink the downtown business district."*

Tad responded that Teddy needed to find another line of work, that if his lifework was negative, then his life would be, too.

"Look," Teddy exclaimed one day, "I know you want me to go out passing out tracts with you, but I've got a reputation to think about. My bosses expect me to be a rational person. I can't go around embarrassing them."

"Why do you think we're here on Earth?" asked fourteen-year-old Tad, softly.

"I really don't know," answered Teddy truthfully.

"How long is eternity?" asked Tad.

"Forever," said Teddy.

"How long is a human's life?" asked Tad.

"Seventy, maybe 100 years."

"Which is longer? Which one is going to take up more of our existence?"

"Huh?"

"Are we going to be on Earth longer or are we going to be in heaven or maybe hell longer?"

"Aw, come on, Tad."

"Think about it."

Bicycling with Tad was like going to a rock concert with him. He carried religious materials and little New Testaments and passed them out to joggers, children and policemen. At stoplights, he moved up the line of cars, giving out pamphlets while Teddy fidgeted at the corner.

He was an excellent public speaker. He was a hard worker. He was an efficient organizer. He was in intense demand to work and speak at summer camps, neighborhood fellowships, weekend retreats, youth rallies. He got frequent accolades, where his personal history was related—usually inaccurately—and his and Teddy's orphan status applauded.

Only occasionally did either bother to give what they called "the full explanation:" that they weren't actual brothers, that both were illegitimate and were not orphans in the strict definition of the word—that only Tad's mother was dead.

Seldom did they go into Teddy's blighted past.

Although at school Tad was considered by his peers more than a bit eccentric, such seemed to enhance his popularity. He was elected president of the freshman class.

If nothing else, Tad was a novelty.

He was an enthusiastic, inspirational, kind, gentle, peaceful, trusting kid with an incredible drive to do whatever he felt God was guiding him to do.

One never knew what that would be.

The first thing Tad did as freshman president was appoint a chaplain and launch a petition drive for the administration to provide a place for a before-school prayer meeting.

The chaplain position was immediately abolished and the prayer meeting idea was turned down. The school board had a policy that providing school facilities for religious meetings might put damaging psychological pressure on young skeptics.

"They're so ignorant," ranted Tad. "It doesn't matter that we're all under pressure to stay high, to kill ourselves playing football, to work ourselves to death so we can pay for motorcycles and cars, to think about nothing but having sex, to cheat so we can make good grades. That's different. We can talk about any of that. But, we sure can't run the risk of harming somebody who might feel bad because he doesn't want to come to our prayer meeting."

As their financial situation improved, Teddy offered to enroll him in one of Albuquerque's booming private Christian schools. "Naw," said Tad. "Somebody's got to stick around. It's just going to get worse. They won't let you teach Jesus, yet they're always pitching un-Christian philosophies and their ever-changing theories on evolution—each time acting like they've finally got it right this time. Somebody's got to stay. Me."

He jokingly compared staying in the public schools to volunteering to stick around after the Rapture—the event prophesied in the Book of Revelation where Christians will be taken into heaven while the heathen fight it out on earth.

"What's really depressing is some of my teachers really believe that they're teaching us—that the Earth just happened, that we're all related to frogs." Tad chopped up a head of lettuce. "It takes more faith to believe their baloney than to accept the truth: that God was looking at our corner of the universe and said, 'Hmmmmmmm. Let's do something interesting here.'"

Teddy snickered.

"I've got one teacher," said Tad, "who sat me down in her office and started lecturing me about my giving out tracts down in the smoke hole. She said that God isn't the answer for the dopers. She said they need to find that unless they believe in themselves, nothing is worth doing. Can you believe that? I couldn't get her to see that if all we believe in is ourselves, then there is absolutely no point to anything.

"She told me I'm nuts. Poor lady. I'm really praying for her."

  ✐   ✐   ✐

A crowd of teens from church filed into seats in the Albuquerque Civic Center.

"This is going to be great," whispered Kathy, a girl Teddy had met at Tad's Sunday School.

Down three rows, Tad sat down with a buxom cheerleader named Evelyn. But his attention was on the group. That Spring, Tad had become the assistant youth minister at the largest church in Albuquerque.

Teddy sang in the church choir, attended a neighborhood Friday night fellowship and helped Tad on outings.

That is, he helped on outings that did not require him to pass out tracts on the street corner. He approved of Tad doing it if he felt led. But Teddy felt no such leading. He had had do-gooders thrust pamphlets at him when he was twelve and thirteen. He could remember the times he had needed them to offer him real help, the times he had expected them to be interested in talking to him to see if he was hungry or to offer him somewhere to stay.

But the ones he had encountered were only interested in saving his soul. And most of them had seemed to have more problems than he.

"Okay," Assistant Youth Minister Tad said, standing and leaning against the back of a seat. The Albuquerque Heights church kids all got quiet. The large auditorium continued to fill. "There are several parts of this that I just don't approve of and you'll see why."

They had come to see a revival of the old Broadway musical "Godspell"—in which Jesus Christ is played by a kind-hearted clown.

"This was written to appeal to people in the world," said Tad. "And it's very good in that respect. But it falls short of really lifting Jesus up."

Tad had been particularly irritated with a section that seemed to glorify Mary Magdeline as a happy hooker.

"I think you're too sensitive about prostitutes," drawled Teddy. "You know what happened when I was a little snot and somebody called me an s.o.b.?"

"What?"

"I was really surprised. I wondered how they knew."

Tad grimaced. As the musical went into its second act, Kathy leaned back against Teddy. Automatically, he lifted his arm around her. Then, his eye was caught by the back of a head—a very familiar head down ten or more rows.

And, as he stared in disbelief, a girl turned. It was Angie, a girl he'd liked at the ranch. She looked right at him. Their eyes held for long moments. "What are you doing HERE?" she mouthed.

Teddy grinned. He glanced up at the exit. She nodded.

"Uh, Kathy, do you want any popcorn?"

"No thanks. I'll take a Dr. Pepper, though."

"What are you doing in Albuquerque?"

"Oh, Teddy." Angie melted against him, her head on his chest. "My husband works for a hotel here."

"Your *husband?*" Teddy pulled away.

"He's a drummer in a nightclub orchestra. He's really good."

"Yeah? How long have you guys been married?"

"Three years. I met him right after...after you left Fayetteville. Teddy, I thought I was going to die. I married him because he reminds me of you. You could be twins. But he's not you. He's not kind. I'm so miserably unhappy. I still love you so."

Uncomfortably, Teddy looked around, expecting to see this "twin" slamming into the lobby, looking for his wife.

"Uh," Teddy said, not knowing how to respond.

"I got him to come to Albuquerque, hoping I'd find you," she whispered, clutching his hand. "We were in Vegas. I've been desperate, just hoping God would send me to you."

Teddy winced. "You could have called or something. We could have talked it out."

"We can't afford a phone. Musicians don't have anything. What money he makes, he spends on better drums and nice stage clothes."

"Well, what are you doing with yourself?" he asked.

"I teach ballet at the YMCA," she said. Gently, she touched one finger to his chest. "I've missed you so."

"Hey, this is really something, us running into each other," he said, clearing his throat. "Some coincidence, huh?"

"Oh, no. It's God's guidance," she whispered. "I've missed you so."

Teddy stared at her. God wouldn't guide some looney ex-girlfriend to run into him so she could run off from her husband. "Let's get out of here," she suggested.

"You don't know what you're saying," he exclaimed. "Angie, you're married. I'm very happy for you. I'd like to meet him sometime. But, I can't take off with you. I think we ought to cool it, you know?"

Shaken, Teddy sank back into his seat beside Kathy. "Where's my Dr. Pepper?" she asked.

"Uh, I...hey, I need to talk to my brother."

Teddy got up and circled over by Tad's seat. The cheerleader was adjusting his tie and giggling. Teddy, standing in the aisle, leaned against the armrest.

"Tadpole," he whispered. "Remember Angie?"

Tad looked up, startled. "Huh? From the ranch?"

Teddy snickered, nodding. "I just ran into her."

"Oh yeah? What'd she have to say?"

"Ask me about it later."

On stage, the cast was singing "Day by Day."

✐　　　✐　　　✐

"Teddy?" The voice on the phone was Angie's.

"Just a minute," said Tad. "He's parking the truck. We just got back from taking the kids at church to a musical. Is this Angie? This is Tad. How are you doing? How's your husband?"

There was an awkward silence, then a click as she hung up.

           🖋   🖋   🖋

Over ten thousand bicyclists showed up for the second annual World's Greatest Bicycle Ride. On a New Mexico football field crowded with tents and bicycles, the two brothers sat in the camper on the back of their pickup. His eyes closed, fifteen-year-old Tad picked his guitar and softly sang along with music from his earphones.

"Alleluia, alleluia, alleluia...alleluia," he whispered.

Teddy pecked away at a computer terminal.

"The roller coaster route twisted out of the Sacramento Mountains National Forest, veering straight up at times, then plummeting back, catapulting the thousands on the second annual World's Greatest Bicycle Ride toward azure bays and gravel beaches thirteen nerve-wrenching times.

"Exhausted from the climb, scores stumbled into the Norwood Mountain Grocery and Bait, where free cookies, brownies and lemonade were being served by the entire Contarez clan, which included wide-eyed kids in bib-overalls and a pregnant daughter-in-law slicing summer sausage onto Waverly wafers."

"Hey," said Tad, "Call Phoebe."

"Huh? Naw, that's long over."

Tad smiled mysteriously. Teddy returned to his keyboard.

"Just a holler off, another crowd of multiaged bicyclists from as far away as Switzerland, South Africa, Australia and East Orange, N.J., crowded into Francie Fite's general store. Excited Navajo neighbor kids stood in the middle of the road, waving cardboard welcome signs and yelling at riders that they had to stop and have a ten-inch chocolate chip cookie or a Norwood Mountain T-shirt.

"Miles ahead and beyond, attorneys, retired geologists, computer programmers, telephone repairmen, Southern Bap-

tist pastors, Santa Fe firefighters, Gallop oil executives and twenty-year-old schoolteachers from Farmington crawled up, then careened off the mountain...."

"What are you writing, Bear?" asked Tadpole.

"Story." Ted gazed over the campgrounds. "How you doing?"

Tad put on his earphones. "What do you mean?"

"You having fun?"

The paper was paying the high school sophomore to mark the route each morning before dawn and to meet with officials at the next overnight town. He was the "scout."

"Naw. Doesn't it bother you that we're not accomplishing anything? That we're not doing anything but proving that thousands of people can ride bicycles?"

"No," exclaimed Teddy, surprised at the question and at his own defensiveness. "Hey, I haven't seen you doing anything, either. You're not doing your usual wild-eyed evangelizing. What did you do with all your tracts?"

"I gave away all 1,500 the first day. People just threw them on the ground. These are cynical people, Bear. One Pueblo guy said he was going to scalp me if I preached to him. Your bicycling buddies are hard."

Teddy puttered with the terminal. "You know what?"

"What?" monotoned Tad, warily.

"If I were you, I'd try to quit talking so much and start showing people what you believe."

"That's a cop-out. Jesus didn't tell His disciples to go forth and hope all nations would notice what nice guys they were."

Teddy didn't say anything.

"I should have brought my megaphone."

"Gosh," drawled Teddy. "I don't know whatever possessed me to sneak it out of your luggage."

✐   ✐   ✐

Teddy sank into his chair on the *Albuquerque Daily World*'s city desk.

"What'd you do for dinner?" asked City Editor Susan Billingsley.

"I went to choir practice. At my church."

"Yeah, sure." Susan laughed, tapping away at her terminal.

"Hey, no kidding. That's where I went."

"Sure, Ted. Where'd you go? Over to the Press Club?"

"No kidding. Choir practice." Teddy mulled his screen.

"You really believe in all that stuff, don't you?"

"Sure. Why not?"

She stared at him with a wry grin. "I had an aunt who was a Holy Roller. She'd been a good church member like the rest of my family, then she got weird and kept the family all upset from then on. Don't you think that most of that stuff is just hysteria?"

"No."

"Well, what is it?"

"Why don't I introduce you to my little brother?"

"No, I want to hear it from you."

Teddy grinned. He shrugged.

"Teddy. Line five," interrupted the state editor.

✎   ✎   ✎

Teddy looked up from his computer terminal. He was working on a badly written story the new education writer had cranked out on a school board meeting.

The reporter couldn't even spell. The phone rang. "Yeah. City desk," Teddy said into the phone.

"T.B.?" asked a nervous voice. It was Angie.

✎   ✎   ✎

"I shouldn't have come," Teddy said, glancing around the restaurant. "I only came so we could talk this out."

"Teddy, why didn't you ever tell me why you just never called again? Was it my friends? Was it me? All these years, I've wondered what I did, why you just rejected me suddenly and never even had the decency to tell me why."

"Why don't we sit down?" Teddy caught the eye of the maitre d'. Then, he spotted a nine- or ten-year-old busboy, a little black kid sitting on a barstool by the cashier. The kid gave him a winning smile.

Teddy stared at the kid.

"I've decided to leave David," she said, sipping a cocktail. "Is there room in your life for me? Once we had something very special."

"Look," Teddy said. "My church doesn't believe in divorced people remarrying. Even if I wanted to, I couldn't marry you. Plus, it's been years. Uh...We don't have anything but a very nice memory. Let's just leave it that way. You need to stay with your husband and just work at making your life with him."

"You don't mean that."

"I do mean that."

She fumbled with her drink's straw. "I stayed up last night so I could see my favorite movie on the late show—*Same Time Next Year* with Alan Alda. Have you seen it?"

Teddy shook his head.

"It's this story of two lovers who meet every year just for one day. Both of them are married and have other lives. But just once a year, they meet at a remote resort and have a special weekend. It's the funniest movie."

Teddy winced. "Great. A comedy about adultery."

"That's not a very nice way of putting it."

"That's what it is."

Angie stared at him. "Maybe you and I ..."

"It could be nice," he said softly. "But I can't."

"Why not?"

"I've changed."

"You can't have changed that much."

"Oh, yes, I did. I've found myself. Actually, I'm still finding myself. But there's no point in me getting into what would be a real mistake."

"What are you talking about?"

"I'm religious, Angie. I found God."

"You're kidding."

"Nope. I done seen the light, honey bunch."

She stared at him in alarm. "What a waste." She touched the inside of his leg with her shoe.

          ✐   ✐   ✐

Teddy was sipping fruit punch at a Los Cerrillos church reunion when his Uncle Willem suddenly left the room looking particularly grim.

"Teddy," said his Aunt Minnie, coming up behind him. "Go help your uncle."

Teddy frowned.

"It's Hans," she whispered. "He's outside, drunk. Can you get him out of here?"

"Hans?" Teddy exclaimed.

Hans, his baseball-nut cousin.

Hans, who had gone a little crazy after Janny was killed.

Who had lived with Mrs. Cuminsky and then had gone off looking for Teddy.

The stringy-haired twenty-five-year-old was surrounded by calm deacons who were issuing platitudes and wondering if they were going to have to physically restrain him.

"Hans!" shouted Teddy, running across the porch.

"Wha—?" bellowed the drunk irritatedly. "Lemme talk to my mother!"

Whooping, Teddy galloped through the deacons and embraced his skinny cousin. Dull eyes, nervous with fear, glanced him over. The drunk shook his head vehemently.

"Who are you?" he slurred. Teddy shook with emotion. He looked just like Janny would have.

"Come on, you know me!"

"You're J.P.!"

J.P. was an older brother in Oregon.

"No! Come on!"

"Oh, I know. You're that stinkin' Kenneth Hillman." Hans began swearing, denying something Teddy didn't comprehend.

"No, I'm Teddy Bear."

"Oh," said Hans, relieved. "You used to live with us when you were a little snot. You got this weird thing for bicycles."

Teddy took him home. But he began to realize that Hans wasn't—and never had been—Janny. In the first hour, Hans alternated between hyperactive, sleepy and belligerent. He constantly requested money.

Teddy had no desire to search him, but could tell that he was popping exotic combinations of pills.

One of the first things he did was explore Teddy's medicine cabinet. "What do these do?" he asked, holding up a prescription bottle.

"I was having trouble with my knee," said Teddy.

"Do they make you high?"

"No."

"Why do you take 'em, then?"

Tad was fascinated. "Hans. Do you want to be free from drugs, really free?"

Hans stared at him dully. "Why?"

"Jesus wants you to be free."

Hans chortled and suggested Tad attempt something sexual that was gymnastically improbable.

"Jesus wants you back, Hans," said Tad, unperturbed. "He'll help you."

Hans expressed an obscene curiosity about Christ.

Tad stared at him. "I love you, Hansie," he said, hugging him suddenly. "And Father God, in the name of Jesus, I bind these demons possessing Your chosen son Hans and I command them to depart and flee, for Hans is Yours. Get thee hence!"

There was a shriek. The next thing Teddy saw was Tad being hurled into a bookcase and Hans diving out the door.

Tad began crying, dropping to his knees and pleading with God to intervene, to free Hans, to heal him, to restore him.

Teddy didn't quite know what to do.

He sat on the floor with his brother and quietly listened to the prayers and beseechings. Exhausted, Tadpole paused. "He won't be back, Teddy," Tad whispered.

"Sure he will."

Tad shook his head. "I failed. God help me, I failed."

"No, I think you scared him to death, but he'll be back—if nothing else out of curiosity."

And in the night, Teddy remembered the Janny who had been his best friend, whom he'd taught to cuss and smoke, for whom he'd begged shots of whiskey, for whom he had found somebody at school selling marijuana.

The sarcastic Hans had always been watching, curious. If anybody was responsible for the path he had chosen, it was Teddy. Sometimes it's hard to undo your mistakes.

✐   ✐   ✐

In the hallway, the phone rang.

Teddy moaned and squinted in the darkness. Tad was already up. "Hello?" he said. There was a long silence, then "Hey, wait, I'm Tad," he said. "You want to talk to Ted."

"Teddy," he said, leaning in the dark doorway. "She hung up again."

Teddy switched on his light and squinted in the brightness. "What'd she say this time?"

"She's found you a publisher for your novel. She was all excited."

Teddy's heart skipped a beat. "That's incredible. How did she know I was still working on it?"

"Teddy, she's bad news."

"I know. But, dang, Tadpole, what if she could get *Wild-Eyed Pentecost* published? She's been living in Los Angeles. She's got connections with publishers. Wow."

"Teddy," said Tad softly. "I think she's possessed by Satan."

"Oh, come on, Tadpole."

"How else did she know you're still working on your book? Have you been seeing her?"

"Not exactly." Teddy shrugged. Then, he became serious. "Tad, I'm sorry. You've got every right to ask me that. No. I've quit seeing her. She's got a screw loose. Plus, I just can't handle her being the big M, you know: married."

Tadpole squinted. "Listen, you need to call Phoebe. She's still crazy about you. I know what I'm talking about."

Teddy grinned at the boy. "Right. Thank you for your imput."

Tad glared at him.

      ✐   ✐   ✐

"Teddy Bear, how can you stand not accomplishing anything for Jesus Christ?"

"I wish you would quit asking me that."

In frustration, Tad yanked open the refrigerator, puttered around, then slammed it shut. "Let's go to Israel. You and me."

"Israel? There's nothing for us there. You belong here. You're accomplishing all sorts of stuff with your job as youth minister. Why do you want to go to Israel?"

"The Lord told me to go show His love to His people."

"A buncha Jews?"

"Yes. They're His chosen people. He called them first."

Teddy grimaced. "What would we do there?"

"The Lord will provide."

"I'm sure He will. But, uh, I'd like to know what I'm going for, how I'm going to support myself, where I'm going to stay."

"It is written, 'Man shall not live by bread alone, but by every word that proceeds from the mouth of God,'" said Tad.

"Don't preach to me."

"I'm not," exclaimed Tad. "I'm just telling you that we don't have to worry about that stuff. You believe the Bible, don't you? It says 'Stop being perpetually uneasy about your life, what you shall eat or what you shall drink and about your body, what you shall put on. Is not life greater in quality than food and the body far above and more excellent than clothing? So, don't worry and be anxious, saying "What are we going to have to eat?" or "What are we going to drink?" or "What are we going to wear?" Why be like heathens? They crave after all these things. But seek first of all His kingdom and His righteousness and then all these things taken together will be given you besides.'"

"Are you finished?" asked Teddy, stoically.

"No. That durn newspaper is ruining you," yelled Tad. "You've changed, Teddy Bear. We got work to do, you and me and it's not printing a newspaper. It's doing what Jesus said. And He said *'Go and preach. The Kingdom of heaven is at hand! Heal the sick, raise the dead, cleanse the lepers, drive out demons. Freely you have received and without charge you must give.*

Take no gold, nor silver, nor even copper money in your purse. And do not take a provision bag for your journey, nor two undergarments, nor sandals, nor a staff, for the workman deserves his support, his living, his food.'"

Teddy exhaled loudly. "Why do you stick around here if I'm such an irritation? Why don't you just take off?"

"Because you're supposed to go with me. And I think you're supposed to patch things up with Phoebe, too. I think she's supposed to go with us."

"Tad, you're going daffy on me. I ain't going nowhere, particularly to Israel. They don't want you there. You'll be arrested if you try to preach on your megaphone."

Tad stared at Teddy as if for the first time.

"I've lost you, haven't I?" he said softly.

"Hey, I haven't changed, you have," retorted Teddy. "Why don't you just accept the fact that you're a kid and let me try to be a newspaper editor."

"Will you at least call Phoebe?"

"What? NO."

Tad shrugged. But, he smiled, knowingly.

✐   ✐   ✐

Tad and about fifty kids waited outside the entrance to the city auditorium. Inside, a rock concert was going full blast.

"Where's your brother?" asked Ed Johnson, youth pastor at Jemez Pueblo Faith Fellowship.

"Huh?" asked Tadpole. "This isn't his type of ministry."

The minister snorted. " His newspaper hates Christians. They made us look like a bunch of savages. Most of it was lies."

Tad fumbled with his megaphone. "Like what?"

"Your brother didn't bother to talk to a lot of people who could have told him the truth."

"The only reason my brother would write a lie is if he was quoting somebody and didn't know they were lying. Did he write the story?"

"No, Tad, but it was some reporter who writes for your brother. On and on and on he quoted some New York civil rights activist who was trying to get us to pass an ordinance allowing homosexual marriages. Then he put in the story that the only reason we're trying to get a snorkel fire truck is so the council can ride it in the Christmas parade."

"My brother wrote that?"

"No, but his reporter did."

"Yeah? So, what is it my brother did?"

"Tad, you know what they did—what they always do, come out and stir up things, making people upset with some crazy stuff to make good people look stupid while the liberals come out looking open-minded and mistreated."

"Hey," said Tad. "Do you hate homosexuals?"

"Yes! Of course. Perverts—they're all trying to destroy our nation."

"God loves homosexuals."

"Yeah, right, I know, but that doesn't mean that I have to love their sin and their evil. They are an abomination before the Lord."

Tad squinted. "Do you ever show your church kids the movie *Chariots of Fire?*"

'Sure! It's a classic. A fine Christian movie."

"Did you know the guy who played the hero died of AIDS?"

"You're kidding."

"I guess that ruins the movie, huh?"

"What do you mean?"

"That you've got a really stupid attitude," said Tad. "God loves gossips and chronic complainers and thieves and murderers and people who try to stir up trouble between brothers—and he loves homosexuals, too."

The Jemez Pueblo youth minister grunted. "I heard your brother was a boy prostitute when he was young. Your brother isn't a Christian, is he? Isn't it hard for you living with a sweet guy like that?"

Tad's eyes narrowed. "My brother is one of the most super devout Christians I've ever met. He's got one fault: he's dead-set on being the most honest, efficient, caring, accurate journalist around. He's going to be one of the best editors God has ever had working for Him."

"An honest newspaper man?" Johnson chuckled.

Tad nodded solemnly. "I think the Lord wants him to do something else—I feel a real call for us two to be missionaries in Israel. But, Teddy thinks I'm nuts. However, as you should know, God doesn't force us. And if we seek Him, He blesses whatever we do. So, I guess I'm stuck with the Lord helping my brother become a famous newspaperman instead of a devoted missionary."

Johnson clutched his Bible. The rock concert inside was winding down. Kids were beginning to filter out.

"How come he doesn't get married? How old is he? I don't think it's natural, him being single. He ought to settle down and get a wife."

Tad stared at the man. He bode a surprising anger.

"You may not believe this," he drawled. "My brother's only twenty-three. Sometimes he looks about ten years older, but we had a rough time growing up. He was on his own when he was ten years old. He's never had any parents. He's never had anybody but me. And he's not gay. He's got some emotional things that he's still working through.

"Maybe you don't know this: But because of my brother Teddy Bear, I am what I am. Only God in heaven, my invalid grandmother and my brother Teddy Bear have cared about me since I was six years old."

Tad glanced over the youth minister's shoulder. There was a crowd coming out of the assembly center.

"He dates. He almost got married. He's always falling for girls from really tight-knit families. At least one time that I know of, his fiance, a girl named Phoebe, was really close to her dad, who told Ted that I'd have to go back to the boys' ranch, that his daughter wasn't marrying both of us.

"He was a flake. But Ted really loved his daughter. However, guess who he stuck by? *Me.* He never said a thing, but her little brother, who was my age told me what their dad had said." Tad clutched his megaphone. "Here they come."

"Yo," Tad yelled at the other kids from his church. They fanned out and began handing out tracts.

"Enter ye in at the narrow gate!" Tad began to preach on his megaphone. *"For wide is the gate and broad is the way that leadeth to destruction and many there be who go in that way, because narrow is the gate and narrow is the way which leadeth unto life and few there be that find it ... "*

⌇   ⌇   ⌇

Angie leaned back on the park bench and sighed.

"Oh, Teddy," she sighed. "It is so beautiful out here. Isn't spring great?"

He grinned. "What did your uncle say?"

"He says your novel would never sell like it is."

"What?"

"It needs sex, Teddy. Good kinky stuff. Things you wouldn't know anything about." She giggled.

Teddy blinked. "Sex? In *Wild-Eyed Pentecost?* It's about little kids who close their eyes and move anywhere they want in space and time."

"You are so naive, Teddy. What do you say we change it so they're real horny teens and can only move in time and space while they're naked or maybe having crazy sex with aliens?"

Teddy snickered and shook his head. "You mean there's nobody out there who reads wholesome literature anymore?"

Angie smiled. "Wholesome, yes. Boring, no." She wrinkled her nose at him. "I think you need help with your research." Angie rubbed his back. "It's good! It just needs some sex. We've got to make it appeal to the mass market."

    ◇   ◇   ◇

"I'm going to Israel," said Tad, standing in the doorway to Teddy's bedroom. "Without you."

"Hey, I'm your legal guardian until you're 18. You ain't going nowhere for at least another two and a half years."

"If you'd ever go to church anymore, you'd know this isn't just my idea."

"I know. In the last week, I've had about six of your preacher buddies and former burned-out hippies and that guy that used to be the Catholic priest call me up and want to go eat lunch. They say that God has spoken to them and that you're supposed to go to Israel. You're sure doing a number on me. They act like I'm some sort of heathen."

Tad frowned. "This guy from Chicago was there Sunday morning and he had a prophecy. It went something like that there was one among us who has heard a call and could not go because his brother won't let him. He said that the burden will be lifted."

"Lovely. Okay, say I let you go off to get yourself kicked out of Israel, what are you going to do, drop out of high school? I'm sure Israel is just dying to get fifteen-year-old Americans with megaphones who haven't even finished the tenth grade. They're not even going to let you in. And how are you going to pay for it? You don't have any money."

"I own half of the pickup."

"Super, let's cut the truck in half. But, hey, I thought you told me that you believed you're not even supposed to take any loose change with you, didn't you quote me that Scripture?"

"I've applied for a program called Christian Kibbutzim. I can go to school there and work on a state-owned kibbutz. They need workers and would even pay me. All I need is my airfare. My half of the pickup would pay for it."

Teddy stared at him. "Come here," the 23-year-old said, sitting down on the rug.

Tad sat down beside him. Teddy leaned back against the bed, then awkwardly put his hand around the fifteen-year-old's shoulder.

Just like when he was a little kid, Tad leaned back against his brother's chest. Teddy hugged him. "I know that it's not too far off that I've got to let you go. But I'm not looking forward to that. I gotta look out for you and one way I'm doing that is making you finish school."

Tad didn't say anything.

"Tad, think of all the people who just went and died on me. It's unnatural. I lost my grandmother, I lost Jan. We lost your mom and our grandma. I hardly think it's safe to let you out of the house, much less go to Israel."

Tad nodded silently.

"Is it that important that I let you go off half-cocked to a dangerous part of the world where you're not even wanted? Is it going to ruin your life to just stay here in Albuquerque and be a megaphone preacher?"

Tad sniffled. "I wish we hadn't grown up," he said. "It was more fun when we were little kids, wasn't it?"

Teddy closed his eyes. He sighed, deeply.

"Bear, I gotta do what God tells me to do," said Tad.

"I know."

Neither said anything for several minutes.

"Why don't you go with me? We're a great team. You look after all the details and I look after all the souls."

"Naw. You need to start learning about details, too."

"Why don't you at least spend all that vacation you have to ride your bicycle around Israel? You could help me get moved in and see where I'm gonna be."

"Naw. I want to ride around Poland. Or maybe Australia. Or South America."

✐   ✐   ✐

"Oh, Angie. Hi." With the telephone to his ear, Teddy leaned against the wall.

"Well?" she asked. "Are we running off to Los Angeles together?"

"Angie." Teddy paused. "Tell your uncle to forget about *Wild-Eyed Pentecost*. I'll just put it in a drawer and let it age. I'm a newspaperman, not a porno novelist. I might as well admit it."

"Did you talk to your preacher...about *us?*"

Teddy sighed. "There's no point."

"What do you mean?" Her voice was strained.

"I mean that I don't need to ask any preacher whether I should be messing around with a married woman. I think it's rather obvious."

There was a startled sob on the other end. "Teddy," she whispered. "I love you."

"Angie," he said, softly. "You *liked* me. I was a kid. You don't even know me now. I'm different. There are things I believe in now that are very important to me. They make me what I am.

If I give up on them, I'm not what I've spent 23 years learning to be."

"I could accept your church," she whispered. "I'd want our kids to go with you."

Teddy didn't say anything.

"Let's both go talk to your preacher," she whispered.

"Angie, you're not even divorced yet. I don't know how I ever even considered it. Even if you were divorced, I could not marry you if you left him to come to me. And even if you weren't ever married, Angie, I can't gamble on marrying somebody who isn't a Christian. Angie, I only get one shot at it—marriage. I'm not going to blow it."

"That's the biggest bunch of bull I've ever heard in my life. I am willing to join your church."

"That's between you and God. Angie, let's end this right now."

The front door opened and Tad wandered in. "Bear!" he yelled, his megaphone slung over his shoulder. "I'm home."

"Teddy, we love each other. We were meant to be together. It was a silly, immature thing of me to marry David. He was so much like you. I love you, Teddy Behre."

"Angie," whispered Teddy. "Quit it."

"You're the coldest, meanest person I've ever met," she sobbed. "I don't know why I love you so. You're just going to reject me again? You're going to banish me from your life? Teddy, you're the only thing in the world I care about. Don't send me into the darkness."

"Angie ..." whispered Teddy.

Tad strolled into the hallway. "Who are you talking to? Hey, Kathy! When are you going to get this big lunk to get back in church? Oh, excuse me, Dawna, I mean Laurie."

There was silence on the other end.

"Teddy. Let's run away tonight," she said.

"Look ..." he said.

Tad turned. He looked at Teddy strangely. Then, he came back down the hallway.

Suddenly—loudly—"Father," Tadpole prayed. He grabbed Teddy's arm. "Protect Teddy Bear. In the name of Jesus, I come against this oppression. Teddy is *yours,* Jesus. The enemy cannot touch him. In the name of *Jesus,* I command Satan to flee. Be gone! Leave my brother. *Leave him alone!*"

On the other end of the line, there was a quiet click.

Irritated, Teddy felt like slugging the little fanatic. He hung up and stumbled down the hall. When he opened his eyes, he was sprawled on the hallway floor. Tad had the palms of both hands on his head and was praying with incredible intensity.

"Tad." Teddy grasped Tad's arm. "What happened?"

"It was her, wasn't it?"

"What?"

"It was Angie. She was trying to break you, wasn't she?"

"I don't understand," Teddy rasped.

"Yeah, you do."

"Tadpole, I don't even believe that kind of stuff. It's too crazy. It's not even civilized." But Teddy was trembling.

"Pray with me, Bear," whispered Tad. "Father, open my brother's eyes. Show him that Satan can appear as an angel of light. Give him faith, Father, guide his steps."

     🖉   🖉   🖉

"Okay," said Teddy.

"What?" Tad leaned over a Bible at the desk in his room. School would be out in two weeks.

"If you'll go to school in that Christian Kibbutz deal and promise me you'll stick with it and graduate, you can go to Israel."

Tad sat up, startled.

"You mean it?"

"Yeah."

"Praise God!" Tad leaped to his feet. "Praise Jesus!" he yelled. "I gotta call a bunch of people."

He dashed out of the room.

       ✐   ✐   ✐

Teddy pulled their little white Toyota pickup into the loading zone in front of bustling Albuquerque airport's ticket counters.

Tad jumped out, fumbled with his ticket and passport, then jammed them in his back pocket. He grabbed his backpack out of the truck bed.

"I'll go find somewhere to park, then I'll be right back," said Teddy.

"Right!" barked the sixteen-year-old.

When Teddy jogged back to the ticket counter, Tad had already gone down the concourse to the loading gate. And there, Teddy found about sixty kids and adults from church hugging Tad and shaking his hand. Several of the women were crying.

Behind the boy towered none other than Leroy MacDonald. He was handing him an envelope, apparently a special offering that kids in Arkansas had taken up.

A line of high school girls sniffled on the edge of the crowd.

"Hi, Jenny," said Teddy. The Santana High School girls' basketball team captain fumbled with a Kleenex.

"Why'd you give him permission?" she demanded softly. "I'm never going to see him again."

A wail went up from a fat girl next to her. Teddy tried not to snicker. This brother of his, the Albuquerque Heights church's youngest assistant youth minister ever, had made considerably more impact than he thought.

Tad whispered something to a college kid and the guy stood on a chair and began leading the crowd in a Christian chorus.

Tad dodged around to where Teddy stood.

"Bear," he said. "Let's take a walk."

The two strolled down the long concourse.

"I know you don't like to get emotional in front of people and stuff," mumbled the sixteen-year-old. "So, I want to tell you goodbye here."

Teddy gritted his teeth. He'd sworn he wouldn't cry.

"So, goodbye," said Tadpole. He hugged Teddy quickly, then stepped back.

For the last three weeks, Teddy had been laying down rules and regulations. Tadpole had been balking, agreeing, then coming up with rules of his own for Teddy.

"Hey, you ain't goin' away for good," said Teddy. Awkwardly, he shrugged. "You just go off to Israel and grow up, then you come back. I need my brother to look after me."

Tad laughed through tears.

And suddenly, Tadpole was hugging his brother again and crying openly. And he was sobbing, a lonely first grader scared of monsters in the dark. He clutched Teddy tightly and laid his head on the older boy's shoulder.

"You're too big for me to pick up anymore," said Teddy, softly. He ignored people staring. Gently, he touched Tad's sandy hair. "Hey, get tough, guy."

"Come with me, Bear. I need you bad. We need each other. We're a team, Bear."

"Naw. This will be good for us or something. You gotta do what you think God is after you to do. And I've got to follow my dreams."

"Dumb newspaper." Tad hugged him once more, then awkwardly turned. "I love you, Bear."

"Damn right."

"Quit cussin'. Do you love me or not?"

"Yeah. I love you."

For a long time, the big plane just sat on the runway. Teddy stared after it, not knowing if Tad could see him or not.

Then, it began to move.

Teddy waved, hoping Tadpole was watching.

The plane rolled down to the end of the runway, then sped skyward and was gone. For a long time, Teddy stared after it. And he was alone again.

This time, he was more incredibly alone than ever before.

✐   ✐   ✐

In a dream that night, a foreign army helicopter of some kind lifted off from a soccer field behind and hovered over a tropical city square. *"Your temptation will be far, far greater than mine!" proclaimed Quetzalcoatl. "You are the fulfillment of the great prophecies. You will be the mighty one who leads great Lucifer's final victory!"*

"No," vowed the Teddy, his voice a terrified whisper. "No. Not me. I will not rebel against the One who created me and all that is. I am a warrior angel of the company of Michael. I am a loyal and obedient servant of the Most High!"

✐   ✐   ✐

"Teddy Bear CARES About Them," blared the headline across a full-page color photo of the grinning, tanned twenty-four-year-old standing before a sea of bicyclists. In the picture, his blond curls shone in the sunshine. The excited bicyclers seemed to mirror admiration.

Irritated, suppressing fury, he ignored the Saturday front page rumpled on his motel bed.

Outside, still more thousands of bicyclists poured into tiny White's City, New Mexico. Cars loaded with racing bikes, discount store ten-speeds and rusting 3-speeds packed the two lanes of U.S. 62 for miles. On the blacktop shoulders, festive early arrivals pedaled the opposite direction faster than traffic. In sprawling temporary campgrounds, nervous families in sparkling new bike helmets dutifully stood in long lines at portable toilets.

On the road, laughing international race teams attempted English on giggling teen-age girls hanging out windows of dusty church buses with upside-down bikes lashed to the roof.

Big-city bicycle club members sat in open doorways of RVs and Airstream trailers offering beers and hailing old friends. Along a mile of civic club concession stands lining the road up to Carlsbad Caverns National Monument, nervous junior high schoolers sported brand-new "World's Greatest Bicycle Ride" T-shirts emblazoned with "Teddy Behre CARES about ME."

Teddy ran his fingers through his sun-bleached hair. A scarred bicycle leaned against the wall. A TV flickered mutely, its sound turned down. A portable computer terminal sat silent, its screen a soft green.

He stared blankly at the wall, then, impatiently yanked open the door and was hit with the din of the vast crowd and the wilting heat of late afternoon—the dusty blast of southern New Mexico in June.

Ignoring college students unloading their station wagon into the motel room next to his, Teddy shoved his bike onto the porch, then pedaled across the courtyard and into the noisy throng in the wide Main Street. Overhead, a long banner bore a grinning caricature of Teddy and *I'm Glad You're Here and So Is the Albuquerque Daily World.*

He caressed his handlebars and waxed philosophic, telling himself there was no point in blaming himself over a female's inability to make up her mind, no point in kicking himself for something over which he had no control. He pedaled through the midst of the bicyclists, his deep frustration, his disappointment pushed aside as he looked over the throng.

A swell of pride, a thrill of accomplishment, a rush of success filled him. Then, Teddy ducked his head, hoping not to be recognized. But it was too late.

"There's Ted Behre!" yelled somebody.

Teddy looked up and grinned winningly. He picked up speed.

"Teddy!" hailed a total stranger. Teddy waved, but knew better than to stop and shake the man's hand. He'd be stuck for an hour, being polite to faceless people who somehow considered him a close friend. He had yet to understand what strange void was filled when they fell for the newspaper's odd promotional stunt of turning a cynical young feature writer into a celebrity.

Teddy didn't care about these staring, gawking people. Well, that wasn't totally accurate. This was his baby. This was the *Albuquerque Daily World's* Greatest Bicycle Ride. His face was on the T-shirts, the pamphlets, the promotional posters: Teddy CARES about YOU.

On both sides of U.S. 62, tent cities filled acres of yucca and mesquite, filled with people who trusted him. On the right-of-way, chartered tour buses from New York City, Des Moines, Los Angeles and Atlanta idled empty or disgorged bicyclists and boxed bikes. They, too, had heard about Teddy's legendary bike ride.

Despite his irritated embarrassment, he would drive himself to exhaustion in his determination not to disappoint them.

His head down, he shot up the center of Main Street where the Rotary Club was selling 50-cent tickets for hot showers. That had been his idea back on WGBR II. Small town groups always fell for them on the money-making and public relations angles. In three circus tents under the town's small aerial tramway, Carlsbad church members parcelled out dinners to growing lines of riders. That, too, had been his brainchild back during WGBR II: get locals during WGBR III to feed the bicyclists—and reap the annually increasing monetary rewards.

"T.B.," barked a little walkie-talkie in Teddy's handlebar bag. "Hello, T.B.? Hello, T.B. You out there, T.B.? I wish he'd carry his radio with him. If anybody spots Ted Behre, tell him to get over to the photo truck."

The voice was that of *Albuquerque Daily World* photographer Olav Lutzow.

Teddy grabbed the radio and looped in the middle of the packed street, cutting right in front of a line of racers whose jerseys proclaimed they were from Illinois. The sprinters swerved. "Watch out, you idiots!" yelled a white-haired man on a custom-designed bicycle-built-for-two.

A young girl in the seat behind him, maybe his granddaughter, grabbed his waist and dropped an ice cream bar. She glared at the racers, then recognized the radio-clutching Teddy and poked excitedly at the old man. He braked and peered.

But Teddy was gone. He locked his bike to the bumper of the photo truck and knocked on the back door.

"Go away, we're processing!" yelled the rotund Olav.

"Little pig, little pig, let me come in," returned Teddy on the radio. He growled and waited.

The door swung open.

"Well, where have you been hiding?" greeted pink-faced Lutzow, his rubber apron streaked with darkroom chemicals. "All the motels in Carlsbad, Artesia and Hobbs are *FULL!* In Carlsbad, the city parks are overflowing, according to the police. They said they don't know where they're going to put anybody else and the restaurants are running out of food. I told them that the big crowd won't get here until tomorrow."

Teddy grinned. "Tell them not to worry. There's not even 10,000 here yet."

He sat down at a computer terminal.

There was a tap on the door.

"We're processing! Go away!" yelled Olav.

"Teddy!" yelled an angry voice. "Olav, I saw Teddy Behre go in there. This is Ortega."

Lutzow inquiringly lifted one eyebrow at Teddy.

"Hey, Gene," Ted greeted, leaning over and opening the door.

In the harsh sunlight, "Have you seen this?" bellowed the burly half-Navajo police detective—Teddy's former probation officer—wearing full bike gear. The wide chest of his gold jersey was emblazoned with "The Santa Fe Bicycling Society." As he climbed into the camper, his bicycling cleats clattered on the metal steps. He gripped the front page of the *Albuquerque Daily World* Saturday afternoon edition.

"Have you read this trash?" he repeated

Fear and Loathing on WGBR! announced the headline. Teddy squinted in concern and began reading.

"(Wilson Lang's column this morning was found on tattered, soggy paper, stuffed in a tequila bottle along the WGBR route near White's City.)" the column began.

"To whomever discovers this: I am tired, out of booze, there are no lemonade stands and I am alone on the road.

"This is partially because the World's Worst Bicycle Ride No. 3 hasn't officially begun yet. This is the only time this week I am going to be able to pedal along a dusty highway not having to evade cheerful children trying to sell me lemonade. This humid evening, I do not need to dodge draft lines of Communist racers, chattering, hotdog-munching cheerleaders, fourteen-year-old studs trying to pedal and stand on their heads at the same time or placid grandmothers riding under beach umbrellas or five-year-olds passing me on tricycles.

"I'd like to set the record straight on one thing: WGBR has not yet won the Richard Nixon Bad Housekeeping Seal of

Approval. Neither is it a week of drug-crazed orgies. (See, Teddy, I can say nice things.)

"Oh, you say your relatives in White's City phoned, telling you that there were a lot of people in the cactus Friday night having a good time without their clothes on?

"You say your sweet young nephew reported that he saw the note on the White's City campgrounds message board, from a boy to a girl:

"'I'm sorry for the way I acted on the bus,' he says it read. 'I was stoned. I promise there will be no more animal acts. Please come to my tent.'

"Well, yes, I saw it too. So, now you know about the other side of WGBR. By day, thousands of wholesome folks from all over the globe will be pedaling their wholesome little hearts out next week, downing all the wholesome lemonade that Teddy Behre can find, nibbling wholesome homemade cookies from all the wholesome churches that Behre seems determined to infest this ride with and wholesomely talking of (sheesh!) the joys of exercise.

"But by night, most of these hypocrites—especially your fifteen- to-twenty-eight-year-old sons and daughters—mass in the bars, seeking just the right person with which to share a sleeping bag.

"'Come on, if it weren't for the whoopee side of WGBR, I wouldn't be here,' a Santa Rosa matron told me as she sipped a beer in the trash-strewn back patio of Carlsbad's El Gringo Bar last night.

"Well, I'll have to tell you, I didn't believe a word of it, and neither will Behre. He'll pop off with something like 'How can there be so much sex with so many cold showers?'

"Let me tell you about ol' Theophilus Johnson Behre. (He hates for people to call him that.) He is a very bright young man, but rather naive. I know for a fact that he is a direct

descendant of European royalty and that he skipped the fourth, fifth and seventh grades when he went to school in Los Cerrillos. (What else was there to do in a ghost town?) And he never got a chance to hang out at the corner gas station swapping lies.

"*But you stay tuned and I'll tell you the REAL story of WGBR.*

"*(TO BE CONTINUED).*"

Teddy chuckled, folding the paper in half and handing it back to Ortega. "You ought to sue that guy," yelled Gene.

Teddy squinted at his former juvenile officer.

"You mean," Teddy asked softly. "I should sue somebody who says I was smart enough to skip whole grades? That I'm royalty? That I was protected?"

"Bear, he's gonna ruin this ride."

"Naw. I'll get him in Sunday's paper. I'll write something hilarious. Maybe it's time to tell that we have to send somebody out to retrieve him each evening."

"That won't bother him!" exploded Ortega. "Teddy, we're going to have people driving down here to rescue their kids. Divorces are going to result from his sort of publicity. Is that what you want?"

"Nobody believes Wilson. You don't think he actually saw that on the message board."

"EVERYBODY believes Wilson! Dang it, for an ex-J.D. you ARE protected. That guy's destroying our months of hard work. This is a family event. That sort of story is going to attract motorcycle gangs."

"What's a ex-J.D.?" asked Ragnhild, Olav's seventeen-year-old daughter and darkroom assistant.

"Former juvenile delinquent," said Teddy, not turning.

There was a rap on the door.

"Olav?" yelled a voice. "This is Holt! The president of the Carlsbad Chamber of Commerce is trying to find Behre. You seen him?"

"I'm right here!" Teddy called, opening the door.

"T.B.," greeted Dallas Holt, the disheveled, six-foot-three president of the Albuquerque Bike Club. He dug for a cigarette. "Oh, hi, Gene. Teddy, this here is Hector Herrera with the chamber of commerce. Hector, this is Ted Behre, the assistant city editor of the *Albuquerque Daily World*, which sponsors the ride. Ted, we were just watching the official portable toilets come in. How many have we got this year?"

"We should have ten trucks each carrying twenty," said Teddy, shaking hands with Herrera. "And three honey wagons to clean them out daily. What's the problem?"

"Oh, no problem," said Holt. He chuckled, fumbling for a cigarette lighter in the hip pocket of his long bike shirt. He grinned.

In the distance, they could hear a growing chant. "Porta-POTTIE! Porta-POTTIE! Porta-POTTIE!" whooped hundreds of young riders swarming to greet the convoy.

"Teddy, have you seen the T-shirt Porta-Pottie's going to be selling?" volunteered Ragnhild, glancing quizically at Ortega. "It's got WGBR in the shape of a bicycle and a cartoon of you riding it, saying, 'Keep on Going with Porta-POTTIE!'"

"Uh, Teddy," said Holt. "Hector and I and Dr. Campbell were wondering when we are going to meet tonight. I don't think you've ever met Doc's all-girl ambulance crews or the nurses with the Life Flight helicopter. It, uh, would be worth your time to drop by the first aid tent and introduce yourself."

"How many riders do you think we've got, Teddy?" asked Olav conversationally.

Glancing at Ortega, Teddy forced a grin. "Who knows? They'll be straggling in all night."

Holt turned toward Herrera. "I hope you've warned your volunteers that the traffic won't thin out until about 1 a.m. and then will pick up again around 4 a.m. C'mon, Teddy, are we going to meet this evening or not? Doc is worried about water and nobody's seen the gal in charge of lemonade stands."

"The lemonade stands will take care of themselves," said Teddy. Each year, scores of kids and civic groups made thousands of dollars along the route quenching riders' thirsts and sating ravenous appetites. "What do you say we meet around 5 p.m.? Dallas, Gene, you got your radios?"

Holt looked blank. Gene muttered something and yanked his out of a jersey pocket.

Ragnhild leaned over to a bank of walkie-talkies recharging on the side of the camper clothes closet.

"Here," she said. "And," she added coyly, "Teddy, this year, turn yours on, what do you say?"

Teddy pulled out his little transceiver and pushed the transmit button. "Hello, NMHP? This is Behre. Testing. This is Behre. You reading me, NMHP?"

"Hey, Teddy Bear," crackled a woman's voice. "This is the New Mexico Highway Patrol. How's it going?"

Suddenly Gene Ortega wadded the newspaper, threw it at Teddy, shook hands with Herrera again, glanced back—grinning at Teddy—and crowded his way out of the cramped camper. "See you, Gene," called Teddy. Then, into the radio, "Hey, Lindy, I was afraid you weren't running things this year. What's up?"

"What was wrong with that guy?" asked Herrera as Gene slammed the door.

"Nothing," drawled Olav. "We all just got the pre-ride jitters." He pulled out a camera and began checking the shutter release.

"Everything's crazy as usual," Lindy was telling Teddy on the radio. "You think I'd miss all the fun? No way. This is the greatest week of the year. You really don't want to know what's going on, do you? Cars stalled, a little old lady with heat stroke. Some stoned high school boys. It could get depressing."

"Just keep on keeping it under control," said Teddy, glancing up at the increasingly concerned chamber of commerce president, "like you always do."

"You betcha," crackled Lindy. "Hey, Teddy, we've got twenty troopers out here this year and it looks like we'll have a buncha local sheriffs and police each day. And did you know about the challenge between the New Mexico Sheriff's Association and the patrol brass?"

"No." Teddy grinned winningly at the confused Herrera, then at Holt, who suddenly realized the need to force a smile.

"Our state commander," Lindy's voice crackled, "and the state director of the department of public safety are out here on a radio-equipped bicycle-built-for-two. They've challenged the president and vice president of the New Mexico Sheriff's Association to make the full ride. Hey, Teddy, did the National Guard find you?"

"Sure didn't."

"They've got their mobile showers set up over by the lake at Temporary Campgrounds Five. Man, I've heard that the water is really cold. Everybody's loving it. Hey, gotta go."

"Talk to you later," said Teddy. Glancing at Holt and Herrera, "Without that lady, we'd be in big trouble," he said.

"Is Jenny Wellington helping us this year?" asked Holt, his cigarette hand trembling.

"She's my scout again and she's running the sag wagons," said Teddy. Each year, empty "sag wagon" tour buses from MK&O lines wandered along the route, picking up the tired and hot—and offering water along desolate stretches.

"Jenny's got a new leapfrog system all worked out," volunteered Olav. "Did you know MK&O sent ten buses and drivers this year? Plus, they recruited tourist trams from the national parks at Chaco Canyon, Gran Quivira and Frijoles Canyon, I think. I don't know how they pulled that off. And Arlie's Bicycle Shop in Albuquerque came up with ten flatbed trailers for the buses to pull to carry bikes. I don't know how that's going to work. I've never seen a tour bus pulling a trailer."

"Did you see the repair trucks, Hector?" offered Holt. "Over by the Cavern Inn swimming pool, there are six from Arlie's Bike Shop in Albuquerque and they've got more business than they can handle.

"None of these folks ever get their bikes ready before this thing. You wouldn't believe the bikes some of them expect to ride, rattling, $69.95 discount store specials their kids throw paper routes on. It's incredible."

Actually, more than twenty bike shops from all over the Southwest sent repair trucks. The big Albuquerque shop was only the most visible—and set the standard of charging only for parts, no labor, unless the bike was in derelict shape.

"How do you supply water to these people out in the boonies?" asked Herrera.

"Hey, that's incredible—" said Holt.

Teddy held up his radio.

"Hello, Howard, you got your radio on?"

There was silence, then a long string of mumbled cursing.

"HELLO!" bellowed a voice.

"Howard?" asked Teddy. "Hey you doing any business?"

"Boss, I done sold a zillion T-shirts," crackled the newspaper's errand boy. "And these pretty ladies you got helping me brought me some ice cream."

"Good deal," said Teddy. "Hello, Jenny, you listening in yet?"

There was no response.

"Want me to keep trying for her?" asked Lindy, breaking in.

"I'd appreciate it," said Teddy. He sighed and looked around at Holt and Olav. "I better get over to the motel. I've got a lot of work to do."

Holding his trademark grin as they pooh-poohed his dedication, Teddy opened the door, then shook hands again with the anxious Herrera.

"Teddy," called Ragnhild, stepping out and closing the camper door behind her. She clutched two of her dad's cameras. "When do we all get to meet this Angie of yours?"

Teddy sighed. "That's over." His voice was hoarse.

Ragnhild tried to look sympathetic, but it came across more like delight. "Oh, Teddy. Why?"

He jammed his walkie-talkie into his handlebar bag. "She came to her senses." He grinned wryly.

"I'm SO sorry," Ragnhild offered, almost too cheerfully. "Is she going to divorce her husband?"

Teddy shrugged curtly, looking away. "I don't know. I hope not on my account. I'm not going to marry her."

Ragnhild watched him disappear into the crowd.

She had heard all about the mystery Angie, the beautiful girl from the boys' ranch who had trapped herself into a tragic marriage although she really loved Teddy.

"What's she doing in Los Angeles?" Ragnhild had asked, leaning against Teddy's desk back at the newsroom. "Why doesn't she come live with you?"

"Because I am not interested in shacking up with a married woman," said Teddy absently, puzzling over a note from the managing editor.

"Did you really tell Darla that Angie was the most beautiful girl you'd ever met? That she stunned you the first time you ever saw her?"

"Huh? Yeah. Took my breath away. But I was only thirteen years old."

Now, staring into the crowds of bicyclists from the doorway of the camper, Ragnhild's eyes moistened. Losing her must hurt more than the impassive Teddy let on. Ragnhild had heard of Teddy's incredible past—arrested repeatedly before he turned eleven, jailed at thirteen for armed robbery, spending years at a boys' ranch.

He had told Debbie Arnold, the state editor's daughter, that as a kid, Angie had been extraordinary. The two had found they shared all sorts of dreams, feelings and experiences. She needed him, he had told Debbie, and he needed her.

But he had told Debbie that learning she was married had been sheer hell. Ragnhild bristled. It was *so* tragic.

Once he had told Deb that as a kid shuffled between foster homes and boys' ranches, being let down by people he depended on was something he just got used to. Early on, he had gotten used to stepfathers, relatives, best friends not living up to their promises, not carrying through on their noble, dramatic commitments. His mother had abandoned him at birth.

Once Teddy had told Dina Clark, who typed in engagement and wedding announcements for the Women's Section, that as a little boy, there had been dark, lonely nights when he had longed to have somebody else—anybody—care.

He had said that being unable to talk to anybody when you're ten and all alone is hard, but becomes acceptable. That sometimes it's years between times that you have anybody to tousle your hair, to dry your tears, to tell you that everything's gonna be okay. And that then, the people you finally care about always go away.

Ragnhild leaned in the door. Now, it had to be worse for him. After years of cynical acceptance, he must have actually believed it was going to be different.

He had loved this Angie.

He had wanted to marry her.

Now, he couldn't. And he needed somebody.

Ragnhild sighed dreamily. And she knew she was not going to let an opportunity like this slip by.

      ✎   ✎   ✎

His head down, Teddy pedaled through the mass of riders and retreated to his motel. In the dark, he flipped on the computer terminal set up on his dresser. He opened a wire story at the top of his personal directory.

"AM:Israel 06-twelve 0387

"AM:Israel,380

"American volunteers Missing in Raid

"With ISRAELRAID Bjt

"KIBBUTZ DAGANI (AP)—Israel said four Americans were among twenty farm workers missing when Palestinian guerrillas overran this farm near the Syrian border Saturday only two days after twenty-four Israeli children were massacred near the Lebanese frontier.

"Named as missing were Americans Jon Moffett, 18, of Peoria, IL, Michael Stohler,17, and Jackie Ray Moss, 16, both of Norfolk, VA, and Thaddeus Behre, 17, of Albuquerque, NM.—"

Numbly, Teddy re-read the story, then cleared it and began looking for other stories in the system on the raids. There was nothing else about Tad. He picked up the phone and dialed.

"City desk," answered a voice.

"This is Behre."

"Hang on, I'll get Travis."

The newspaper's managing editor came on the phone. "Ted," he said, his voice grim. "Did you see the story on the wire?"

"Yes, I did. What do you have? Do you know if he's okay?"

"No. I'm terribly sorry. That's it." Teddy's boss paused. "I was hoping you could fill in the pieces about his background. We need something for a story. We've got a couple of clips, but nothing recent. Are you his only family?"

"Yeah." Teddy's mind raced. His hand trembled, clutching the phone to his ear.

"You want to talk to a reporter?" Travis' voice was uncharacteristically gentle.

"Naw." Teddy tried to sound nonchalant. "I'll just punch in something here."

"Okay."

Teddy hung up. His eyes filling with tears, he stared at his screen. "NS CITY, TAD.BEHRE," he typed in too quickly, jamming the keys. He sighed and tried again. He blinked back the unwelcome moisture in his eyes.

"I first met my brother when I was thirteen and he was six," Teddy typed. *"We were roommates at a boys' ranch in Arkansas. Nobody wanted either one of us. He was terrified of the dark. I tried to stay aloof of him, a dumb little kid who meant nothing."*

Teddy stared at the screen.

He frowned, then erased the paragraph.

He tried again:

"Thaddeus Behre, seventeen, is the assistant director of an Albuquerque religious organization 'Kibbutzim for Christ,' which places American volunteers on communal farms, assisting the labor-poor Jewish state."

Teddy paused.

"His brother, Ted Behre, twenty-four, is assistant city editor of the Albuquerque Daily World and director of the newspaper's annual 'World's Greatest Bicycle Ride.'"

He hit the SEND button.

Then, he began scrolling through the foreign wire again. An updated story on the raid was at the top of the directory. He scanned it.

There was nothing new.

A MESSAGE signal glowed at the top of his screen. Teddy called up the message. "Bear," it read. "How about something a little longer. Weren't you guys in a lot of trouble with the law? When did your brother go to Israel? I thought his name was Tad. Where did he go to high school? Wasn't he in jail?"

Teddy sighed. He pulled up his story, looked it over, then made some additions:

"An enthusiastic religious tract-passer and former president of the ninth grade at Santana High School, Tad was once a familiar sight at local rock concerts, preaching over a megaphone with teams of youths from the 'Shelter' coffeehouse.

"He has been in Israel less than a year, planning to finish high school there. He has written home in letters of having difficulty adjusting to Israel's no-proselytizing laws, but has participated in several massive Christian crusades in Jordan and did evangelistic work in Cyprus, where laws are less strict.

"He is the former youth pastor at Albuquerque Heights Church in Albuquerque. As a youngster, he was given the nickname Tadpole by his brother and goes by 'Tad.' He was born Thaddeus Gray, but legally took the name Behre after the death of his mother, Jeanne Anderson, when he was eleven."

Teddy scowled at the screen, then signed off.

He thought about phoning Israel. But he knew no one to call. He thought about flying to Israel. The urge would not go away.

✐   ✐   ✐

"You look dead," whispered Jenny Wellington as Teddy walked into the Cavern Inn's crowded conference room.

"I need to go to Israel. I've got to get there." His voice was emotionless. "I intended to ride every inch this year. But I don't know." Teddy sighed heavily. His world was caving in around him and he had no idea what to do about it. Back in his room after the meeting, he checked the wire services for word on Tad. But there was nothing else new. Teddy signed off the terminal with no apparent emotion. He pushed his bike out the door. Inconspicuously, he rode through the throng and up to Carlsbad Caverns' ampitheater at the entrance to the caves.

Teddy took a seat on the back row and spotted a dour-looking Ragnhild standing by the center stairs, her neck draped with cameras.

He'd heard the ranger's lecture before. As the pot-bellied man rambled on about fruit bats, sonar, vampires and DDT, Teddy tried to catch Ragnhild's eye and wave her over.

But, in midlecture, the evening's first bats fluttered—seemingly dazed—out of the mouth of the caverns. Within minutes, a spiraling black cloud of the tiny creatures was arching off over the horizon. The ranger was quiet, cautioning the audience to be careful not to alarm the thousands of tiny mammals.

The first time Teddy had seen the bat flight, Tad had been eleven. He and Teddy had sat on the front row.

Teddy leaned back as the sunset faded, as the bats winged north in search of bugs, as the crowd got up to go.

"Excuse me," said a woman who had been sitting down the row from him. "Aren't you Teddy Behre?"

Ted grinned and nodded, mischievously. He held one finger to his lips. Nonetheless, a gawking crowd began to gather. A little girl pushed up, tentatively offering an autograph book.

"Oh," said the woman, embarrassed, glancing around. "I just wanted to tell you that we're REALLY looking forward to this year's ride. This is our third time to come all the way from New Jersey. We always have such a good time. But—" She glanced around at the growing crowd and seemed to gain courage. "—why didn't you take the route back up to Sunspot again? And aren't we ever going back to Shakespeare?"

"We try to change the route a little every year," said Teddy, signing the little girl's book and accepting pieces of paper now being thrust at him by adults and teen-agers.

Under a gray sunrise, the thousands filled White's City Main Street. Hoping to be inconspicuous, Teddy pedaled in the midst, reluctantly greeting a few who recognized him, hailing a few riding buddies from the Santa Fe bike club, then carrying his bike up onto a big flatbed truck at the starting line. A cheer went up. Teddy grinned his trademark winning smile.

Already hundreds of riders were on the road. Lindy had reported that the Romanian racers were already in Hagerman, the next overnight stop.

As Teddy shook hands with the governor and checked details with one of the chief executive's aides, Dallas Holt hovered nearby, scanning the sky.

"Teddy, we're a half hour away from letting them go, but it's gonna start raining hard any minute," he worried under his breath, shaking ashes from his cigarette. "Why don't we get things started?"

Teddy scanned the crowd for TV cameras. The governor would stall until cameras were rolling.

"Okay," he said. The governor would go at the last of the brief program anyway—officially riding off at the head of the mob. The TV crews would arrive by then, he hoped. If not, they could stage something on down the road.

"Teddy." It was Ragnhild, all made up and wearing a sun dress, looking like she was ready to go to a party, not to photograph a bicycle ride. She smiled from the edge of the stage.

"What's up?" he asked, stooping on one knee.

"I'm real sorry about Tad," she said, eyes flashing.

"Yeah. Well, those things happen."

Teddy started to stand. It was time for things to start.

"Teddy, are you going to ride today?"

Teddy looked back at her. She smiled sweetly.

"Sure am," he said. "Aren't you going to get your clothes ruined dressing up like that? I think it's gonna rain cats and dogs."

"Do I look nice?"

"Yeah, for a kid. How old are you now, anyway? Fourteen? You're sure getting great big."

"What do you mean GREAT BIG?" she exploded.

Teddy rolled his eyes and feigned innocence. He stepped to the podium and tapped on the microphone, then winked at her.

A cheer went up.

Ragnhild stared daggers at him. She spun and stalked away. Teddy stared over the vast crowd. A thrill rippled through him. These were his bicyclists. These were his people.

This was his WGBR.

But waxing poetic would just come across as maudlin. Teddy interrupted his thoughts, glancing over his clipboard.

"Howdy!" he spoke into the microphone, his voice echoing into the distance. Again the throng cheered its approval. He glanced at his clipboard.

Teddy knew that it all could go to his head very quickly. It didn't matter who stood at the microphone or whose picture was on the t-shirts. These people were excited about the adventure that lay ahead.

"Welcome to the World's Greatest Bicycle Ride," he said, leaning into the microphone. "I'm real glad you're here. This is going to be the most incredible week of your life."

Again they whooped, ecstatic, enthusiastic—very much into the excitement of what was about to begin.

"I want to remind you of what you already know," he said. Large loudspeakers were hanging from telephone poles, carrying his voice into the distance. Riders were still wheeling into the back of the crowd.

"This is no race. Take it easy and you'll surpass your goals. If you push hard and ignore what your body tells you, you won't be there when we make it to Los Alamos."

He paused. "It's too far not to slow down and smell the honeysuckle."

A cheer went up. These were the familiar opening words.

"How many have ridden every WGBR so far?" asked Teddy.

Hands sprouted in the crowd. Teddy smiled, recognizing riders he had written about in past years, fifty-year-old attorneys who had been there at the first, chubby sixteen-year-old girls who had determinedly pedaled every inch back on WGBR I when they were in junior high.

"We've got a bunch of people to thank," said Teddy. "Everyone of us knows that without them we wouldn't even attempt this trek. They're the reason that you don't have to pay a cent to come to New Mexico and ride in the greatest lackadaisical wander in the world."

There was another cheer. WGBR was absolutely free. Riders were responsible only for their own food and repairs.

Teddy began introducing the club presidents, bike shop owner Arlie, the president of MK&O Bus Lines, the Porta-Pottie corporate chief, local officials. Many took the microphone and talked too long. The riders grew impatient.

The president of the Farmington Chamber of Commerce climbed onto the stage, wearing a "Next Year: WGBR VII in Farmington" T-shirt. He gave Teddy a shirt and tried to get him to promise to bring the ride there the following year. Then, girls in bikinis emerged from behind the stage and began giving the shirts out to the crowd.

"Next year: FARMINGTON!" yelled the man. "Next year: FARMINGTON!" A chant went up. Teddy grinned. He took the microphone back and said they would study the roads.

"Hey," said the president, leaning into the microphone. "We'll BUILD roads."

The TV cameras had arrived. It began to sprinkle.

Teddy welcomed the governor, who greeted everybody, rambled on about the nobility of their quest, then looked at Teddy, inquiringly.

"Yessir!" said Teddy.

The governor stared out over the crowd. "Ladies and gentlemen!" he intoned, his voice echoing over the thousands. "Let the World's Greatest Bicycle Ride across the glorious state of New Mexico BEGIN!" And they were off.

The cameras rolled as the governor was helped off the stage and onto Teddy's bike. And off he went in the throng, Dallas Holt's fourteen-year-old son, Billy, patiently helping him get his feet in the toe clips, then staying with him as the chief executive made his first gear change.

Teddy watched anxiously. But the governor had been practicing. Down the road, waving at the cameras, he pedaled, doffing his WGBR cap to elderly ladies on adult tricycles, then stopping and helping a child who had tumbled over.

Teddy shook hands with Herrera and a score of Carlsbad and White's City dignitaries who he had forgotten to introduce. He wrote down their names, promising to mention them in the paper. Teddy looked at the sky.

✐   ✐   ✐

"You don't belong at that silly newspaper," one letter from Israel had read. "I need you here. We need somebody who can administrate, who can get people to work for him.

"It looks like we're going to have to take over four orphanages in southern Lebanon run by a friend of mine who is an Armenian Orthodox priest. They're having big problems. "I need you here, Bear. Your crazy bike ride will run itself." Teddy peered at the sky, his eyes not really focusing.

In the morning stillness, Tad and Teddy sprinted into the city park. A two-mile-long loop drive circled three or four large playing fields. "Race you," the boy had challenged Teddy.

A heavily panting man jogged toward them. Automatically, Tad stuck his hand in his handlebar bag and pulled out a tract. He intercepted the man, then riding alongside him, handed him the religious pamphlet. "I hope you'll read this and come to know Jesus as your personal savior," he said.

The panting man nodded, grasping the tract.

Tad turned away, looking pleased.

"Why did you do that?" asked Teddy.

"Do what?"

"Hassle that guy."

"What do you mean? I was witnessing to him about Jesus."

"Don't you think you could find a better time and place? The poor guy is out here trying to run."

"What better time is there than God's time? I was led by the Spirit to share Jesus with that man. Should I quench the Spirit? Should I disobey?"

Teddy growled. The jogger collapsed on a bench and began reading the tract. When he saw what it was, he threw it down.

"Look," said Teddy. "He just threw it away."

"I did my part," said Tad. "I planted a seed."

"You don't even understand what I'm saying, do you?"

"I understand somehow you are able to ignore Jesus' commandment that we go forth preaching and making disciples."

Teddy snorted. Now in Olav's camper, he leaned over the computer keyboard. Something caught his eye.

"Dang," he exclaimed.

"AM-Israel-Lebanon 3rd-Writethru a1038 06-16 1045
"Eds: New grafs, 1-eleven updating with Americans, conflicting reports from Israeli military authorities on cause; Pick up 12th graf pvs, beginning 'Lebanese rescue.'

"MA'ALOT MAS'ADAH, Lebanon (AP)—Queen Beatrix of the Netherlands appealed Sunday to Palestinian leaders for the safety of a young American related to the Dutch royal family.

"The *Times of London* disclosed Sunday morning that Thaddeus 'Tadpole' Behre, age nineteen, is an American nephew of the Baroness of Friesland, Maud Behre, who as a girl was a prominent figure in the Netherlands' World War II resistance against the Nazi occupation army.

"We appeal as a neutral state and longtime advocate of human rights that those holding all hostages honor the Netherlands' longstanding mutual friendship with the Palestinian peoples," the royal statement said in part.

"Meanwhile, 32 Israeli commandos died here Sunday morning in a powerful predawn blast that destroyed an ancient landmark. Sources said the unit was attempting to rescue four Americans kidnapped by Palestinian guerrillas Saturday.

"Under cover of darkness, the commandos had assaulted an old Phoenician prison where the four reportedly had been held only hours earlier. Lebanese soldiers were searching the rubble Sunday morning, but it was not believed the Americans were still in the stone tower's underground tunnels during the blast.

"The Israeli military command in Tel Aviv issued a communique saying thirteen Israelis were killed and 41 wounded. A Lebanese army medic at the scene, Dr. Arieh Raman, said he had counted thirty-two Israeli bodies.

"The military command was silent on the reason for the raid, but sources said the Americans had been seen there Monday and Tuesday.

"There remained no word about the whereabouts of Behre and the other Americans, Jonathan Moffett, 18, of Peoria, IL, Michael Stohler, seventeen, and Jackie Ray Moss, 16, both of Norfolk, VA The four were volunteer farm workers at Kibbutz Dagani near the Syrian border.

"The French news agency, *Agence France-Presse,* said it received a letter in Damacus Sunday in which a shadowy organization calling itself the 'Army of Armed Palestine' offered the release of the Americans in exchange for Israeli withdrawal from the Golan Heights and Jerusalem. Israeli officials discounted the letter as a hoax ..."

Teddy turned off the terminal. "I gotta go to Israel," he whispered. There was a knock on the camper door.

"Hi," said a familiar face.

"Phoebe," exclaimed Teddy. "Phoebe Jane!"

The dark-haired girl from Tulsa glared at him, fumbling with a tape recorder and notebook. "I didn't know you were Dutch!" she said. "Have you heard anything from your brother? Do you mind if I come in?"

Teddy stared at her. "Phoebe!" he sputtered. "Sure. What are you doing here? Come on in." He opened the door.

Olav peered out from the back.

"Are you Dutch royalty?" she exclaimed. For the first time, Teddy saw that she wore a Cable News Network windbreaker.

"I don't know," Teddy shrugged. "I can remember people talking about some of these names, but I don't think so."

Grinning, Olav surveyed Phoebe, then winked at Teddy.

"Uh, let's go somewhere else to talk," Teddy suggested.

At a picnic table, Phoebe tried to launch into a cold and professional interview. Teddy stared at her, amused. "What are you doing?" he asked.

"You're big international news," she said. "First your bike ride and now Tadpole. I had no idea that you were cousins of the Queen of Holland."

Teddy snickered. "I don't know where that's coming from. I think somebody goofed." Hestared at her. "How have you been?"

"Fine," she said. "Listen, I don't like being here any more than you like having me here. I never wanted to see you again."

"Wait a minute." Teddy grinned broadly. "You don't know how glad I am to see you. How did you get on working for CNN?"

"I have a great deal of respect for people who live up to their commitments," Phoebe spat. "I'm...I'm very...I don't understand people who just walk away from—" Her eyes flashed. "From—"

Teddy squinted at her. "From the ones they love?"

Phoebe's eyes filled with tears.

"Have you heard anything from your brother?"

"No. Nothing more than what was on the wire services a few minutes ago."

"When did Dutch authorities first contact you?"

"They haven't. I don't know what's going on. What did they tell you?"

"You didn't even know you were Dutch?"

"Well, yeah, I mean, my Uncle Willem has kind of a funny accent and all my cousins have names like Hans and Julian and Janny. But I never thought much about it. All Americans are part something or other. I'm part Dutch."

Phoebe jotted that down.

Teddy chuckled. "What are you doing?" he asked.

"Our *AM America* is broadcasting live from your campgrounds tomorrow," snarled the girl. "A remote anchor was my brilliant idea a month ago—since I thought I could spend some time with you.

"Now that I realized that never wanted to set eyes on you again, *guess what?* Corporate loves it. Our morning anchor loves it. Advertising loves it. World's biggest bike ride has a sensational angle on the hostage crisis. A great, heart-tugging angle: *An American prince and the pauper story.* I mean, the Queen of Holland is pleading with the baddies not to touch her little American missionary nephew.

"Meanwhile, you—the missionary's brother—are an orphan raised at a boys ranch and who scrapped his way to the top of a major newspaper's management. A beautiful Horatio Alger story. And unknown to everybody, you're also a prince or a baron or something. This is great stuff, Teddy Bear. Sensational stuff. Americans love royalty. And *AM America* has an exclusive, an inside scoop since you and I are so—" she snorted derisively. "Such dear friends.

"So, here I am—doing the dirty work so the news readers will have something fantastic to ask you tomorrow on camera."

Teddy grinned.

"I work up briefing sheets," said Phoebe, "I am a researcher. I suggest questions that the big guns may or may not ask you. But after this, I may have a shot at, say a substitute Headline News anchor or the Sunday early morning slot."

"You do all the work. While the anchors get all the glory."

"Right. Tell me, how did you get into this?"

"Into what?"

"This bicycle ride. I mean, there are 20,000 people out there on the roads, aren't there?"

"We sent CNN a press packet, didn't I? It tells the history of the ride. I'm the assistant city editor."

"But you run the ride, don't you?"

"Nah. Most of the work is done by volunteers." Teddy began listing off names, bike clubs, the repair shops....

"I have all that in the packet," she said. "What I want to know is more about you. Tell me about you and your brother. You're not really brothers, are you? You never have been. That was just something you two worked up to con people at summer camp."

"Not at all," defended Teddy.

"Where are you from? What does Leroy MacDonald think of Tad being in Israel? Did he know you two were Dutch royalty?"

"Uh, I don't know about this Dutch stuff," said Teddy. "If you'll go off the record, I'll give you a little background."

Phoebe glanced over her notes, then put down her pen.

"Off the record?" asked Teddy.

"Yes."

"He was my roommate at the boys' ranch."

"I know all about that. Have you forgotten our long talks on our rock beside the river? Who adopted you?"

"Uh...nobody. His mother was killed when I was eighteen and he was eleven. I became his legal guardian and he started using my name. He is legally Thaddeus Behre now. That's what it says on his new passport and on his Social Security card. But he was born Grey—I guess for his father. Sometimes he went by Thaddeus Julian, however, since that was his mother's maiden name. Why don't you write this: *When he was in the fifth grade, he decided he wanted to be a missionary. He never changed his mind about it. You'll have to understand that at six, he was as mature mentally as somebody twice his age. At eight, he was light years beyond me and received what in our church we call spiritual 'renewal' and he was responsible for me doing the same.*

"You can write this: *I owe most of what I am to him. He taught me how to care about somebody other than myself.*

"He came to live with me while I put myself through the University of Arkansas. We raised each other and although I have relatives here in New Mexico and even know where my mother is, he's the only real family I've ever had. I love him very much." He squinted at the girl.

There were tears in her eyes. "I know," she said.

Teddy grinned.

"I've already talked with your uncle," she said. "The Rev. Willem Behre, in Los Cerrillos, and with people at the Albuquerque Heights church where Tad was youth minister. Okay, tell me about this royalty thing."

"Hey, I don't know much. Tad found something when he was in school, but I never took it very seriously." Teddy squinted.

She scribbled on her pad. "So, this is the World's Greatest Bicycle Ride. This is the biggest one in the world, isn't it? The governor is going to be with us live tomorrow, too. He's really sold on you. And the editor-in-chief of your newspaper speaks very highly of you. He told my producers quite a tale, that you had been a petty thief at age eight and in street gangs in New York City and that you were snatched out of the Kansas State Prison by one of the bicycle club members in what was a dramatic story and that you went off to Leroy's boys' ranch and completely rehabilitated yourself."

Teddy winced. "Well, you know that's not exactly right." He grinned nervously.

Phoebe smiled. "He said that you grew up in jails all over the United States and Canada."

"I hope they will talk about the bike ride tomorrow and not that kind of garbage."

"No, I think America would like to know about all this. It's fascinating. What sort of heinous crimes did you commit that you never told me about?"

"Come on," said Teddy. "I never really did anything. I told you everything. I was never convicted of anything. And it was all expunged from my record when I turned twenty-one."

"Don't be so defensive," she snapped. "I'm not out of line. You're a newsman. You know I have a job to do."

Teddy shrugged. "Come on, Phoebe, I'll introduce you to some of the bike club officials."

"Why were you really in jail?"

"You know about the credit card thing. Come on —"

"No thank you. I remember what you told me when we were going through our little puppy love thing as kids that you were involved as a little boy in homosexual prostitution."

Teddy stared at her. "Is this still off the record?"

Phoebe shrugged, her eyes flashing.

"I hustled a john one time and you know everything there is to know about it. I robbed him before I had to do anything weird. Frankly, I am not really sure he was a john. Sometimes when I think back about it, he may have just been a nice old man trying to help a messed-up kid. Stealing his wallet is what got me in jail. Look, it was years and years ago."

"How was Tadpole involved in that sort of thing?"

Anger welled in Teddy. "He wasn't," he said evenly. "He lived with his grandmother until she put him in the boys' ranch. He's never been in any trouble. I busted my butt making sure Tadpole never had to do any of the things that I went through."

"Who did you kill?"

"My cousin. But it was an accident. He was my very best friend. I took him on a ride to the Grand Canyon with the Santa Fe bike club when we were both eleven and he fell off a cliff."

"You pushed him?"

"No. But I believed I could have saved him and didn't."

"How does a kid stay alive on his own? Did you have a pimp?"

"Look," said Teddy. "I wasn't a prostitute. I got into some wild stuff, but that was just because I didn't know any better. I was an abandoned child. The one time that I tried hustling, I couldn't go through with it. So, I just robbed the guy."

Phoebe scribbled away. Teddy sighed.

"How many people did you rob?"

"Nobody really. Mostly I'd just shoplift stuff and swipe clothes out of laundromats. Ever heard of dumpster diving?"

"No."

"You dig for really good food that high-class restaurants throw away. You'd be surprised what you can find."

She looked repulsed.

"There's all sorts of ways to stay alive," said Teddy. "You call up a pizza parlor and order some really noxious combination, say anchovies and pineapple. When nobody comes to get it, they throw it in their dumpster. Then, you go get it."

"Ugh," she said. "Didn't you get sick eating spoiled food?"

Teddy shrugged. "Look, your stomach gets used to it."

She smiled. "Are you bisexual?"

"What?" exploded Teddy.

"Do you like having intercourse with either gender?"

"Look," said Teddy, wincing. "You aren't going to believe this." He glanced around nervously.

Attentively, Phoebe waited.

"I, ah," said Teddy. "I'm a virgin."

"Ha!" exclaimed Phoebe, laughing. "You?"

"Really," said Teddy. "With AIDS and incurable herpes and venereal diseases and—and the streets full of throwaway kids who don't have any idea of who their fathers are, I believe very strongly that I am supposed to wait until I find the right woman…and then I am going to love her for the rest of my life and be completely faithful…and teach our kids to do the same."

Their eyes held for a long moment.

"Once," he said, softly. "I swore to myself that you were that wonderful girl. I wrote it in my diary. And not a day has gone by in the last five years that I haven't thought about you and wondered where you are."

She fumbled with her pad. "Did you love me? No, don't answer. Listen. I have never known anybody else quite like you."

Teddy didn't say anything.

"You're not bisexual—attracted to either boys or girls?" asked Phoebe. "I've seen you look at boys. I was jealous."

"Look at boys?" mused Teddy. "I...hmmmm. Yeah, I think I sense something when I see little guys who are in trouble or need somebody to pay attention to them and help them get themselves together. So, yeah, when I see a kid like that, it turns my head." He squinted in thought. "But, Phoebe, I am very attracted to women—particularly women with beautiful hearts and spirits."

He stared out over the campground. "As a kid, I used to be worried that I might be attracted to other boys. I was really worried about it. But I never took advantage of a great number of opportunities because I knew it was wrong, because I knew it would hurt people I loved, and because I knew that it wasn't what I wanted for my life. Phoebe, I want to be a righteous man. It just didn't fit into my self-image. It's not what I am determined that I will be."

"Is homosexuality a sin?"

Teddy winced. "What do you want from me?" he asked softly. "I'm not Anita Bryant. I don't need the National Gay Task Force picketing me and denouncing me as a bigot."

"Do you hate fags?"

"Phoebe, Jesus Christ hung around with prostitutes and tax collectors. He didn't hate anybody—but had incredible scorn for self-righteous people trying to stir up trouble betweeen sisters and brothers."

"You're pretty wishy-washy," accused Phoebe.

Teddy stood. He scratched his nose. "Phoebe, I don't hate homosexuals. I believe differently than some of them—I believe that anybody who is tempted to become homosexual can refuse. I was tempted from about fourteen different directions. But I guess I'm just too culturally hetero. Or maybe my moral fiber is too strong. Or maybe I'm a closed-minded jerk. Take your pick. It wasn't for me. I happen to think it's wrong. And I sure didn't want to get AIDS."

"Then you're a latent homosexual?"

"Phoebe, there is no such thing. Every male goes through doubt. And darn near every adult man — if he's honest — will admit one time of dabbling in the darkness of his deepest fear. That doesn't mean anything except that we're normal human beings — with the ability to choose right or wrong."

"So, you're a psychologist, too?"

"No, but I think I know something about this one."

Teddy turned, but did not say anything.

"Why didn't you call?" Phoebe asked.

Teddy studied her. "I did."

"Why didn't you keep it up?"

He shrugged and turned away. Then, he turned back. "I'm sorry," he said.

"Me, too."

Hesitantly, as if he were back at church camp, he held out his hand. Carefully, she slipped her palm into his.

And they stared silently into the years of each other's eyes — mourning for the good times they had stupidly missed.

✐   ✐   ✐

Back in the camper, Teddy showed her how to call up the Associated Press foreign wire on his portable computer. They scrolled the other wires, too, but found nothing about Tad.

"What has the state department told you?" asked Phoebe.

"I haven't heard a thing from them."

"There was a really nice profile on you two guys on the *CBS Morning News* back in our motel."

"Oh yeah? What'd they say?"

"The Dutch royal family says that you're one of theirs. Did you have an Aunt Maud? Apparently, she was the granddaughter of some famous World War II baronness. Anyway, they know all about you and they're pulling out all the diplomatic stops to get Tad released.

"Anyway, CBS also got some tape from one of the local stations of Tadpole at some church coffeehouse, preaching on a megaphone. They're really piling it on—the teenage missionary, an American prince, held hostage."

"What'd they say about me?"

"Oh, the usual, about you guys adopting each other at the boys' ranch and bringing up each other. Hey, they don't know you guys aren't really brothers."

Teddy winced.

"I don't get it," he whispered. "Let's say I am related to the Dutch. You know, I think I do remember my grandmother talking about something like that. She always had a thing about Hans Brinker. But still, Tad's not a Behre—not really. I was only his guardian. He had his name changed on documents and stuff, but he's not related to me."

Phoebe shrugged.

Teddy frowned. "It sounds like your *AM America* guys are out for my scalp, you know, to tell the 'real story' of the juvenile delinquent waifs."

"Naw," said Phoebe, grinning guiltily. "That was just me. You'll have to admit, it was a great revenge opportunity. But that's not how they're going to be playing it. This American prince stuff is too big to foul up with a scandal. They're making your nutty little brother out to be Albert Schweitzer, Mother Theresa and Little Lord Fauntleroy all rolled into one."

Teddy looked unconvinced.

"Hey, what can they do?" asked Phoebe. "You never did anything too bad."

Teddy winced. "Do you think I ended up at a boys' ranch because I was a good little tyke? I was *SENT* there."

"They already told all about that. They even had some woman named Sarah Van Arsdale who says she was your foster parent when you lived in New York City."

"Sarah? Really? I wonder where they found her. She wasn't my foster anything. She was a bag lady."

Phoebe snickered.

"Listen," said Teddy. "If they want to, they can make out that I was some kind of pervert."

"That's all in your head. They've built Tadpole up bigger than life, volunteering at a kibbutz and now being held by the big, bad Palestinian crazies. They're not going to ruin the effect."

That evening, Teddy skipped out on the WGBR banquet and sent Arlie, Olav and Ragnhild in his place.

Instead, he and Phoebe found a quiet little cafe 25 miles off of the bike route. And they spent most of the evening out under the stars atop a windswept butte away from the madding crowd.

🖉   🖉   🖉

The Monday morning sun was just peeking over the horizon, but the stream of riders had begun. Many were newcomers.

Around 6:15, Teddy and Phoebe reported to the *AM America* set at the campgrounds. She was wearing a WGBR cap and biking shorts.

"You don't know how glad I am to see you!" exclaimed her boss. Teddy went into a trailer, where his paper's editor-in-chief and the governor were being made up.

"Your highness!" chuckled the editor, Martin Garrett. "So, you finally decided to get up! Hey, these folks are great!"

Phoebe hovered as Teddy had makeup applied, then rushed him outside. She glanced at her watch. "They're on a commercial break. Come on."

An earplug tucked up under his curly locks, Teddy sat down, then stood and shook hands with the weatherman. The man, too, was wearing a WGBR cap and t-shirt.

"So, how's it going?" asked the weatherman, smiling, jolly. He was much shorter than Teddy had expected.

"Great," said Teddy, the adrenaline flowing. Nervously, he glanced around. Ragnhild was standing behind the lights. Dallas and Olav leaned back in chairs by a weather map. The governor spotted Teddy and gave a leisurely salute.

"You'll hear New York on your earplug," instructed a technician, clipping two tiny microphones to Teddy's WGBR jacket. A makeup man fussed with the weatherman's toupe. "Watch that monitor there."

On the screen, ancient Mikey was spooning up Life cereal while his brothers stared in disbelief.

Then, "Good MORNING, New York and everybody across America," enthused the weatherman. "I'm standing here with Teddy Behre. That's really his name, John, no kidding. Teddy, don't you go by Ted?"

"That's right." Teddy grinned into the camera.

"Well, Tom, I wish you could see the beautiful sunrise we've got. It's clear and already 82 degrees in Albuquerque north of the World's Greatest Bicycle Ride. It's going to be a scorcher today. Teddy here is the director of the World's Greatest Bicycle Ride, which he likes to call the largest lackadaisical family bicycle ramble in the world. How long have you been doing this, Teddy? Ten years?"

Teddy flashed his shy trademark grin. "Not quite that long."

"Ol' Teddy here pulled a fast one on us this morning," said the weatherman, beaming. "He didn't want to have to get up at 3 a.m., so he sent Dallas and Will and the other presidents of the bike clubs that we've been talking to.

"Back to you, Tom."

And on the monitor, Teddy watched as the newsman back in New York began recapping news headlines.

"Stand by, Mr. Behre," said a voice in Teddy's ear. Then, there was a familiar voice. "Mr. Behre, this is Jim Mitchell in New York. In a few minutes, I'm going to be giving an update on the story in Amsterdam as well as in Lebanon and we'll cut away to some footage we have of the Israeli commandos being returned to Israel. I'm going to ask you to tell us why your brother was in Israel."

Teddy nodded, listening.

On the monitor, a newswoman in London was talking about an economic summit.

Then, over his earplug, Teddy could hear the audio of the *AM America* show.

On the monitor, Mitchell talked with the Dutch ambassador to the United Nations, who refused to divulge details of private discussions with the governments of Iran and Syria to get Tadpole's release.

Next, Mitchell talked with a Palestinian spokesman in Tunis, who said that he believed the boys were being held in Syria by pro-Iranian zealots.

Then, there was film of the Israeli commandos. Mitchell told the latest death count.

"Standing by in Albuquerque, on the route of the World's Greatest Bicycle Ride, we've been talking with Ted Behre, brother of one of the most prominent American hostage, nineteen-year-old Christian missionary Tad Behre. Ted, just what was Tad doing at Kibbutz Dagani when he was taken captive?"

"Ever since Tad was little," said Teddy, talking slowly, his voice carefully low, "he's had a missionary-type concern for Israel. I think the first time he told me he wanted to go to Israel to preach was back when he was still in junior high school. The spring that he turned seventeen, I couldn't keep him here anymore and he became a volunteer farm worker at a kibbutz near Haifa. Israel has strict laws against traditional Christian evangelism, so he just worked as a kibbutznik. His letters home told about digging sugar beets, working in a shoe factory and witnessing his faith to his co-workers. He lived in a dorm with the other teen-agers and went to school at night. That was part of the deal he and I made. He could go if he would finish school."

"You're his only immediate relative, aren't you, Teddy? I mean, that's what you thought. I'm told that you had no idea that the two of you are Dutch princes."

Teddy winced. "I don't know much about that," he said. "This is really brand new. It's *possible*. I mean, I lived in Holland as an infant. It's entirely possible that I'm related to the royal family, but it's a bit of a surprise. Nevertheless, I am very grateful to them for what they're doing. I've read *Hans Brinker* and Corrie ten Boom's *The Hiding Place* and Brother Andrew's *God's Smuggler* and, of course, *Diary of Anne Frank*. So, if it turns out that I'm Dutch, then I have a great deal to be very proud of."

"Ted, as Tad's legal guardian, why would you let Tad, your only brother, go off to Israel by himself?"

"It was the fervent desire of his heart to go to Israel. I was pretty nervous about it, but it was all he could think about. And he loves it there. On weekends, he participates in evangelistic crusades in Jordan and Lebanon and travels throughout the land where Jesus lived, just talking with the people, like Jesus did. He's learned fluent Arabic and Hebrew and in his last letter, he wrote that he was learning a Druse dialect."

"Didn't you ever feel a little anxious, knowing that something like this could happen to him? On the one hand, you have the element of orthodox Jewish extremists who take a rather militant attitude toward Christian proselytizing. On the other hand, you have of Moslem hardliners, who see missionaries as CIA agents and representatives of U.S. imperialism. And there's the threat of a kibbutz in northern Israel being the target of terrorist actions or Palestinian raids. Didn't you worry about Tad?"

"Sure. But, this isn't the first time he's been in hot water over there. Once, he spent three weeks in a Syrian jail for giving away little New Testaments in downtown Damascus. Tad's specialty is preaching on street corners with a battery-powered megaphone. Unfortunately, the Syrian authorities didn't approve."

Mitchell chuckled.

"You two aren't the average sort of brothers, are you?"

Teddy grinned warily. "I love my little brother very much. I don't think some brothers are forced to depend on each other like we were. We were all each other had. Tad and I had it hard some years. It was rough, for example, when he was in the eighth grade and we couldn't afford for him to play junior high football. I was still at the University of Arkansas and working three jobs. He had three or four paper routes, but still, we just couldn't afford for him to give up the routes and play football."

"Tell us how you met Tadpole, Teddy."

Teddy smiled, the lights hot. "I was thirteen and he was six. His mother had, ah, left him with an elderly grandmother, who when he was in the first grade, had to enter a nursing home. So, he ended up at Ouachita Hills Boys' Ranch and Christian School near Fayetteville, Arkansas."

"How did you end up at the ranch? You had been in a little trouble with the law, I believe.

"You could say that. I had been on my own since I was ten. But, I was lucky. God was watching over me. And I had people who believed in me, significantly, my probation officer, a Santa Fe police detective named Gene Ortega. He arranged for me to be sent to the ranch. He's here, on the ride. He's the president of the Santa Fe Bicycling Society."

"I understand you were a street child, that you raised yourself."

"Oh, I lived in all sorts of places. For awhile I traveled with my mother. I was on my own a lot between the time I was ten years old and when I turned thirteen. I was sent to a Wyoming state school for delinquents when she ran off on me when I was ten. When I was nine or ten, we got back together and she and I were picked up in Galveston, Texas, and she went to prison for car theft and prostitution, among other things. When I was thirteen, I very nearly became the youngest person ever sent into the Kansas State Prison System. There were some rocky times, but I survived."

"Tell us about Tad. Don't you call him Tadpole?"

Teddy grinned, his blond hair shining under the lights.

"He's a special kid. They don't make many like him. He taught me everything I know about caring about other people. I was all he had."

"Thank you, Teddy. We'll be talking with you some more this morning. Teddy Behre, assistant city editor of the *Albuquerque Daily World,* director of the World's Greatest Bicycle Ride and very worried foster brother and legal guardian of seventeen-year-old Thaddeus Behre, one of four Americans being held hostage by terrorists somewhere in northern Israel, southern Lebanon, or if reports from the PLO are to be believed, in Syria. This is Jim Mitchell for *AM America.*"

Behind the lights, beaming Santa Fe Bicycle Club members gave Teddy thumbs up.

And then, he did the interview again.

This time, they asked about the Dutch connection and let Teddy talk by video hookup to Crown Prince Willem-Alexander, who was in Florida playing polo.

"Well, hello, Cousin," said the Crown Prince in a warm greeting that would be replayed on all the networks all day, "Theophilus, at The Hague, our people have been studying the many reports concerning Thaddeus. My mum—Her Royal Majesty—wants you to have her and my family's assurance: *If this boy is good enough for you, he's good enough for us.* Although we now understand there is no bloodline to our family, that becomes unimportant, all things considered.

"We shall honor your devotion to this young lad. Diplomatic efforts are continuing and shall continue on an international scale. We Dutch have our ways."

Teddy's eyes misted. "But ..." he mumbled. "Isn't all this rather embarrassing to you, I mean —"

The Crown Prince began to laugh. "Theo," he chuckled. "Your rather checkered past gives my family and the people of the Netherlands new richness and pride. You, a son of Holland, have distinguished yourself nobly, which is one reason why we cannot but affirm that your blood is indeed blue and certainly very Dutch. No one else could have survived and thrived amid all this but a true Dutchman. Look at you, you're the editor of a prestigious American newspaper and the founder of a world-famous bicycle race. We welcome you, our American cousin."

Teddy mumbled thanks and accepted an invitation to come to Amsterdam.

Then, he watched as the newscaster told of Tad's being the youngest youth pastor ever at Albuquerque's largest church and asked Teddy for details about how Tad had gotten out of Damascus jail for preaching on his megaphone.

They wanted to know all about the Christian Kibbutzim program. They asked all about Ouachita Hills Boys' Ranch.

And then it was over.

On the back of bicycle-built-for-two borrowed from Arlie, Teddy and Phoebe biked off down the route to the NBC News lemonade stand. Teddy talked with them for fifteen minutes and watched Crown Prince Willem-Alexander's statement on tape. Wiping makeup off of his face, the humbled Teddy climbed in Olav's camper.

"Look at this!" declared Ragnhild, her eyes flashing at Phoebe. On a little portable TV, an incredibly aged Trixie was blowing smoke rings and telling a San Francisco talk-show host about how the brutal authorities had separated her from her beloved little boy.

"Listen," said Phoebe, "I've got to get back. See you tonight?"

"Sure," said Teddy. The two exchanged a quick peck on the lips—which the alarmed Ragnhild did not miss. She glowered in the back of the camper as Teddy silently watched Phoebe hail a repair truck back to the CNN broadcast.

He turned to Olav's portable computer terminal. On the wires was a recap of what had been happening on TV.

The exhausted Teddy stepped outside the camper.

He grabbed Ragnhild's bike and disappeared down the route.

Not a mile away, he stopped under a large, spreading oak. No riders were in sight—the main body of bicyclists was miles ahead. He pushed his bike up to the roadside fence, laid it down in the tall weeds, then slowly walked over the hill—out of sight of the road.

And he sat down in the warm sun. It was all beyond his comprehension. Phoebe was back. Tad was in trouble. Or was he? And were they Dutch royalty? If so, what did that mean?

Teddy plopped back in the high grass and stared at the sky. *Dutch royalty?* He sighed.

He closed his eyes and tried to think.

Instead, he fell into an unexpected sleep.

And he dreamed:

Sitting at a computer terminal, Teddy pulled up a story that told how the Americans' bodies had been found in shallow

*graves near the kibbutz—that apparently they'd been tortured
and killed the same day they were captured.*

*In the dream, everybody was sympathetic, even his solemn
Uncle Will.*

*And Teddy didn't want to do anything but go to Israel and kill
Palestinians.*

*In a vengeful fury, he raised his hands to heaven. The sky
dimmed, then turned scarlet. Beside him, "Now, you know who
you are," smiled the old man, Quetzalcoatl. "But it is far, far
more than this. Soon you will lead the greatest battle!"*

*"No!" wept Teddy. He raised his hands to heaven again, his
heart breaking.*

He woke with a start, upset that he could have felt such evil
depths of vengeance—such a lust for blood. Standing up, he
found himself shaken with emotion, believing that Tad was
really dead—little Tad, six years old and riding around on his
shoulders, telling people they were brothers—Tad. The only
person who had ever cared enough about Teddy to try to
understand his secret hurts, his deep confusion and his incredible, hidden anger. Placid, secure Tad, thirteen years old and
smuggling his junior high school band into the University of
Arkansas commencement exercises, tooting out *The Impossible Dream* as Teddy walked up to get his diploma.

Tad, sixteen years old and standing on Albuquerque street
corners preaching on a megaphone, trying to give tracts to
dodging passersby.

Teddy's eyes misted.

Calmly, he sat up.

"God," whispered Teddy in the morning sun. "Thank you for
sending Phoebe back to me. Now, please take care of Tadpole,
Father. Protect him. Shield him, Father, wherever he is. Help
him. Don't let anything happen to him."

He shook with deep emotion, filled with memories of the boy he loved. And now, Teddy gripped his fists tight.

"God, You know I'd go to Israel if I thought You wanted me there. But, I can't, God. It's in Your hands. You hold Tad in Your hands."

He began crying softly. Sinking to his knees, "He's Your devoted servant. I have never known anybody so consumed with a desire to do Your will," Teddy prayed. "He changed me. He taught me what it is to love. And he showed me what life is really all about. Lord, I have no right to want to hold onto him. Maybe You want him with You. Maybe he has earned his place among the archangels. He loves You so. He has no fear of dying. To him it means being with You and out of this crummy world."

Teddy stared up at the sky

"But, Father, I plead with You that I need him here. You are the Master of the Universe. But I need him here."

Teddy shook with unexpected intensity.

And, bewildered, he felt great peace.

Slowly, he fell to his knees, his eyes closed, his hands raised to heaven, trembling. And it was as if he could see Tad in a rocky field, laughing and preaching, unafraid, praying for a commander in military fatigues.

The man pulled a pistol. Tad laughed and raised his hands to heaven as the barrel was leveled at his head.

"Father, we cannot accept this defeat, can we?" Tad yelled—in Arabic. "Yes, I would come to be with You! But, would You let me come when I have unfinished business here? Father, don't close Your eyes to this man who so loves his people and wants them to live in *PEACE!* Show this devoted man that Jesus *LOVES* him!"

The commander angrily jammed the barrel against the seventeen-year-old's temple.

Without a bit of remorse, the man pulled the trigger.

But the gun did not fire.

Tad turned, staring him in the face, smiling like some sort of beatific martyr. "Lord," the boy prayed unafraid, "show him that You want to *END* all his years of oppression and bitterness! Show this man whom You love the way to free his people, the real key to peace and security and JOY!"

Angrily, the commander gripped the gun with both hands and pulled the trigger again. Again, the gun did not fire. "Father God, our mighty Creator, show him that even in a refugee camp —" proclaimed Tad. His face seemed aglow, like some sort of saint, "— Lord, show him that *nobody* can take away from him what *you* can give him right now."

Furiously, the commander pounded the gun with his hand. He pointed it skyward and fired three quick shots. Then, he leveled it at the seventeen-year-old American again.

Tad did not pause. "O Lord, help my hurting comrade!" prayed the boy. "He wants to *know* peace—Your peace that will not leave him even when the politics of war swirl around him, killing his people, destroying their lives. Help this man to truly lead his people to a new day! To *YOUR* way!"

The commander pulled the trigger again.

And the gun refused to fire.

As the man wept aloud, "Thank You, Lord!" exclaimed Tad. "You have chosen to spare my life as a sign to this fine commander. Open his eyes, Lord! Show him that it was the hand of the Almighty God that would not let him kill me! Open his heart, Lord! Let him see that Jesus Christ is Lord!"

Screaming and dancing in fury, "Get him out of here!" yelled the commander. But around him guerrillas threw down their weapons and sank to their knees.

"Thank You, *Jesus!*" laughed Tad. "Hear the prayer of Your servants kneeling here before You. But, do not stop with them. Now, let their good, dedicated commander know *YOUR* way and let him see what he MUST do to end his fear and hate and despair! He already knows that You are God. Now, don't let him turn away when he finally has the answers to all this! He KNOWS that You would use him!"

Shrieking, the commander grabbed an assault rifle. He slammed the butt into Tad's face. But the boy was untouched.

"See and know the power of Jesus!" proclaimed Tadpole.

Stunned, the commander looked around him as all the guerrillas groveled face-down, weeping, praying with Tad, thanking the God that they still called Allah that this imperialist American had been given to them to show them God's will for them. The commander stared over them in shock. His aide dropped into the traditional head-down Moslem prayer posture, wailing to God.

"Go to the devil!" screamed the commander at Tad. "Leave us in peace! Go bedevil the Zionists!"

"I have been sent to *you!*" declared Tad. "God loves you! He loves your people! He loves your little son, back home in Amman. Pull out your pistol and kill me and you will *STILL* know the truth. Your God cared enough to send His only Son, Jesus Christ, to die for you. And today, He sent me to tell you about it. You know within you that I speak the truth you've searched for. Right, now, ask Jesus to come into your heart and change you. Ask Him to show you the true way for your people. There will be peace in Palestine and it will be a glorious peace of Jesus Christ!"

In fury, the man shrieked, then began ordering his men to their feet.

"You fool!" answered a lieutenant, shedding an ammunition belt. "Allah has sent us a great prophet!"

"No, your commander is no fool. He knows the truth!" declared Tad. "I am no prophet. I am a servant. I am a boy, a boy that God loves, just like He loves you!"

And Tad knelt with the lieutenant, then with another guer-rilla with one arm, praying with them in Arabic as they wept and prayed.

His eyes terrified, the commander jammed his pistol into its holster. And running, he vanished into the woods.

"Bring him back, Father!" Tad was yelling. "Don't let him leave this place. He is *Yours!* He longs for Your truth!"

Stunned, Teddy sank face-first into the New Mexico weeds. There was no doubt of what he had just seen.

But, he whispered to himself: *he didn't even believe in visions.*

But, what he had seen was too real.

He had heard Arabic and understood it.

And he knew in the depths of his soul that Tad was safe. The peace that filled Teddy was not the product of any hallucination, of any disturbed imagination.

Tad was safe.

"Tuesday marks the third day of captivity for the 4.3 million hostage bicyclists trapped on this Dutch Royal prayer march across New Mexico," began Wilson Lang's column in the morning paper.

"Everyone knows there's only 200-300 riders out here, but the crowd estimates get more and more ridiculous as the trek sloshes on. So, let's be really absurd.

"The 27.3 million riders claim they've been treated well by His Royal Majesty the Maharajah Teddy of Behre.

"But me? My head hurts from my forgetting to fill both of my bike's water bottles with straight tequila. For reasons that escape me, last night at the campgrounds I filled them with water. Nasty stuff.

"I made friends with a rowdy bunch of Mississippi bicyclists who were mixing what they called Garbage Can Surprise. This delicate cocktail is not for the short of breath.

"'You take six or eight bottles of whatever you have on hand,' instructed Otto Scruggs, 27, veteran of smaller bike rides across Georgia, Ohio, Kansas, Oklahoma and Iowa, as he pulled a plastic, green trash barrel from the back of the group's over-sized pickup truck. 'Then, you add two gallons or so of Everclear, a case of beer, some Pepsi, whatever fruit juices that you've shoplifted from small groceries and three bottles of Grenadine.'

"The result Saturday night was twenty gallons of pomegranate-flavored dragster fuel. The only way to drink it, I was advised, was to fill a soft plastic bike bottle full of half-thawed orange juice concentrate and squirt the syrupy citrus into your mouth before the Surprise hits your stomach.

"I was leaning over a lavatory at the White's City Phillips 66 gas station some befogged hours later when I met Travis Phelps, 16, of Albuquerque, who showed me how to do one's laundry while on WGBR.

"He'd stuffed three pairs of grimy socks, two sweat-stiffened t-shirts and his only pair of underwear into a small nylon camp sack. Carefully, he doused the contents with liquid dish soap. Then, firmly grasping the bag's drawstring, he lowered it all into the toilet bowl.

"'You just keep flushing until there's no suds,' the boy instructed.

"Mom, it's worse than you feared.

"Indeed, the most important thing your precocious sixteen-year-old boy needs is not a bike at all—if he is to be successful on this ride.

"'Nope, whatcha need's a purty tent,' a young Cassanova advised, walking me around his $760 dome tundra special. The tent, he bragged, was equipped with 'good music, good refreshments and good dope.'

"'Last year, my daddy come out to the campgrounds in Clovis,' he confided. 'And I had dis big bag of really good sinsemilla marijuana out on the picnic table. He picked that sucker up and asked me what it was. I just looked him in the eye and told him it was that gorp that Teddy Behre's always tellin' ever'body to eat. (Daddy, gorp is nuts and raisins and, occasionally, chocolate chips.)

"'So, my daddy, he took this big ol' bite and spit it out on the ground and said it was TERRIBLE, how could I eat that stuff?'

"A shocking tale. I, myself do not believe a word of it."

"I got up at 8:15 Monday morning, determined to get an early start on the 52 miles of solid lemonade stands into some unknown little town where we were to spend the night. But, when I stuck my head out of my tent, it looked like a Twilight Zone scene where The Rebel Colonel returns to The Plantation after The War only to find that his family has been abducted by Martians.

"Only a few pieces of paper blew across the campgrounds giving evidence that just hours before, the dusty field had been a seething mass of semihumanity.

"I started out as the last person and steadily lost ground all morning. I knew I was in big trouble when buzzards started circling just as I made it to the Red Oak Cub Scouts Breakfast Jamboree. They were out of food.

"Their pack mother told me she knew a good shortcut into town, but I turned her down. I knew the road she was suggesting and it goes much too close to my mother's house.

"My relatives believe I'm a war correspondent off covering civil strife in Central America. I can't let them see me on a bicycle. Their kids will visit me from now on.

"I never did find a lemonade stand with anything left. Ye, GADS! Has all of New Mexico gone mad, left their homes and *families to come ride these last days across the Land of Enchantment?*

"To think once upon a time only a few hundred made this jaunt and there was more lemonade than you could flush down your septic tank. Incredibly, I've developed a taste for the noxious stuff.

"Well, I'm going to stick this column in the front door of the local newspaper office as I ride past. Jesse (our local circulation agent), if you don't hear from me again, please send a message to my wife:

"'The life insurance policy is in the safe deposit box. I never hated your mother. Don't let Gerald drive the car. Ever. Don't let him on a bicycle either. And do not let him buy a tent. Make him walk and take buses like nature intended.'

"I think if I just head south, maybe I can be first on next year's WGBR. I'll buy up all the lemonade and let next year's 561.2 billion riders taste some of their own medicine.

"Oh, yes: Hey boss. I broke the portable computer terminal. I punched it out. I'm not sorry.

Farewell."

The phone line to Israel crackled. "Tad?" asked Teddy.

"Bear," rasped an excited kid. "Where are you?"

"New Mexico. Some little town. Where'd you think I was?"

"I was hoping you were at the airport or needing us to come get you at the bus station."

"No. Sorry about that. How are you doing?"

"Oh, just fine." Tad was obviously disappointed.

The phone line was silent. "Well, which airport should I fly into?" asked Teddy. "If I come?"

"Tel Aviv," exclaimed Tadpole. "All right!" He put his hand over the receiver, but Teddy could hear him anyway "Hey! My brother is coming! My brother! Bear's coming!"

Teddy sighed impatiently.

"When?" demanded Tad.

"Well," Teddy's voice was distant. "As soon as I can get out of here. It may be a few days. I have responsibilities here, you know."

"You have people who *love* you here," said Tad.

Teddy was silent. "Okay," he said.

"What are you going to do?"

"I'm coming to Israel. I'll call you as soon as I know what flight and all that."

"Buy a one-way ticket. I need you to stay."

Teddy groaned, grinning. "I'm no missionary," he said. "I have no idea what I am going to do in Israel."

"Right," snickered Tad. "See you."

"Hey," said Teddy.

"What? "

"I love you."

"Yeah, I know. And I love you and I need you to get over here and help me out."

"Right. Bye."

As his jet crossed the Mediterranean Sea, Teddy dozed off.

"I will not rebel against the One who created me and all that is. I am a warrior angel of the company of Michael. I am a loyal and obedient servant of the Most High!" proclaimed the boy atop the ancient pyramid.

"You know who you are!" his father rasped.

"I don't care!" exclaimed Teddy. *"An obscure Dutch prince. Big deal. It'll get my picture on the cover of People magazine, then that'll be that."*"

"Dutch?" exclaimed his father. *"That is only the beginning. You are the fulfillment of great and ancient prophecies."*

"What do you mean?" asked Teddy.

"You are Xocoy. You are Wolf. You are Theophilus Behre, not bound by a human soul, a great angelic warrior sent among

*men. Immortal! Yet, you are also human, too—made an
incarnate mortal just like the first Christ. The blood of czars
and kaisers runs in your human veins. You are the second
Christ.*

"*What?*" *exclaimed Teddy.* "*You mean Antichrist!*" *He guffawed, not believing.*

"*They will come to you—joyfully. Your temptation is far, far
greater than mine, Teddy Bear! You will be the mighty one who
leads the final war against the Tyrant. All nations will draw
unto you. Europe belongs to Theophilus. The United States
belongs to Wolf. The great ancient American empires belong to
Xocoy. And Babylon will rise behind your little brother. The
two of you will stand at the reins of a new age as we march
triumphant through the gates of the Tyrant's Holy City!*"'"

"*No,*" *rasped Teddy, his voice a calm whisper.* "*Not me. I may
participate in the last battle, but I will not be leading anybody.
I will serve the One Creator who has made me one of His
beloved humans and has allowed me to call Him my Father!*"

"*You will have no choice!*" *exclaimed the old man, his voice
shrill.*

"*We'll see,*" *snickered Teddy.*

He awoke.

He looked around him.

Below him were the plains of Israel. He grinned, knowing
Tadpole was waiting at the airport—excited, enthusiastic and
ready to conquer the world.

He leaned back in his seat. Beside him, Phoebe read over her
notes, then smiled and squeezed his hand.

And Teddy wondered just what had been a dream.

And what had not.